ESSAYS ON LORD CLIVE AND WARREN HASTINGS

Owing to the antiquity and rarity of this book, certain pages are regrettably absent, and readability is compromised due to the blurring of the original text. If you possess any insights regarding the availability of these missing sections, kindly inform us. Your assistance is crucial in ensuring the completion of this significant work for the benefit of future generations.

ESSAYS ON LORD CLIVE AND WARREN HASTINGS

BY
THOMAS BABINGTON MACAULAY

GYAN

Published by

Gyan Publishing House
5, Ansari Road
Daryaganj, New Delhi-110002
Phone: 011-47034999, 9811692060
E-mail: books@gyanbooks.com

Distribution Network
gyanbooks.com
India, USA, Canada, UK, Australia

ISBN: 978-93-6208-525-2 (PB)
First Published, 1909

2nd Impression 2024

Printed at: Gyan Press, Delhi.

ESSAYS ON LORD CLIVE AND WARREN HASTINGS
Author: THOMAS BABINGTON MACAULAY

Merrill's English Texts

ESSAYS ON LORD CLIVE AND WARREN HASTINGS

BY
THOMAS BABINGTON MACAULAY

EDITED WITH AN INTRODUCTION AND NOTES BY CORNELIA BEARE, INSTRUCTOR IN ENGLISH, WADLEIGH HIGH SCHOOL, NEW YORK CITY

NEW YORK
CHARLES E. MERRILL CO.
44–60 EAST TWENTY-THIRD STREET

CONTENTS

PUBLISHERS' NOTE

Merrill's English Texts

THIS series of books will include in complete editions those masterpieces of English Literature that are best adapted for the use of schools and colleges. The editors of the several volumes will be chosen for their special qualifications in connection with the texts to be issued under their individual supervision, but familiarity with the practical needs of the classroom, no less than sound scholarship, will characterize the editing of every book in the series.

In connection with each text, a critical and historical introduction, including a sketch of the life of the author and his relation to the thought of his time, critical opinions of the work in question chosen from the great body of English criticism, and, where possible, a portrait of the author, will be given. Ample explanatory notes of such passages in the text as call for special attention will be supplied, but irrelevant annotation and explanations of the obvious will be rigidly excluded.

CHARLES E. MERRILL CO.

INTRODUCTION

BIOGRAPHICAL SKETCH

Thomas Babington Macaulay, whose father was Zachary Macaulay—famous for his advocacy of the abolition of slavery, was born at Rothley Temple, in Leicestershire, towards the end of 1800. From his infancy he showed a precocity that was simply extraordinary. He not only acquired knowledge rapidly, but he possessed a marvelous power of working it up into literary form, and his facile pen produced compositions in prose and in verse, histories, odes, and hymns. From the time that he was three years old he read incessantly, for the most part lying on the rug before the fire with his book on the ground, and a piece of bread and butter in his hand. It is told of him that when a boy of four, and on a visit with his father, he was unfortunate enough to have a cup of hot coffee overturned on his legs, and when his hostess, in her sympathetic kindness, asked shortly after how he was feeling, he looked up in her face and said, "Thank you, madam, the agony is abated." At seven he wrote a compendium of Universal History. At eight he was so fired with the *Lay* and with *Marmion* that he wrote three cantos of a poem in imitation of Scott's manner, and called it the "Battle of Cheviot." And he had many other literary projects, in all of which he showed perfect correctness both in grammar and in spelling, made his meaning uniformly clear, and was scrupulously accurate in his punctuation.

With all this cleverness he was not conceited. His parents, and particularly his mother, were most judicious in their treatment. They never encouraged him to display his powers of conversation, and they abstained from every kind of remark that might help him to think himself different from other boys. One result was that throughout his life he was free from literary vanity; another was that he habitually overestimated the knowledge of others. When he said in his essays that every schoolboy knew this and that fact in history, he was judging their information by his own vast intellectual stores.

At the age of twelve, Macaulay was sent to a private school in the neighborhood of Cambridge. There he laid the foundation of his future scholarship, and though fully occupied with his school work—chiefly Latin, Greek, and mathematics—he found time to gratify his insatiable thirst for general literature. He read at random and without restraint, but with an apparent partiality for the lighter and more attractive books. Poetry and prose fiction remained throughout his life his favorite reading. On subjects of this nature he displayed a most unerring memory, as well as the capacity for taking in at a glance the contents of a printed page. Whatever caught his fancy he remembered, as well as though he had consciously got it by heart. He once said, that if all the copies of *Paradise Lost* and the *Pilgrim's Progress* were to be destroyed, he would from memory alone undertake to reproduce both.

In 1818 Macaulay went from school to the university—to Trinity College, Cambridge. But here the studies were not to his mind. He had no liking for mathematics, and was nowhere as a mathematical student. His inclination was wholly for literature, and he gained various high distinctions in that department. It was unfortunate for him that he had no severe discipline in scientific method; to his disproportionate partiality for the lighter sides of literature must be attributed his want of philosophic grasp, his dislike of arduous speculations, and his want of courage in facing intellectual problems.

The private life of Cambridge had a much greater influence on him than the recognized studies of the place. He made many friends. His social qualities and his conversational powers were widely exercised and largely developed. He became, too, a brilliant member of the Union Debating Society, and here politics claimed his attention. Altogether he gave himself more to the enjoyment of all that was stirring around him than to the taking of university honors. In 1824, however, he was elected a Fellow, and began to take pupils. Further, he sought a wider field for his literary labors, and contributed papers to some of the magazines—mostly to *Knight's Quarterly Magazine.* Chief among these contributions are "Ivry," and "Naseby" in spirited verse, and the conversation between Cowley and Milton, in as splendid prose.

When Macaulay went to Cambridge, his father seemed in affluent circumstances, but the slave-trade agitation engrossed his time and his energy, and by and by there came on the family commercial ruin. This was a blow to the eldest son, but he bore up bravely, brought sunshine and happiness into the depressed household, and proceeded to retrieve their position with stern fortitude. He ultimately paid off his father's debts.

Though called to the bar in 1826, he did not take kindly to the law, and soon renounced it for an employment more congenial—literature. Already in 1824 he had been invited to write for the *Edinburgh Review*, and in August, 1825, appeared in that magazine his article on Milton, which created a sensation, and made the critics aware of the advent of a new literary power. This first success he followed up rapidly, and besides giving new life to the periodical, he soon gained for himself a name of note. In 1828 he was made a Commissioner of Bankruptcy, and in 1830 was elected M. P. for Calne. In the Reformed Parliament he sat for Leeds.

He entered Parliament at an opportune period, and was in the thick of the great Reform conflict. His speeches on the Reform Bill raised him to the first rank as an orator, and gained for him official posts. It was while burdened with these severe public labors that he wrote thirteen (from Montgomery to Pitt) of the *Edinburgh Review* Essays. Thus he went on for four years, but the narrow circumstances of his family induced him to accept the lucrative post of legal adviser to the Supreme Council of India. This necessitated his going to India, which was clearly adverse to his prospects at home; yet the certainty of returning with £20,000 saved from his large salary was sufficient inducement to make the sacrifice, and he sailed February 15, 1834.

In India he maintained his reputation as a hard worker. Besides his official duties as a Member of Council, he undertook the additional burden of acting as chairman in two important committees, and it is in connection with one of these—the committee appointed to draw up the new codes—that he has his chief title to fame as an Indian statesman. The New Penal Code was in great part his work, and proves his wide acquaintance with English Criminal Law. He also took great part in the work of the Committee of Public Instruction, and was chiefly instrumental in introducing English studies among the native population. But he was not popular in Calcutta. Certain changes he helped to introduce roused the feeling of the English residents against him, and he was attacked in the most scurrilous way.

In 1838 he was back in England. Meanwhile he had written two more essays for the *Edinburgh,* one on Mackintosh and one on Bacon, and he was hardly home when there appeared another, that on Sir W. Temple. After spending the winter in Italy, he reviewed in 1839 Mr. Gladstone's book on *Church and State,* and might have settled down to purely literary life, but once more he was drawn into politics. Elected as Member for Edinburgh, he was soon admitted into the Cabinet as Secretary-at-War to the Whig Ministry of Lord Melbourne. The position, however, was no gain to Macaulay. He purposed to write "*A History of England,* from the accession of King James II, down to a time which is within the memory of men still living," and his official duties forced him to lay this project aside for the present.

Fortunately Lord Melbourne's ministry did not last long; it fell in 1841, and Macaulay was released from office. Still retaining his seat for Edinburgh, and speaking occasionally in the House he was free to follow his natural bent.

His leisure hours were given as usual to essay-work for the *Edinburgh,* and he wrote in succession "Clive," "Hastings," "Frederick the Great," "Addison," "Chatham," etc. But in

1844 his connection with the *Review* came to an end, and he wrote no more for the Blue and Yellow, as it was called. In 1841 he had put forth a volume of poems—the *Lays of Ancient Rome*—not without misgivings as to the result. But the fresh and vigorous language at once carried the volume into popularity, and it had an enormous sale.

On a change of government in 1846, Macaulay, at the request of Lord John Russell, again became a Cabinet Minister, this time as Paymaster-General of the Army, and having to seek re-election from his constituents, went down to Scotland for the purpose. After a severe contest, and notwithstanding a growing unpopularity, he was successful. But at the general election of the following year the forces in opposition to him redoubled their energy, and he was defeated.

This was the real end of his political life. Although pressed to contest other seats, he resolutely declined, and for the next few years worked "doggedly" at his *History*. In 1848 appeared the first two volumes, which had an immense success, 13,000 copies being sold in less than four months. The same year he was elected Lord Rector of Glasgow University. By 1852 the people of Edinburgh had repented the rejection of their famous Member, and took steps to re-elect him free of expense; and so thoroughly was the scheme carried out that Macaulay, without having made a single speech, and without having visited the city, was returned triumphantly at the top of the poll. Through the length and breadth of the land the news was hailed with satisfaction, as an act of justice for an undeserved slight in the past. The result was very flattering to Macaulay, but he never really returned to political life as in his younger days. Moreover, forty years of incessant intellectual labors had begun to undermine his health, and he was now unequal to the fatigues that formerly were a pleasure to him. Accordingly in 1856, after having brought out the third and fourth volumes of his history, of which in a few months 25,000 copies were sold, he resigned his seat, and yielding too late obedience to all interested in his welfare, gave himself up to the enjoyment of that ease which he had faithfully earned. Then in 1857 he was created a Peer—Baron Macaulay of Rothley, his birthplace. Still struggling on with his *History* in the intermissions of his malady, he died suddenly on December 28, 1859. He was only fifty-nine—the victim of an appetite for work, insatiable and unfortunately too long ungoverned.

CRITICAL OPINIONS

"I always prophesied his greatness, from the first moment I saw him, then a very young and unknown man. There are no limits to his knowledge, on small subjects as well as great. He is like a book in breeches."—*Sydney Smith*

"His learning is prodigious; and perhaps the chief defects of his composition arise from the exuberant riches of the stores from which they are drawn. When warmed in his subject, he is thoroughly in earnest, and his language, in consequence, goes direct to the heart."—*Alison*

"The exact style, the antitheses of ideas, the harmonious construction, the artfully balanced paragraphs, the vigorous summaries, the regular sequence of thoughts, the frequent comparisons, the fine arrangement of the whole—not an idea or phrase of his writings in which the talent and the desire to explain does not shine forth."—*Taine*

"Behind the external show and glittering vesture of his thoughts—beneath all his pomp of diction, aptness of illustration, splendor of imagery, and epigrammatic point and glare—a careful eye can easily discern the movement of a powerful and cultivated intellect, as it successively appears in the well-trained logician, the discriminating critic, the comprehensive thinker, the practical and far-sighted statesman, and the student of universal literature."—*E. P. Whipple*

"Macaulay's essays, are remarkable for their brilliant rhetorical power, their splendid tone of coloring, and their affluence of illustration with a wide range of reading, and the most docile and retentive memory. He pours over his theme all the treasures of a richly-stored mind, and sheds light upon it from all quarters. He excels in the delineation of historical characters, and in the art of carrying his reader into a distant period and reproducing the past with the distinctness of the present."—*George S. Hillard*

PRINCIPAL WORKS

Macaulay excelled as a POET, ESSAYIST, ORATOR, and HISTORIAN.

As a Poet: Of the first fruits of our author's poetical genius perhaps the most admired are *The Battle of Ivry* and *The Spanish Armada*. In 1842, Macaulay gave to the world his *Lays of Ancient Rome*, consisting of the soul-stirring narrations of "Horatius Cocles," "Battle of the Lake Regillus," "Death of Virginia," and "Prophecy of Capys."

As an Essayist: Macaulay's essay on Milton, published in the *Edinburgh Review* for August, 1825, was followed by essays, in all about forty, from the same pen for nearly a score of years, articles unsurpassed in varied and accurate learning, and in fervid eloquence and brilliancy, by any composition of the kind in the English language. The following is a list of the principal essays, with the years of publication, for the most part published in the *Edinburgh Review:* "Milton," 1825; "Machiavelli," 1827; "Dryden," 1828; "History," 1828; "Hallam's Constitutional History," 1828; "Southey's Colloquies on Society," 1830; "Montgomery's Poems," 1830; "Southey's Edition of Bunyan's The Pilgrim's Progress," 1830; "Moore's Byron," 1831; "Boswell's Life of Dr. Johnson," 1831; "Nugent's Hampden," 1831; "Lord Burleigh and his Times," 1832; "Mirabeau," 1832; "War of the Spanish Succession," 1833; "Horace Walpole," 1833; "Earl of Chatham," 1834; "Sir James Mackintosh," 1835; "Lord Bacon," 1837; "Sir William Temple," 1838; "Church and State," 1839; "Lord Clive," 1840; "Ranke's History of the Popes," 1840; "Comic Dramatists of the Restoration," 1841; "Lord Holland," 1841; "Warren Hastings," October, 1841; "Frederick the Great," 1842; "Madame D'Arblay," 1843; "Joseph Addison," 1843;

"Earl of Chatham," 1844; "Barère's Memoirs," 1844; "Athenian Orators;" "Mitford's Greece," and "Mill's Essay on Government."

Biographies of Dr. Johnson, Bunyan, William Pitt, Goldsmith, and others, written for the eighth edition of the *Encyclopedia Britannica* (1857–1858), were among the latest productions of Macaulay's pen.

As an Orator: Macaulay's speeches, parliamentary and miscellaneous, number nearly one hundred, generally held to be some of the most eloquent and instructive ever delivered before the English public.

As a Historian: In 1848 appeared the first two volumes of Macaulay's *History of England*, "from the accession of King James the Second down to a time which is within the memory of men still living." The third and fourth volumes were issued in 1855. The success of these volumes was great and immediate. A fifth volume, comprising all that he left ready for the press, and bringing the work down to the end of the year 1701, was published after his death. The great work thus remains a fragment of that originally projected.

REFERENCES

For any desired information concerning Macaulay and his writings, consult, besides the ordinary reference books, Trevelyan's *Life of Macaulay*, a work of the deepest interest and full of all manner of details about the personal life of England's great historian. There is a little book by Adams, called *Life Sketches of Macaulay*, interesting from its anecdotes and sketches of Macaulay's personal career. E. P. Whipple has written one of the ablest criticisms of Macaulay's characteristics as an essayist which has ever been published. This article, from which we quote elsewhere, and for which Macaulay expressed great admiration, can be found in the first volume of Whipple's *Essays*. See also a scholarly essay by Peter Bayne; consult very full articles in *Allibone*, the *Encyclopedia Britannica*, and the numerous references in Poole's *Index to Periodical Literature*.

HISTORICAL SKETCH OF INDIA

British India includes Hindustan and several provinces on the eastern shore of the Bay of Bengal. Its extent from the great mountain barrier on the north to Cape Comorin, its southern extremity, is about 1800 miles; and from the western boundary of Scinde to Pegu, about 1900 miles. Its area is about 1,000,000 square miles, with a coast line of nearly 4500 miles; and it contains a population of about 156,000,000. The king bears the title of Emperor of India, conferred for the first time January 1, 1877. Besides the actual dependencies under direct British administration, there are the "Native States" under the protection of the British government, and acknowledging the paramount sovereignty of the crown. These include about one hundred and fifty feudatory states and principalities, containing nearly half a million square miles and about 52,000,000 inhabitants.

The Indian executive government is administered by the viceroy or governor-general appointed by the crown, and acting under the control of the secretary of state for India. The viceroy is appointed by the crown for a term of six years, and is assisted by a council of five ordinary members, three appointed by the secretary of state, two by his Majesty's warrant. Each of them has charge of a department of the executive. The commander in chief may be constituted an extraordinary member of the council. The legislative council is composed of the members of the executive, together with from six to twelve other members, one-half of whom must be unconnected with the public service. They are nominated for two years by the viceroy.

The oldest history of India is entirely legendary. It is shrouded in mythical narratives, which, though of the highest interest from a religious and archæological point of view, do not enlighten us as to the dates of the personages concerned, or as to the reality of the facts which they record.

The Sultan Mahmud, sovereign of the small state of Ghizni, was the first conqueror who permanently established the Mohammedan power in India. In 1186 the House of Ghizni became extinct, and the Hindu princes fell one by one before a succession of Mohammedan dynasties, whose names and dates are as follows:

Slave Kings of Delhi (1206–1288). One of these sovereigns, Altmish, who ascended the throne in 1211, added the greater part of Hindustan proper to his dominions, and in his reign the Mongol Genghis Khan devastated the northeastern parts of India. In Balin's reign the Mongols made a second irruption into Hindustan, but were totally defeated by the monarch's eldest son, the heroic Mohammed, who fell in the action.

The Khiljis and House of Toghlak (1288–1412). In 1290, the Mongols made their third and last great irruption into Hindustan, but were almost annihilated by Zafir Khan, whose name became so proverbial among the Mongols that when their horses started they would ask them if they saw the ghost of Zafir Khan. In 1397, during the reign of the last of the Toghlak kings, the Tartar Timur, or Tamerlane, sacked Delhi, and proclaimed himself emperor of India.

The Syuds (1412–1450). The House of Lodi (1450–1526). To the kings of this dynasty succeeded the Great Moguls or House of Timur (1526–1707).

Baber, who had for twenty-two years been sovereign of Cabul, invaded India, for the fifth time, towards the end of the year 1525, and after doing battle with Sultan Ibrahim on the plain of Paniput, April, 1526, entered Delhi in triumph, and established himself as emperor of the Mohammedan dominions in India, in right of his ancestor Timur. He died in 1530, and was succeeded by his son Humayun. The celebrated Akbar, son of Humayun, became emperor in 1556, and reigned for nearly twenty-five years. His son ascended the throne in 1605, and his grandson, Shah Jehan, in 1627. In 1658 Shah Jehan was imprisoned by his son, the famous Aurungzebe, who usurped the imperial power. This remarkable man raised the Mogul empire to the highest pitch of greatness and splendor; and was the ablest and most powerful, as well as the most ambitious and bigoted, of his race. The death of Aurungzebe took place in 1707, and the decay of the empire, which had begun a few years before then, proceeded rapidly.

A succession of nominal sovereigns, sunk in indolence and debauchery, sauntered away life in secluded palaces. Viceroys of the Great Mogul formed their provinces into independent states; whilst Hindu and Mohammedan adventurers carved out kingdoms with the sword. The dismemberment of the Mogul empire opened a wide field for ambition and enterprise to the nations of Europe. The Venetians, the Genoese, the Portuguese, and the Dutch had by turns traded with India; and in 1602 the English appeared on the scene.

In 1653 Madras was raised into a presidency, and in 1668 the Island of Bombay—which was the dowry of Charles II's queen, the Infanta Catherine of Portugal—was transferred by the crown to the East India Company. The invasion of the Persian, Nadir Shah, in 1738, who sacked Delhi, slaughtered its inhabitants, and carried away the Peacock Throne and vast treasure, hastened the fall of the Mogul empire.

Great jealousy existed between the English and French, who also had established themselves in India. On the declaration of war between England and France, hostilities commenced in the Madras presidency, nor were they terminated by the peace of Aix-la-Chapelle in 1748. The struggle in the Carnatic was continued with ardor, under pretext of supporting the claims of rival native princes to sovereignty. Clive, the first and most famous name on that great muster-roll of British soldiers and statesmen who have thrown such luster on the British occupation of India, laid the foundation of his country's supremacy in the East. His memorable defense of Arcot in 1751, and his subsequent victories. broke the spell of French invincibility. For a more detailed account of Clive's conduct in India the student is referred to the following historic Essay by Macaulay.

PEOPLES OF INDIA

At the time of the formation of the East India Company India was already inhabited by two contending peoples—the Hindus and the Mohammedans. The Hindus comprised first of all the aboriginal peoples,—Bhils, Gurkhas, Hill-men as they are called to-day,—the original owners of the land, as shown by the fact that even yet, when some of the native princes are vested with the government of their principality, the ceremony is not complete until sealed by a mark made in blood drawn from the veins of a Bhil. Next came the Aryan Hindus, the people of culture, possessing one of the best civilizations in the world. Finally there was added, in the early days of the Christian Era, the Scythian element, the last to be absorbed in the Hindu race. After the rise of Mohammed's power in Arabia, and its check on the field of Tours, the Mohammedan hordes invaded India, and after long wars established there a Mohammedan state; allied finally with the Tartar Moguls, whose power lasted until the death of Arungzebe, although the title of Mogul emperor did not become extinct until the death of Mohammed Bahadin Shah in 1857.

REFERENCES ON INDIA

Hunter. *Brief History of Indian Peoples* (Rulers of India Series), —Clive, Hastings, Dupleix.

Plimblett. *How the British Won India.*

McCarthy. *History of Our Own Times.*

J. R. Greene. *Short History of English People.*

LORD CLIVE

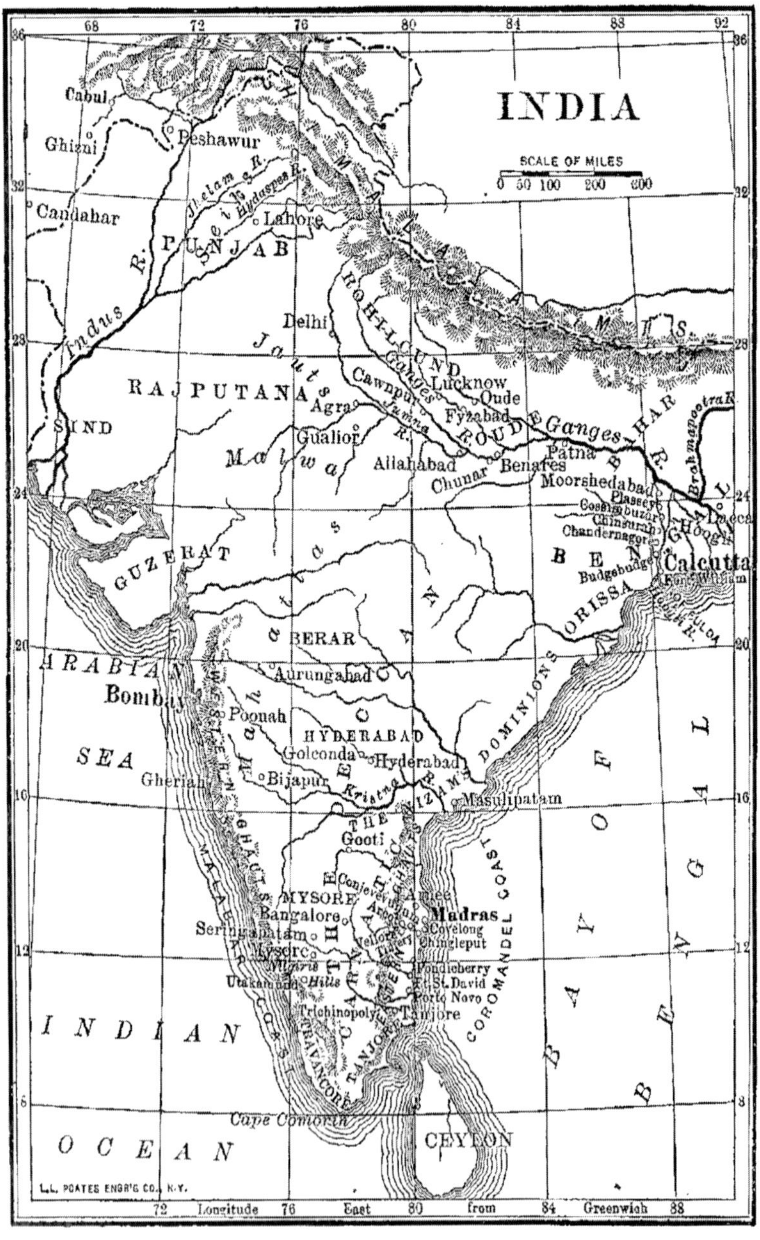

INDIA
SCALE OF MILES
0 50 100 200 300
Cabul
Ghizni
Peshawur
Candahar
Jhelam R.
Hydaspes R.
Lahore
PUNJAB
Indus R.
Delhi
ROHILCUND
Lucknow
Oude
Cawnpur
Ganges
Jumna R.
Agra
RAJPUTANA
SIND
Gualior
Malwa
Allahabad
Fyzabad
OUDE
Ganges
Patna
Benares
Chunar
BAHAR
Brahmapootra R.
Moorshedabad
Plassey
Chinsurah
Chandernagore
Hoogly
Dacca
Calcutta
Fort William
Budgebudge
BENGAL
ORISSA
GUZERAT
BERAR
ARABIAN
SEA
Bombay
Aurungabad
Poonah
HYDERABAD
Golconda
Hyderabad
Bijapur
Gheriah
Kristna R.
Masulipatam
DOMINIONS
THE NIZAM
THE DECCAN
Gooti
MYSORE
Arnee
Madras
Bangalore
Seringapatam
Mysore
Covelong
Chingleput
Nilgiris Hills
Utakamund
Pondicherry
Ft. St. David
Porto Novo
Trichinopoly
Tanjore
TANJORE
TRAVANCORE
MALABAR COAST
COROMANDEL COAST
CARNATIC
BAY OF BENGAL
INDIAN OCEAN
Cape Comorin
CEYLON
L.L. POATES ENGR'G CO. N.Y.
Longitude East from Greenwich

LORD CLIVE

We have always thought it strange, that while the history of the Spanish empire in America is familiarly known to all the nations of Europe, the great actions of our countrymen in the East should, even among ourselves, excite little interest. Every schoolboy knows[1] who imprisoned Montezuma,[2] and who strangled Atahualpa. But we doubt whether one in ten, even among English gentlemen of highly cultivated minds, can tell who won the battle of Buxar,[3] who perpetrated the massacre of Patna,[4] whether Surajah Dowlah[5] ruled in Oude or in Travancore, or whether Holkar[6] was a Hindoo or a Mussulman. Yet the victories of Cortes were gained over savages[7] who had no letters, who were ignorant of the use of metals, who had not broken in a single animal to labor, who wielded no better weapons than those which could be made out of sticks, flints, and fish-bones, who regarded a horse-soldier as a monster half man and half beast, who took a harquebusier[8] for a sorcerer, able to scatter the thunder and lightning of the skies. The people of India, when we subdued them, were ten times as numerous as the Americans whom the Spaniards vanquished, and were at the same time quite as highly civilized as the victorious Spaniards. They had reared cities larger and fairer than Saragossa or Toledo, and buildings more beautiful[1] and costly than the cathedral of Seville. They could show bankers richer than the richest firms of Barcelona or Cadiz, viceroys whose splendor far surpassed that of Ferdinand the Catholic,[2] myriads of cavalry and long trains of artillery which would have astonished the Great Captain.[3] It might have been expected that every Englishman who takes any interest in any part of history would be curious to know how a handful of his countrymen, separated from their home by an immense ocean, subjugated, in the course of a few years, one of the greatest empires in the world.[4] Yet, unless we greatly err, this subject is to most readers, not only insipid, but positively distasteful.

Perhaps the fault lies partly with the historians. Mr. Mill's book,[5] though it has undoubtedly great and rare merit, is not sufficiently animated and picturesque to attract those who read for amusement. Orme,[6] inferior to no English historian in style and power of painting, is minute even to tediousness. In one volume he allots, on an average, a closely printed quarto page to the events of every forty-eight hours. The consequence is, that his narrative, though one of the most authentic, and one of the most finely written in our language, has never been very popular, and is now scarcely ever read.

We fear that the volumes before us will not much attract those readers whom Orme and Mill have repelled. The materials placed at the disposal of Sir John Malcolm by the late Lord Powis[7] were indeed of great value. But we cannot say that they have been very skilfully worked up. It would, however, be unjust to criticise with severity a work which, if the author had lived to complete and revise it, would probably have been improved by condensation and by a better arrangement. We are the more disposed to perform the pleasing duty of expressing our gratitude to the noble family to which the public owes so much useful and curious information.

The effect of the book, even when we make the largest allowance for the partiality of those who have furnished and of those who have digested the materials, is, on the whole, greatly to raise the character of Lord Clive. We are far indeed from sympathizing with Sir John Malcolm, whose love passes the love of biographers,[1] and who can see nothing but wisdom and justice in the actions of his idol. But we are at least equally far from concurring in the severe judgment of Mr. Mill, who seems to us to show less discrimination in his account of Clive than in any other part of his valuable work. Clive, like most men who are born with strong passions and tried by strong temptations, committed great faults. But every person who takes a fair and enlightened view of his whole career must admit that our island, so fertile in heroes and statesmen, has scarcely ever produced a man more truly great either in arms or in council.

The Clives had been settled, ever since the twelfth century, on an estate of no great value, near Market-Drayton in Shropshire. In the reign of George the

First this moderate but ancient inheritance was possessed by Mr. Richard Clive, who seems to have been a plain man of no great tact or capacity. He had been bred to the law, and divided his time between professional business and the avocations of a small proprietor. He married a lady from Manchester, of the name of Gaskill, and became the father of a very numerous family. His eldest son, Robert, the founder of the British empire in India, was born at the old seat of his ancestors,[1] on the twenty-ninth of September, 1725.

Some lineaments of the character of the man were early discerned in the child. There remain letters written by his relations when he was in his seventh year; and from these letters it appears that, even at that early age, his strong will and his fiery passions, sustained by a constitutional intrepidity which sometimes seemed hardly compatible with soundness of mind, had begun to cause great uneasiness to his family. "Fighting," says one of his uncles,[2] "to which he is out of measure addicted, gives his temper such a fierceness and imperiousness, that he flies out on every trifling occasion." The old people of the neighborhood still remember to have heard from their parents how Bob Clive climbed to the top of the lofty steeple of Market-Drayton, and with what terror the inhabitants saw him seated on a stone spout near the summit. They also relate how he formed all the idle lads of the town into a kind of predatory army, and compelled the shop-keepers to submit to a tribute of apples and halfpence, in consideration of which he guaranteed the security of their windows. He was sent from school to school,[1] making very little progress in his learning, and gaining for himself everywhere the character of an exceedingly naughty boy. One of his masters, it is said, was sagacious enough to prophesy that the idle lad would make a great figure in the world. But the general opinion seems to have been that poor Robert was a dunce, if not a reprobate. His family expected nothing good from such slender parts and such a headstrong temper. It is not strange, therefore, that they gladly accepted for him, when he was in his eighteenth year, a writership [2] in the service of the East India Company, and shipped him off to make a fortune or to die of a fever at Madras.

Far different were the prospects of Clive from those of the youths whom the East India College [3] now annually sends to the Presidencies of our Asiatic empire. The Company was then purely a trading corporation. Its territory consisted of a few square miles, for which rent was paid to the native governments. Its troops were scarcely numerous enough to man the batteries of three or four ill-constructed forts, which had been erected for the protection of the warehouses. The natives, who composed a considerable part of these little garrisons, had not yet been trained in the discipline of Europe, and were armed, some with swords and shields, some with bows and arrows. The business of the servant of the Company was not, as now, to conduct the judicial, financial, and diplomatic business of a great country, but to take stock, to make advances to weavers, to ship cargoes, and, above all, to keep an eye on private traders who dared to infringe the monopoly. The younger clerks were so miserably paid that they could scarcely subsist without incurring debt; the elder enriched themselves by trading on their own account; and those who lived to rise to the top of the service often accumulated considerable fortunes.

Madras, to which Clive had been appointed, was, at this time, perhaps, the first in importance of the Company's settlements. In the preceding century Fort St. George had risen on a barren spot beaten by a raging surf; and in the neighborhood a town, inhabited by many thousands of natives, had sprung up, as towns spring up in the East, with the rapidity of the prophet's gourd.[1] There were already in the suburbs many white villas, each surrounded by its garden, whither the wealthy agents of the Company retired, after the labors of the desk and the warehouse, to enjoy the cool breeze which springs up at sunset from the Bay of Bengal. The habits of these mercantile grandees appear to have been more profuse, luxurious, and ostentatious, than those of the high judicial and political functionaries who have succeeded them. But comfort was far less understood. Many devices which now mitigate the heat of the climate, preserve health, and prolong life, were unknown. There was far less intercourse with Europe than at present. The voyage by the Cape, which in our time has often been performed within three months, was then very seldom accomplished in six, and sometimes protracted to more than a year.

Consequently, the Anglo-Indian was then much more estranged from his country, much more addicted to Oriental usages, and much less fitted to mix in society after his return to Europe, than the Anglo-Indian of the present day.

Within the fort and its precincts, the English exercised, by permission of the native government, an extensive authority, such as every great Indian landowner exercised within his own domain. But they had never dreamed of claiming independent power. The surrounding country was ruled by the Nabob of the Carnatic, a deputy of the Viceroy of the Deccan,[1] commonly called the Nizam, who was himself only a deputy of the mighty prince designated by our ancestors as the Great Mogul. Those names, once so august and formidable, still remain. There is still a Nabob [2] of the Carnatic, who lives on a pension allowed to him by the English out of the revenues of the province which his ancestors ruled. There is still a Nizam, whose capital is overawed by a British cantonment, and to whom a British resident gives, under the name of advice, commands which are not to be disputed. There is still a Mogul, who is permitted to play at holding courts, and receiving petitions, but who has less power to help or hurt than the youngest civil servant of the Company.

Clive's voyage was unusually tedious even for that age. The ship remained some months at the Brazils, where the young adventurer picked up some knowledge of Portuguese, and spent all his pocket-money. He did not arrive in India till more than a year after he had left England. His situation at Madras was most painful. His funds were exhausted. His pay was small. He had contracted debts. He was wretchedly lodged, no small calamity in a climate which can be made tolerable to an European only by spacious and well-placed apartments. He had been furnished with letters of recommendation to a gentleman who might have assisted him; but when he landed at Fort St. George he found that this gentleman had sailed for England. The lad's shy and haughty disposition withheld him from introducing himself to strangers. He was several months in India before he became acquainted with a single family. The climate affected his health and spirits. His duties were of a kind ill suited to his ardent and daring character. He pined for his home, and in his letters to his relations expressed his feelings in language softer and more pensive than we should have expected either from the waywardness of his boyhood, or from the inflexible sternness of his later years. "I have not enjoyed," says he, "one happy day since I left my native country;" and again, "I must confess, at intervals, when I think of my dear native England, it affects me in a very particular manner. . . . If I should be so far blest as to revisit again my own country, but more especially Manchester, the centre of all my wishes, all that I could hope or desire for would be presented before me in one view."

One solace he found of the most respectable kind. The Governor possessed a good library, and permitted

Clive to have access to it. The young man devoted much of his leisure to reading, and acquired at this time almost all the knowledge of books that he ever possessed. As a boy he had been too idle, as a man he soon became too busy, for literary pursuits.

But neither climate nor poverty, neither studies nor the sorrows of a home-sick exile, could tame the desperate audacity of his spirit. He behaved to his official superiors as he had behaved to his schoolmasters, and was several times in danger of losing his situation. Twice, while residing in the Writers' Buildings, he attempted to destroy himself; and twice the pistol which he snapped at his own head failed to go off. This circumstance, it is said, affected him as a similar escape affected Wallenstein.[1] After satisfying himself that the pistol was really well loaded, he burst forth into an exclamation that surely he was reserved for something great.

About this time an event which at first seemed likely to destroy all his hopes in life suddenly opened before him a new path to eminence. Europe had been, during some years, distracted by the war of the Austrian Succession.[2] George the Second was the steady ally of Maria Theresa. The house of Bourbon took the opposite side. Though England was even then the first of maritime powers, she was not, as she has since become, more than a match on the sea for all the nations of the world together; and she found it difficult to maintain a contest against the united navies of France and Spain. In the eastern seas France obtained the ascendency. Labourdonnais,[1] governor of Mauritius, a man of eminent talents and virtues, conducted an expedition to the continent of India in spite of the opposition of the British fleet, landed, assembled an army, appeared before Madras, and compelled the town and fort to capitulate. The keys were delivered up; the French colors were displayed on Fort St. George; and the contents of the Company's warehouses were seized as prize of war by the conquerors. It was stipulated by the capitulation that the English inhabitants should be prisoners of war on parole, and that the town should remain in the hands of the French till it should be ransomed. Labourdonnais pledged his honor that only a moderate ransom should be required.

But the success of Labourdonnais had awakened the jealousy of his countryman, Dupleix,[2] governor of Pondicherry. Dupleix, moreover, had already begun to revolve gigantic schemes, with which the restoration of Madras to the English was by no means compatible. He declared that Labourdonnais had gone beyond his powers; that conquests made by the French arms on the continent of India were at the disposal of the governor of Pondicherry alone, and that Madras should be razed to the ground. Labourdonnais was compelled to yield. The anger which the breach of the capitulation excited among the English, was increased by the ungenerous manner in which Dupleix treated the principal servants of the Company. The Governor and several of the first gentlemen of Fort St. George were carried under a guard to Pondicherry, and conducted through the town in a triumphal procession, under the eyes of fifty thousand spectators. It was with reason thought that this gross violation of public faith absolved the inhabitants of Madras from the engagements into which they had entered with Labourdonnais. Clive fled from the town by night in the disguise of a Mussulman, and took refuge at Fort St. David, one of the small English settlements subordinate to Madras.

The circumstances in which he was now placed naturally led him to adopt a profession better suited to his restless and intrepid spirit than the business of examining packages and casting áccounts. He solicited and obtained an ensign's commission in the service of the Company, and at twenty-one entered on his military career. His personal courage, of which he had, while still a writer, given signal proof by a desperate duel with a military bully, who was the terror of Fort St. David, speedily made him conspicuous even among hundreds of brave men. He soon began to show in his new calling other qualities which had not before been discerned in him,—judgment, sagacity, deference to legitimate authority. He distinguished himself highly in several operations against the French, and was particularly noticed by Major Lawrence,[1] who was then considered as the ablest British officer in India.

Clive had been only a few months in the army when intelligence arrived that peace [2] had been concluded between Great Britain and France. Dupleix was in consequence compelled to restore Madras to the English Company; and the young ensign was at liberty to resume his former business. He did indeed return for a short time to his desk. He again quitted it in order to assist Major Lawrence in some petty hostilities with the natives, and then again returned to it. While he was thus wavering between a military and a commercial life, events took place which decided his choice. The politics of India assumed a new aspect. There was peace between the English and French Crowns; but there arose between the English and French Companies trading to the East a war most eventful and important, a war in which the prize was nothing less than the magnificent inheritance of the house of Tamerlane.

The empire which Baber and his Moguls reared in the sixteenth century was long one of the most extensive and splendid in the world. In no European kingdom was so large a population subject to a single prince, or so large a revenue poured into the Treasury. The beauty and magnificence of the buildings [1] erected by the sovereigns of Hindostan amazed even travellers who had seen St. Peter's. The innumerable retinues and gorgeous decorations which surrounded the throne of Delhi dazzled even eyes which were accustomed to the pomp of Versailles. Some of the great viceroys who held their posts by virtue of commissions from the Mogul ruled as many subjects as the King of France or the Emperor of Germany. Even the deputies of these deputies might well rank, as to extent of territory and amount of revenue, with the Grand Duke of Tuscany or the Elector of Saxony.

There can be little doubt that this great empire,

powerful and prosperous as it appears on a superficial view, was yet, even in its best days, far worse governed than the worst governed parts of Europe now are. The administration was tainted with all the vices of Oriental despotism, and with all the vices inseparable from the domination of race over race. The conflicting pretensions of the princes of the royal house produced a long series of crimes and public disasters. Ambitious lieutenants of the sovereign sometimes aspired to independence. Fierce tribes of Hindoos, impatient of a foreign yoke, frequently withheld tribute, repelled the armies of the government from the mountain fastnesses, and poured down in arms on the cultivated plains. In spite, however, of much constant maladministration, in spite of occasional convulsions which shook the whole frame of society, this great monarchy, on the whole, retained, during some generations, an outward appearance of unity, majesty, and energy. But, throughout the long reign of Aurungzebe,[1] the state, notwithstanding all that the vigor and policy of the prince could effect, was hastening to dissolution. After his death, which took place in the year 1707, the ruin was fearfully rapid. Violent shocks from without co-operated with an incurable decay which was fast proceeding within; and in a few years the empire had undergone utter decomposition.

The history of the successors of Theodosius [2] bears no small analogy to that of the successors of Aurungzebe. But perhaps the fall of the Carlovingians [3] furnishes the nearest parallel to the fall of the Moguls.

Charlemagne was scarcely interred when the imbecility and the disputes of his descendants began to bring contempt on themselves and destruction on their subjects. The wide dominion of the Franks was severed into a thousand pieces. Nothing more than a nominal dignity was left to the abject heirs of an illustrious name, Charles the Bald, and Charles the Fat, and Charles the Simple. Fierce invaders, differing from each other in race, language, and religion, flocked, as if by concert, from the farthest corners of the earth, to plunder provinces which the government could no longer defend. The pirates of the Northern Sea [1] extended their ravages from the Elbe to the Pyrenees, and at length fixed their seat in the rich valley of the Seine. The Hungarian,[2] in whom the trembling monks fancied that they recognized the Gog or Magog of prophecy, carried back the plunder of the cities of Lombardy to the depths of the Pannonian forests. The Saracen ruled in Sicily, desolated the fertile plains of Campania,[3] and spread terror even to the walls of Rome. In the midst of these sufferings, a great internal change passed upon the empire. The corruption of death began to ferment into new forms of life. While the great body, as a whole, was torpid and passive, every separate member began to feel with a sense, and to move with an energy all its own. Just here, in the most barren and dreary tract of European history, all feudal privileges, all modern nobility, take their source. It is to this point that we trace the power of those princes who, nominally vassals, but really independent, long governed, with the titles of dukes, marquesses, and counts, almost every part of the dominions which had obeyed Charlemagne.

Such or nearly such was the change which passed on the Mogul empire during the forty years which followed the death of Aurungzebe. A succession of nominal sovereigns, sunk in indolence and debauchery, sauntered away life in secluded palaces, chewing bang,[1] fondling concubines, and listening to buffoons. A succession of ferocious invaders descended through the western passes, to prey on the defenceless wealth of Hindostan. A Persian conqueror [2] crossed the Indus, marched through the gates of Delhi, and bore away in triumph those treasures of which the magnificence had astounded Roe and Bernier, the Peacock Throne, on which the richest jewels of Golconda had been disposed by the most skilful hands of Europe, and the inestimable Mountain of Light, which, after many strange vicissitudes, lately shone in the bracelet of Runjeet Sing, and is now destined to adorn the hideous idol of Orissa. The Afghan soon followed to complete the work of devastation which the Persian had begun. The warlike tribes of Rajpootana threw off the Mussulman yoke. A band of mercenary soldiers occupied Rohilcund. The Seiks ruled on the Indus. The Jauts spread dismay along the Jumna. The highlands which border on the western sea-coast of India poured forth a yet more formidable race, a race which was long the terror of every native power, and which, after many desperate and doubtful struggles, yielded only to the fortune and genius of England. It was under the reign of Aurungzebe that this wild clan of plunderers first descended from their mountains; and soon after his death, every corner of his wide empire learned to tremble at the mighty name of the Mahrattas.[1] Many fertile viceroyalties were entirely subdued by them. Their dominions stretched across the peninsula from sea to sea. Mahratta captains reigned at Poonah, at Gualior, in Guzerat, in Berar, and in Tanjore. Nor did they, though they had become great sovereigns, therefore cease to be freebooters. They still retained the predatory habits of their forefathers. Every region which was not subject to their rule was wasted by their incursions. Wherever their kettledrums were heard, the peasant threw his bag of rice on his shoulder, hid his small savings in his girdle, and fled with his wife and children to the mountains or the jungles, to the milder neighborhood of the hyena and the tiger. Many provinces redeemed their harvests [2] by the payment of an annual ransom. Even the wretched phantom who still bore the imperial title stooped to pay this ignominious blackmail. The camp-fires of one rapacious leader were seen from the walls of the palace of Delhi. Another, at the head of his innumerable cavalry, descended year after year on the rice-fields of Bengal. Even the European factors trembled for their magazines. Less than a hundred years ago, it was thought necessary to fortify Calcutta against the horsemen of Berar, and the name of the Mahratta ditch [3] still preserves the memory of the danger.

Wherever the viceroys of the Mogul retained authority they became sovereigns. They might still acknowledge in words the superiority of the house of Tamerlane; as a Count of Flanders or a Duke of. Burgundy might have acknowledged the superiority of the most helpless driveller among the later Carlovingians. They might occasionally send to their titular sovereign a complimentary present, or solicit from him a title of honor. In truth, however, they were no longer lieutenants removable at pleasure, but independent hereditary princes. In this way originated those great Mussulman houses which formerly ruled Bengal and the Carnatic, and those which still, though in a state of vassalage, exercise some of the powers of royalty at Lucknow and Hyderabad.

In what was this confusion to end? Was the strife to continue during centuries? Was it to terminate in the rise of another great monarchy? Was the Mussulman or the Mahratta to be the Lord of India? Was another Baber to descend from the mountains, and to lead the hardy tribes of Cabul and Chorasan against a wealthier and less warlike race? None of these events seemed improbable. But scarcely any man, however sagacious, would have thought it possible that a trading company, separated from India by fifteen thousand miles of sea, and possessing in India only a few acres for purposes of commerce, would, in less than a hundred years, spread its empire from Cape Comorin to the eternal snow of the Himalayas; would compel Mahratta and Mohammedan to forget their mutual feuds in common subjection; would tame down even those wild races which had resisted the most powerful of the Moguls; and having united under its laws a hundred millions of subjects, would carry its victorious arms far to the east of the Burrampooter,[1] and far to the west of the Hydaspes, dictate terms of peace at the gates of Ava,[2] and seat its vassal on the throne of Candahar.

The man who first saw that it was possible to found an European empire on the ruins of the Mogul monarchy was Dupleix. His restless, capacious, and inventive mind had formed this scheme, at a time when the ablest servants of the English Company were busied only about invoices and bills of lading. Nor had he only proposed to himself the end. He had also a just and distinct view of the means by which it was to be attained. He clearly saw that the greatest force which the princes of India could bring into the field would be no match for a small body of men trained in the discipline, and guided by the tactics, of the West. He saw also that the natives of India might, under European commanders, be formed into armies, such as Saxe or Frederic[3] would be proud to command. He was perfectly aware that the most easy and convenient way in which an European adventurer could exercise sovereignty in India, was to govern the motions, and to speak through the mouth of some glittering puppet dignified by the title of Nabob or Nizam. The arts both of war and policy which a few years later were employed with such signal success by the English were first understood and practised by this ingenious and aspiring Frenchman.

The situation of India was such that scarcely any aggression could be without a pretext either in the old laws or in recent practice. All rights were in a state of utter uncertainty; and the Europeans who took part in the disputes of the natives confounded the confusion, by applying to Asiatic politics the public law of the West, and analogies drawn from the feudal system. If it was convenient to treat a Nabob as an independent prince, there was an excellent plea for doing so. He was independent in fact. If it was convenient to treat him as a mere deputy of the Court of Delhi, there was no difficulty; for he was so in theory. If it was convenient to consider his office as an hereditary dignity, or as a dignity held during life only, or as a dignity held only during the good pleasure of the Mogul, arguments and precedents might be found for every one of those views. The party who had the heir of Baber in their hands represented him as the undoubted, the legitimate, the absolute sovereign, whom all subordinate authorities were bound to obey. The party against whom his name was used did not want plausible pretexts for maintaining that the empire was in fact dissolved; and that, though it might be decent to treat the Mogul with respect, as a venerable relic of an order of things which had passed away, it was absurd to regard him as the real master of Hindostan.

In the year 1748, died one of the most powerful of the new masters of India, the great Nizam al Mulk,[1] Viceroy of the Deccan. His authority descended to his son, Nazir Jung. Of the provinces subject to this high functionary, the Carnatic was the wealthiest and the most extensive. It was governed by an ancient Nabob, whose name the English corrupted into Anaverdy Khan.

But there were pretenders to the government both of the viceroyalty and of the subordinate province. Mirzapha Jung, a grandson of Nizam al Mulk, appeared as the competitor of Nazir Jung. Chunda Sahib, son-in-law of a former Nabob of the Carnatic, disputed the title of Anaverdy Khan.[1] In the unsettled state of Indian law, it was easy for both Mirzapha Jung and Chunda Sahib to make out something like a claim of right. In a society altogether disorganized, they had no difficulty in finding greedy adventurers to follow their standards. They united their interests, invaded the Carnatic, and applied for assistance to the French, whose fame had been raised by their success against the English in the recent war on the coast of Coromandel.

Nothing could have happened more pleasing to the subtle and ambitious Dupleix. To make a Nabob of the Carnatic, to make a Viceroy of the Deccan, to rule under their names the whole of southern India; this was indeed an attractive prospect. He allied himself with the pretenders, and sent four hundred French soldiers, and two thousand sepoys,[2] disciplined after the European fashion, to the assistance of his confederates. A battle was fought. The French distinguished themselves greatly. Anaverdy Khan was defeated and slain. His son, Mohammed Ali, who was afterwards well known in England as the Nabob of Arcot, and who owes to the eloquence of Burke[3] a most unenviable immortality, fled with a scanty remnant of his army to Trichinopoly; and the conquerors became at once masters of almost every part of the Carnatic.

This was but the beginning of the greatness of Dupleix. After some months of fighting, negotiations, and intrigue, his ability and good fortune seemed to have prevailed everywhere. Nazir Jung perished by the hands of his own followers; Mirzapha Jung was master of the Deccan; and the triumph of French arms and French policy was complete. At Pondicherry all was exultation and festivity. Salutes were fired from the batteries, and *Te Deum* sung in the churches. The new Nizam came thither to visit his allies; and the ceremony of his installation was performed there with great pomp. Dupleix, dressed in the garb worn by Mohammedans of the highest rank, entered the town in the same palanquin with the Nizam, and, in the pageant which followed, took precedence of all the court. He was declared Governor of India from the river Kristna to Cape Comorin, a country about as large as France, with authority superior even to that of Chunda Sahib. He was intrusted with the command of seven thousand cavalry. It was announced that no mint would be suffered to exist in the Carnatic except that at Pondicherry. A large portion of the treasures which former Viceroys of the Deccan had accumulated found its way into the coffers of the French governor. It was rumored that he had received two hundred thousand pounds sterling in money, besides many valuable jewels. In fact, there could scarcely be any limit to his gains. He now ruled thirty millions of people with almost absolute power. No honor or emolument could be obtained from the government but by his intervention. No petition, unless signed by him, was perused by the Nizam.

Mirzapha Jung [1] survived his elevation only a few months. But another prince of the same house was raised to the throne by French influence, and ratified all the promises of his predecessor. Dupleix was now the greatest potentate in India. His countrymen boasted that his name was mentioned with awe even in the chambers of the palace of Delhi. The native population looked with amazement on the progress which, in the short space of four years, an European adventurer had made towards dominion in Asia. Nor was the vainglorious Frenchman content with the reality of power. He loved to display his greatness with arrogant ostentation before the eyes of his subjects and of his rivals. Near the spot where his policy had obtained its chief triumph, by the fall of Nazir Jung and the elevation of Mirzapha, he determined to erect a column, on the four sides of which four pompous inscriptions, in four languages, should proclaim his glory to all the nations of the East. Medals stamped with emblems of his successes were buried beneath the foundations of this stately pillar, and round it arose a town bearing the haughty name of Dupleix Fatihabad, which is, being interpreted, the City of the Victory of Dupleix.

The English had made some feeble and irresolute

attempts to stop the rapid and brilliant career of the rival Company, and continued to recognize Mohammed Ali as Nabob of the Carnatic. But the dominions of Mohammed Ali consisted of Trichinopoly alone; and Trichinopoly was now invested by Chunda Sahib and his French auxiliaries. To raise the siege seemed impossible. The small force which was then at Madras had no commander. Major Lawrence had returned to England, and not a single officer of established character remained in the settlement. The natives had learned to look with contempt on the mighty nation which was soon to conquer and to rule them. They had seen the French colors flying on Fort St. George; they had seen the chiefs of the English factory led in triumph through the streets of Pondicherry; they had seen the arms and counsels of Dupleix everywhere successful, while the opposition which the authorities of Madras had made to his progress had served only to expose their own weakness and to heighten his glory. At this moment the valor and genius of an obscure English youth suddenly turned the tide of fortune.

Clive was now twenty-five years old. After hesitating for some time between a military and a commercial life, he had at length been placed in a post which partook of both characters,—that of commissary to the troops, with the rank of captain. The present emergency called forth all his powers. He represented to his superiors that unless some vigorous effort were made, Trichinopoly would fall, the house of Anaverdy Khan would perish, and the French would become the real masters of the whole peninsula of India. It was absolutely necessary to strike some daring blow. If an attack were made on Arcot, the capital of the Carnatic and the favorite residence of the Nabobs, it was not impossible that the siege of Trichinopoly would be raised. The heads of the English settlement, now thoroughly alarmed by the success of Dupleix, and apprehensive that, in the event of a new war between France and Great Britain, Madras would be instantly taken and destroyed, approved of Clive's plan, and intrusted the execution of it to himself. The young captain was put at the head of two hundred English soldiers, and three hundred sepoys, armed and disciplined after the European fashion. Of the eight officers who commanded this little force under him only two had ever been in action, and four of the eight were factors of the Company, whom Clive's example had induced to offer their services. The weather was stormy, but Clive pushed on, through thunder, lightning, and rain, to the gates of Arcot. The garrison, in a panic, evacuated the fort, and the English entered it without a blow.

But Clive well knew that he should not be suffered to retain undisturbed possession of his conquest. He instantly began to collect provisions, to throw up works, and to make preparations for sustaining a siege. The garrison, which had fled at his approach, had now recovered from its dismay; and, having been swollen by large reinforcements from the neighborhood to a force of three thousand men, encamped close to the town.

At dead of night, Clive marched out of the fort, attacked the camp by surprise, slew great numbers, dispersed the rest, and returned to his quarters without having lost a single man.

The intelligence of these events was soon carried to Chunda Sahib, who, with his French allies, was besieging Trichinopoly. He immediately detached four thousand men from his camp, and sent them to Arcot. They were speedily joined by the remains of the force which Clive had lately scattered. They were further strengthened by two thousand men from Vellore, and by a still more important reinforcement of a hundred and fifty French soldiers whom Dupleix despatched from Pondicherry. The whole of this army, amounting to about ten thousand men, was under the command of Rajah Sahib, son of Chunda Sahib.

Rajah Sahib proceeded to invest the fort of Arcot, which seemed quite incapable of sustaining a siege. The walls were ruinous, the ditches dry, the ramparts too narrow to admit the guns, the battlements too low to protect the soldiers. The little garrison had been greatly reduced by casualties. It now consisted of a hundred and twenty Europeans and two hundred sepoys. Only four officers were left; the stock of provisions was scanty; and the commander, who had to conduct the defence under circumstances so discouraging, was a young man of five and twenty, who had been bred a book-keeper.

During fifty days the siege went on. During fifty days the young captain maintained the defence with a firmness, vigilance, and ability, which would have done honor to the oldest marshal in Europe. The breach, however, increased day by day. The garrison began to feel the pressure of hunger. Under such circumstances, any troops so scantily provided with officers might have been expected to show signs of insubordination; and the danger was peculiarly great in a force composed of men differing widely from each other in extraction, color, language, manners, and religion. But the devotion of the little band to its chief surpassed anything that is related of the Tenth Legion of Cæsar,[1] or of the Old Guard of Napoleon.[2] The sepoys came to Clive, not to complain of their scanty fare, but to propose that all the grain should be given to the Europeans, who required more nourishment than the natives of Asia. The thin gruel, they said, which was strained away from the rice, would suffice for themselves. History contains no more touching instance of military fidelity, or of the influence of a commanding mind.

An attempt made by the government of Madras to relieve the place had failed. But there was hope from another quarter. A body of six thousand Mahrattas, half soldiers, half robbers, under the command of a chief named Morari Row, had been hired to assist Mohammed Ali; but thinking the French power irresistible, and the triumph of Chunda Sahib certain, they had hitherto remained inactive on the frontiers of the Carnatic. The fame of the defence of Arcot roused them from their torpor. Morari Row declared that he had never before believed that Englishmen could fight, but that he would willingly help them since he saw that they had spirit to help themselves. Rajah Sahib learned that the Mahrattas were in motion. It was necessary for him to be expeditious. He first tried negotiation. He offered large bribes to Clive, which were rejected with scorn. He vowed that, if his proposals were not accepted, he would instantly storm the fort, and put every man in it to the sword. Clive told him in reply, with characteristic haughtiness, that his father was an usurper, that his army was a rabble, and that he would do well to think twice before he sent such poltroons into a breach defended by English soldiers.

Rajah Sahib determined to storm the fort. The day was well suited to a bold military enterprise. It was the great Mohammedan festival which is sacred to the memory of Hosein, the son of Ali.[1] The history of Islam contains nothing more touching than the event which gave rise to that solemnity. The mournful legend relates how the chief of the Fatimites, when all his brave followers had perished round him, drank his latest draught of water, and uttered his latest prayer, how the assassins carried his head in triumph, how the tyrant smote the lifeless lips with his staff, and how a few old men recollected with tears that they had seen those lips pressed to the lips of the prophet of God.[2] After the lapse of near twelve centuries, the recurrence of this solemn season excites the fiercest and saddest emotions in the bosoms of the devout Moslem of India. They work themselves up to such agonies of rage and lamentation that some, it is said, have given up the ghost from the mere effect of mental excitement. They believe that whoever, during this festival, falls in arms against the infidels, atones by his death for all the sins of his life, and passes at once to the garden of the Houris.[1] It was at this time that Rajah Sahib determined to assault Arcot. Stimulating drugs were employed to aid the effect of religious zeal, and the besiegers, drunk with enthusiasm, drunk with bang, rushed furiously to the attack.

Clive had received secret intelligence of the design, had made his arrangements, and, exhausted by fatigue, had thrown himself on his bed. He was awakened by the alarm, and was instantly at his post. The enemy advanced, driving before them elephants whose foreheads were armed with iron plates. It was expected that the gates would yield to the shock of these living battering-rams. But the huge beasts no sooner felt the English musket balls than they turned round, and rushed furiously away, trampling on the multitude which had urged them forward. A raft was launched on the water which filled one part of the ditch. Clive, perceiving that his gunners at that post did not understand their business, took the management of a piece of artillery himself, and cleared the raft in a few minutes. Where the moat was dry the assailants mounted with great boldness; but they were received with a fire so heavy and so well directed, that it soon quelled the courage even of fanaticism and of intoxication. The rear ranks of the English kept the front ranks supplied with a constant succession of loaded muskets, and every shot told on the living mass below. After three desperate onsets, the besiegers retired behind the ditch.

The struggle lasted about an hour. Four hundred of the assailants fell. The garrison lost only five or six men. The besieged passed an anxious night, looking for a renewal of the attack. But when day broke, the enemy were no more to be seen. They had retired, leaving to the English several guns and a large quantity of ammunition.

The news was received at Fort St. George with transports of joy and pride. Clive was justly regarded as a man equal to any command. Two hundred English soldiers and seven hundred sepoys were sent to him, and with this force he instantly commenced offensive operations. He took the fort of Timery, effected a junction with a division of Morari Row's army, and hastened, by forced marches, to attack Rajah Sahib, who was at the head of about five thousand men, of whom three hundred were French. The action was sharp; but Clive gained a complete victory. The military chest of Rajah Sahib fell into the hands of the conquerors. Six hundred sepoys, who had served in the enemy's army came over to Clive's quarters, and were taken into the British service. Conjeveram surrendered without a blow. The governor of Arnee deserted Chunda Sahib, and recognized the title of Mohammed Ali.

Had the entire direction of the war been intrusted

to Clive, it would probably have been brought to a speedy close. But the timidity and incapacity which appeared in all the movements of the English, except where he was personally present, protracted the struggle. The Mahrattas muttered that his soldiers were of a different race from the British whom they found elsewhere. The effect of this languor was, that in no long time Rajah Sahib, at the head of a considerable army, in which were four hundred French troops, appeared almost under the guns of Fort St. George, and laid waste the villas and gardens of the gentlemen of the English settlement. But he was again encountered and defeated by Clive. More than a hundred of the French were killed or taken, a loss more serious than that of thousands of natives. The victorious army marched from the field of battle to Fort St. David. On the road lay the City of the Victory of Dupleix, and the stately monument which was designed to commemorate the triumphs of France in the East. Clive ordered both the city and the monument to be razed to the ground. He was induced, we believe, to take this step, not by personal or national malevolence, but by a just and profound policy. The town and its pompous name, the pillar and its vaunting inscriptions, were among the devices by which Dupleix had laid the public mind of India under a spell. This spell it was Clive's business to break. The natives had been taught that France was confessedly the first power in Europe, and that the English did not presume to dispute her supremacy. No measure could be more effectual for the removing of this delusion than the public and solemn demolition of the French trophies.

The government of Madras, encouraged by these events, determined to send a strong detachment, under Clive, to reinforce the garrison of Trichinopoly. But just at this conjuncture, Major Lawrence arrived from England, and assumed the chief command. From the waywardness and impatience of control which had characterized Clive, both at school and in the counting-house, it might have been expected that he would not, after such achievements, act with zeal and good humor in a subordinate capacity. But Lawrence had early treated him with kindness; and it is bare justice to Clive to say that, proud and overbearing as he was, kindness was never thrown away upon him. He cheerfully placed himself under the orders of his old friend, and exerted himself as strenuously in the second post as he could have done in the first. Lawrence well knew the value of such assistance. Though himself gifted with no intellectual faculty higher than plain good sense, he fully appreciated the powers of his brilliant coadjutor. Though he had made a methodical study of military tactics, and, like all men regularly bred to a profession, was disposed to look with disdain on interlopers, he had yet liberality enough to acknowledge that Clive was an exception to common rules. "Some people," he wrote, "are pleased to term Captain Clive fortunate and lucky; but, in my opinion, from the knowledge I have of the gentleman, he deserved and might expect from his conduct everything as it fell out;—a man of an undaunted resolution, of a cool temper, and of a presence of mind which never left him in the greatest danger; born a soldier; for, without a military education of any sort, or much conversing with any of the profession, from his judgment and good sense, he led on an army like an experienced officer and a brave soldier, with a prudence that certainly warranted success."

The French had no commander to oppose to the two friends. Dupleix, not inferior in talents for negotiation and intrigue to any European who has borne a part in the revolutions of India, was ill qualified to direct in person military operations. He had not been bred a soldier, and had no inclination to become one. His enemies accused him of personal cowardice; and he defended himself in a strain worthy of Captain Bobadil.[1] He kept away from shot, he said, because silence and tranquillity were propitious to his genius, and he found it difficult to pursue his meditations amidst the noise of fire-arms. He was thus under the necessity of intrusting to others the execution of his great warlike designs; and he bitterly complained that he was ill served. He had indeed been assisted by one officer of eminent merit, the celebrated Bussy. But Bussy [2] had marched northward with the Nizam, and was fully employed in looking after his own interests, and those of France, at the court of that prince. Among the officers who remained with Dupleix, there was not a single man of capacity; and many of them were boys, at whose ignorance and folly the common soldiers laughed.

The English triumphed everywhere. The besiegers of Trichinopoly were themselves besieged and compelled to capitulate. Chunda Sahib [1] fell into the hands of the Mahrattas, and was put to death, at the instigation probably of his competitor, Mohammed Ali. The spirit of Dupleix, however, was unconquerable, and his resources inexhaustible. From his employers in Europe he no longer received help or countenance. They condemned his policy. They gave him no pecuniary assistance. They sent him for troops only the sweepings of the galleys. Yet still he persisted, intrigued, bribed, promised;—lavished his private fortune, strained his credit, procured new diplomas from Delhi, raised up new enemies to the government of Madras on every side, and found tools even among the allies of the English Company. But all was in vain. Slowly, but steadily, the power of Britain continued to increase, and that of France to decline.

The health of Clive had never been good during his residence in India; and his constitution was now so much impaired that he determined to return to England. Before his departure he undertook a service of considerable difficulty, and performed it with his usual vigor and dexterity. The forts of Covelong and Chingleput were occupied by French garrisons. It was determined to send a force against them. But the only force available for this purpose was of such a description that no officer but Clive would risk his reputation by commanding it. It consisted of five hundred newly levied sepoys, and two hundred recruits who had just landed from England, and who were the worst and lowest wretches that the Company's crimps could pick up in the flash-houses [1] of London. Clive, ill and exhausted as he was, undertook to make an army of this undisciplined rabble, and marched with them to Covelong. A shot from the fort killed one of these extraordinary soldiers; on which all the rest faced about and ran away, and it was with the greatest difficulty that Clive rallied them. On another occasion, the noise of a gun terrified the sentinels so much that one of them was found, some hours later, at the bottom of a well. Clive gradually accustomed them to danger, and, by exposing himself constantly in the most perilous situations, shamed them into courage. He at length succeeded in forming a respectable force out of his unpromising materials. Covelong fell. Clive learned that a strong detachment was marching to relieve it from Chingleput. He took measures to prevent the enemy from learning that they were too late, laid an ambuscade for them on the road, killed a hundred of them with one fire, took three hundred prisoners, pursued the fugitives to the gates of Chingleput, laid siege instantly to that fastness, reputed one of the strongest in India, made a breach, and was on the point of storming, when the French commandant capitulated, and retired with his men.

Clive returned to Madras victorious, but in a state of health which rendered it impossible for him to remain there long. He married at this time a young lady of the name of Maskelyne,[2] sister of the eminent mathematician who long held the post of Astronomer Royal. She is described as handsome and accomplished; and her husband's letters, it is said, contain proofs that he was devotedly attached to her.

Almost immediately after the marriage, Clive embarked with his bride for England. He returned a very different person from the poor slighted boy who had been sent out ten years before to seek his fortune. He was only twenty-seven; yet his country already respected him as one of her first soldiers. There was then general peace in Europe. The Carnatic was the only part of the world where the English and French were in arms against each other. The vast schemes of Dupleix had excited no small uneasiness in the city of London; and the rapid turn of fortune, which was chiefly owing to the courage and talents of Clive, had been hailed with great delight. The young captain was known at the India House by the honorable nick-name of General Clive, and was toasted by that appellation at the feasts of the Directors. On his arrival in England, he found himself an object of general interest and admiration. The East India Company thanked him for his services in the warmest terms, and bestowed on him a sword set with diamonds. With rare delicacy he refused to receive this token of gratitude, unless a similar compliment were paid to his friend and commander, Lawrence.

It may easily be supposed that Clive was most cordially welcomed home by his family, who were delighted by his success, though they seem to have been hardly able to comprehend how their naughty idle Bobby had become so great a man. His father had been singularly hard of belief. Not until the news of the defence of Arcot arrived in England was the old gentleman heard to growl out that, after all, the booby had something in him. His expressions of approbation became stronger and stronger as news arrived of one brilliant exploit after another; and he was at length immoderately fond and proud of his son.

Clive's relations had very substantial reasons for rejoicing at his return. Considerable sums of prize money had fallen to his share; and he had brought home a moderate fortune, part of which he expended in extricating his father from pecuniary difficulties, and in redeeming the family estate. The remainder he appears to have dissipated in the course of about two years. He lived splendidly, dressed gayly even for those times, kept a carriage and saddle horses, and, not content with these ways of getting rid of his money, resorted to the most speedy and effectual of all modes of evacuation, a contested election followed by a petition.

At the time of the general election of 1754, the government was in a very singular state. There was scarcely any formal opposition. The Jacobites had been cowed by the issue of the last rebellion. The Tory party had fallen into utter contempt. It had been deserted by all the men of talents who had belonged to it, and had scarcely given a symptom of life during some years. The small faction which had been held together by the influence and promises of Prince Frederic, had been dispersed by his death. Almost every public man of distinguished talents in the kingdom, whatever his early connections might have been, was in office, and called himself a Whig. But this extraordinary appearance of concord was quite delusive. The administration itself was distracted by bitter enmities and conflicting pretensions. The chief object of its members was to depress and supplant each other. The prime minister, Newcastle,[1] weak, timid, jealous, and perfidious, was at once detested and despised by some of the most important members of his government, and by none more than by Henry Fox, the Secretary at War. This able, daring, and ambitious man seized every opportunity of crossing the First Lord of the Treasury, from whom he well knew that he had little to dread and little to hope; for Newcastle was through life equally afraid of breaking with men of parts and of promoting them.

Newcastle had set his heart on returning two members for St. Michael, one of those wretched Cornish boroughs [2] which were swept away by the Reform Act in 1832. He was opposed by Lord Sandwich, whose influence had long been paramount there: and Fox exerted himself strenuously in Sandwich's behalf. Clive, who had been introduced to Fox, and very kindly received by him, was brought forward on the Sandwich interest, and was returned. But a petition was presented against the return, and was backed by the whole influence of the Duke of Newcastle.

The case was heard, according to the usage of that

time, before a committee of the whole House.[1] Questions respecting elections were then considered merely as party questions. Judicial impartiality was not even affected. Sir Robert Walpole was in the habit of saying openly that, in election battles, there ought to be no quarter. On the present occasion the excitement was great. The matter really at issue was, not whether Clive had been properly or improperly returned, but whether Newcastle or Fox was to be master of the new House of Commons, and consequently first minister. The contest was long and obstinate, and success seemed to lean sometimes to one side and sometimes to the other. Fox put forth all his rare powers of debate, beat half the lawyers in the House at their own weapons, and carried division after division [2] against the whole influence of the Treasury. The committee decided in Clive's favor. But when the resolution was reported to the House, things took a different course. The remnant of the Tory Opposition, contemptible as it was, had yet sufficient weight to turn the scale between the nicely balanced parties of Newcastle and Fox. Newcastle the Tories could only despise. Fox they hated, as the boldest and most subtle politician and the ablest debater among the Whigs, as the steady friend of Walpole, as the devoted adherent of the Duke of Cumberland. After wavering till the last moment, they determined to vote in a body with the Prime Minister's friends. The consequence was that the House, by a small majority, rescinded the decision of the committee, and Clive was unseated.

Ejected from Parliament, and straitened in his means, he naturally began to look again towards India. The Company and the Government were eager to avail themselves of his services. A treaty favorable to England had indeed been concluded in the Carnatic. Dupleix had been superseded, and had returned with the wreck of his immense fortune to Europe, where calumny and chicanery soon hunted him to his grave. But many signs indicated that a war between France and Great Britain was at hand; and it was therefore thought desirable to send an able commander to the Company's settlements in India. The Directors appointed Clive governor of Fort St. David. The King gave him the commission of a lieutenant-colonel in the British army, and in 1755 he again sailed for Asia.

The first service on which he was employed after his return to the East was the reduction of the stronghold of Gheriah. This fortress, built on a craggy promontory, and almost surrounded by the ocean, was the den of a pirate named Angria, whose barks had long been the terror of the Arabian Gulf. Admiral Watson, who commanded the English squadron in the Eastern seas, burned Angria's fleet, while Clive attacked the fastness by land. The place soon fell, and a booty of a hundred and fifty thousand pounds sterling was divided among the conquerors.

After this exploit, Clive proceeded to his government of Fort St. David. Before he had been there two months, he received intelligence which called forth all the energy of his bold and active mind.

Of the provinces which had been subject to the house of Tamerlane, the wealthiest was Bengal. No part of India possessed such natural advantages both for agriculture and for commerce. The Ganges, rushing through a hundred channels to the sea, has formed a vast plain of rich mould which, even under the tropical sky, rivals the verdure of an English April. The rice fields yield an increase such as is elsewhere unknown. Spices, sugar, vegetable oils, are produced with marvellous exuberance. The rivers afford an inexhaustible supply of fish. The desolate islands along the sea-coast, overgrown by noxious vegetation, and swarming with deer and tigers, supply the cultivated districts with abundance of salt. The great stream which fertilizes the soil is, at the same time, the chief highway of Eastern commerce. On its banks, and on those of its tributary waters, are the wealthiest marts, the most splendid capitals, and the most sacred shrines of India. The tyranny of man had for ages struggled in vain against the overflowing bounty of nature. In spite of the Mussulman despot and of the Mahratta freebooter, Bengal was known through the East as the garden of Eden, as the rich kingdom. Its population multiplied exceedingly. Distant provinces were nourished from the overflowing of its granaries; and the noble ladies of London and Paris were clothed in the delicate produce of its looms. The race by whom this rich tract was peopled, enervated by a soft climate and accustomed to peaceful employments, bore the same relation to other Asiatics which the Asiatics generally bear to the bold and energetic children of Europe. The Castilians have a proverb, that in Valencia the earth is water and the men women; and the description is at least equally applicable to the vast plain of the Lower Ganges. Whatever the Bengalee does, he does languidly. His favorite pursuits are sedentary. He shrinks from bodily exertion; and, though voluble in dispute and singularly pertinacious in the war of chicane, he seldom engages in a personal conflict, and scarcely ever enlists as a soldier. We doubt whether there be a hundred genuine Bengalees in the whole army of the East India Company. There never, perhaps, existed a people so thoroughly fitted by nature and by habit for a foreign yoke.

The great commercial companies of Europe had long possessed factories in Bengal. The French were settled, as they still are, at Chandernagore [1] on the Hoogley. Higher up the stream the Dutch traders held Chinsurah. Nearer to the sea, the English had built Fort William. A church and ample warehouses rose in the vicinity. A row of spacious houses, belonging to the chief factors of the East India Company, lined the banks of the river; and in the neighborhood had sprung up a large and busy native town, where some Hindoo merchants of great opulence had fixed their abode. But the tract now covered by the palaces of Chowringhee [2] contained only a few miserable huts thatched with straw. A jungle, abandoned to waterfowl and alligators, covered the site of the present Citadel, and the Course,[3] which is now daily crowded at sunset with the gayest equipages of Calcutta. For the ground on which the settlement stood, the English, like other great landholders, paid rent to the government; and they were, like other great landholders, permitted to exercise a certain jurisdiction within their domain.

The great province of Bengal, together with Orissa and Bahar, had long been governed by a viceroy, whom the English called Aliverdy Khan,[1] and who, like the other viceroys of the Mogul, had become virtually independent. He died in 1756, and the sovereignty descended to his grandson, a youth under twenty years of age, who bore the name of Surajah Dowlah. Oriental despots are perhaps the worst class of human beings; and this unhappy boy was one of the worst specimens of his class. His understanding was naturally feeble, and his temper naturally unamiable. His education had been such as would have enervated even a vigorous intellect, and perverted even a generous disposition. He was unreasonable, because no one ever dared to reason with him, and selfish, because he had never been made to feel himself dependent on the good will of others. Early debauchery had unnerved his body and his mind. He indulged immoderately in the use of ardent spirits, which inflamed his weak brain almost to madness. His chosen companions were flatterers sprung from the dregs of the people, and recommended by nothing but buffoonery and servility. It is said that he had arrived at that last stage of human depravity, when cruelty becomes pleasing for its own sake, when the sight of pain as pain, where no advantage is to be gained, no offence punished, no danger averted, is an agreeable excitement. It had early been his amusement to torture beasts and birds; and when he grew up, he enjoyed with still keener relish the misery of his fellow-creatures.

From a child Surajah Dowlah had hated the English. It was his whim to do so; and his whims were never opposed. He had also formed a very exaggerated notion of the wealth which might be obtained by plundering them; and his feeble and uncultivated mind was incapable of perceiving that the riches of Calcutta, had they been even greater than he imagined, would not compensate him for what he must lose, if the European trade, of which Bengal was a chief seat, should be driven by his violence to some other quarter. Pretexts for a quarrel were readily found. The English, in expectation of a war with France, had begun to fortify their settlement without special permission from the Nabob. A rich native, whom he longed to plunder, had taken refuge at Calcutta, and had not been delivered up. On such grounds as these Surajah Dowlah marched with a great army against Fort William.[1]

The servants of the Company at Madras had been forced by Dupleix to become statesmen and soldiers. Those in Bengal were still mere traders, and were terrified and bewildered by the approaching danger. The governor, who had heard much of Surajah Dowlah's cruelty, was frightened out of his wits, jumped into a boat, and took refuge in the nearest ship. The military commandant thought that he could not do better than follow so good an example. The fort was taken [1] after a feeble resistance; and great numbers of the English fell into the hands of the conquerors. The Nabob seated himself with regal pomp in the principal hall of the factory, and ordered Mr. Holwell, the first in rank amongst the prisoners, to be brought before him. His Highness talked about the insolence of the English, and grumbled at the smallness of the treasure which he had found; but promised to spare their lives, and retired to rest.

Then was committed that great crime, memorable for its singular atrocity, memorable for the terrible retribution by which it was followed. The English captives were left at the mercy of the guards, and the guards determined to secure them for the night in the prison of the garrison, a chamber known by the fearful name of the Black Hole. Even for a single European malefactor, the dungeon would, in such a climate, have been too close and narrow. The space was only twenty feet square. The air-holes were small and obstructed. It was the summer solstice, the season when the fierce heat of Bengal can scarcely be rendered tolerable to natives of England by lofty halls and by the constant waving of fans. The number of the prisoners was one hundred and forty-six. When they were ordered to enter the cell, they imagined the soldiers were joking; and, being in high spirits on account of the promise of the Nabob to spare their lives, they laughed and jested at the absurdity of the notion. They soon discovered their mistake. They expostulated; they entreated; but in vain. The guards threatened to cut down all who hesitated. The captives were driven into the cell at the point of the sword, and the door was instantly shut and locked upon them.

Nothing in history or fiction, not even the story which Ugolino[1] told in the sea of everlasting ice, after he had wiped his bloody lips on the scalp of his murderer, approaches the horrors which were recounted by the few survivors of that night. They cried for mercy. They strove to burst the door. Holwell, who, even in that extremity, retained some presence of mind, offered large bribes to the jailers. But the answer was that nothing could be done without the Nabob's orders, that the Nabob was asleep, and that he would be angry if anybody woke him. Then the prisoners went mad with despair. They trampled each other down, fought for the places at the windows, fought for the pittance of water with which the cruel mercy of the murderers mocked their agonies, raved, prayed, blasphemed, implored the guards to fire among them. The jailers in the meantime held lights to the bars, and shouted with laughter at the frantic struggles of their victims. At length the tumult died away in low gaspings and moanings. The day broke. The Nabob had slept off his debauch, and permitted the door to be opened. But it was some time before the soldiers could make a lane for the survivors, by piling up on each side the heaps of corpses on which the burning climate had already begun to do its loathsome work. When at length a passage was made, twenty-three ghastly figures, such as their own mothers would not have known, staggered one by one out of the charnel-house. A pit was instantly dug. The dead bodies, a hundred and twenty-three in number, were flung into it promiscuously and covered up.

But these things, which, after the lapse of more than eighty years, cannot be told or read without horror, awakened neither remorse nor pity in the bosom of the savage Nabob. He inflicted no punishment on the murderers. He showed no tenderness to the survivors. Some of them, indeed, from whom nothing was to be got, were suffered to depart; but those from whom it was thought that anything could be extorted were treated with execrable cruelty. Holwell, unable to walk, was carried before the tyrant, who reproached him, threatened him, and sent him up the country in irons, together with some other gentlemen who were suspected of knowing more than they chose to tell about the treasures of the Company. These persons, still bowed down by the sufferings of that great agony, were lodged in miserable sheds, and fed only with grain and water, till at length the intercessions of the female relations of the Nabob procured their release. One Englishwoman had survived that night. She was placed in the harem of the Prince at Moorshedabad.

Surajah Dowlah, in the meantime, sent letters to his nominal sovereign at Delhi, describing the late conquest in the most pompous language. He placed a garrison in Fort William, forbade any Englishman to dwell in the neighborhood, and directed that, in memory of his great actions, Calcutta should thenceforward be called Alinagore, that is to say, the Port of God.

In August the news of the fall of Calcutta reached Madras, and excited the fiercest and bitterest resentment. The cry of the whole settlement was for vengeance. Within forty-eight hours after the arrival of the intelligence, it was determined that an expedition should be sent to the Hoogley, and that Clive should be at the head of the land forces. The naval armament was under the command of Admiral Watson. Nine hundred English infantry, fine troops and full of spirit, and fifteen hundred sepoys, composed the army which sailed to punish a Prince who had more subjects than Louis the Fifteenth or the Empress Maria Theresa. In October the expedition sailed; [1] but it had to make its way against adverse winds, and did not reach Bengal till December.

The Nabob was revelling in fancied security at Moorshedabad. He was so profoundly ignorant of the state of foreign countries that he often used to say that there were not ten thousand men in all Europe; and it had never occurred to him as possible, that the English would dare to invade his dominions. But, though undisturbed by any fear of their military power, he began to miss them greatly. His revenues fell off; and his ministers succeeded in making him understand that a ruler may sometimes find it more profitable to protect traders in the open enjoyment of their gains than to put them to the torture for the purpose of discovering hidden chests of gold and jewels. He was already disposed to permit the Company to resume its mercantile operations in his country, when he received the news that an English armament was in the Hoogley. He instantly ordered all his troops to assemble at Moorshedabad, and marched towards Calcutta.

Clive had commenced operations with his usual vigor. He took Budgebudge, routed the garrison of Fort William, recovered Calcutta, stormed and sacked Hoogley. The Nabob, already disposed to make some concessions to the English, was confirmed in his pacific disposition by these proofs of their power and spirit. He accordingly made overtures to the chiefs of the invading armament, and offered to restore the factory, and to give compensation to those whom he had despoiled.

Clive's profession was war; and he felt that there was something discreditable in an accommodation with Surajah Dowlah. But his power was limited. A committee, chiefly composed of servants of the Company who had fled from Calcutta, had the principal direction of affairs; and these persons were eager to be restored to their posts and compensated for their losses. The government of Madras, apprised that war had commenced in Europe, and apprehensive of an attack from the French, became impatient for the return of the armament. The promises of the Nabob were large, the chances of a contest doubtful; and Clive consented to treat, though he expressed his regret that things should not be concluded in so glorious a manner as he could have wished.

With this negotiation commences a new chapter in the life of Clive. Hitherto he had been merely a soldier carrying into effect, with eminent ability and valor, the plans of others. Henceforth he is to be chiefly regarded as a statesman; and his military movements are to be considered as subordinate to his political designs. That in his new capacity he displayed great ability, and obtained great success, is unquestionable. But it is also unquestionable that the transactions in which he now began to take a part have left a stain on his moral character.

We can by no means agree with Sir John Malcolm, who is obstinately resolved to see nothing but honor and integrity in the conduct of his hero. But we can as little agree with Mr. Mill, who has gone so far as to say that Clive was a man "to whom deception, when it suited his purpose, never cost a pang." Clive seems to us to have been constitutionally the very opposite of a knave, bold even to temerity, sincere even to indiscretion, hearty in friendship, open in enmity. Neither in his private life, nor in those parts of his public life in which he had to do with his countrymen, do we find any signs of a propensity to cunning. On the contrary, in all the disputes in which he was engaged as an Englishman against Englishmen, from his boxing-matches at school to those stormy altercations at the India House and in Parliament, amidst which his later years were passed, his very faults were those of a high and magnanimous spirit. The truth seems to have been that he considered Oriental politics as a game in which nothing was unfair. He knew that the standard of morality among the natives of India differed widely from that established in England. He knew that he had to deal with men destitute of what in Europe is called honor, with men who would give any promise without hesitation, and break any promise without shame, with men who would unscrupulously employ corruption, perjury, forgery, to compass their ends. His letters show that the great difference between Asiatic and European morality was constantly in his thoughts. He seems to have imagined, most erroneously in our opinion, that he could effect nothing against such adversaries, if he was content to be bound by ties from which they were free, if he went on telling truth, and hearing none, if he fulfilled, to his own hurt, all his engagements with confederates who never kept an engagement that was not to their advantage. Accordingly this man, in the other parts of his life an honorable English gentleman and a soldier, was no sooner matched against an Indian intriguer, than he became himself an Indian intriguer, and descended, without scruple, to falsehood, to hypocritical caresses, to the substitution of documents, and to the counterfeiting of hands.

The negotiations between the English and the Nabob were carried on chiefly by two agents, Mr. Watts, a servant of the Company, and a Bengalee of the name of Omichund. This Omichund had been one of the wealthiest native merchants resident at Calcutta, and had sustained great losses in consequence of the Nabob's expedition against that place. In the course of his commercial transactions, he had seen much of the English, and was peculiarly qualified to serve as a medium of communication between them and a native court. He possessed great influence with his own race, and had in large measure the Hindoo talents, quick observation, tact, dexterity, perseverance, and the Hindoo vices, servility, greediness, and treachery.

The Nabob behaved with all the faithlessness of an Indian statesman, and with all the levity of a boy whose mind had been enfeebled by power and self-indulgence. He promised, retracted, hesitated, evaded. At one time he advanced with his army in a threatening manner towards Calcutta; but when he saw the resolute front which the English presented, he fell back in alarm, and consented to make peace with them on their own terms. The treaty was no sooner concluded than he formed new designs against them. He intrigued with the French authorities at Chandernagore. He invited Bussy to march from the Deccan to the Hoogley, and to drive the English out of Bengal. All this was well known to Clive and Watson. They determined accordingly to strike a decisive blow, and to attack Chandernagore, before the force there could be strengthened by new arrivals, either from the south of India, or from Europe. Watson directed the expedition by water, Clive by land. The success of the combined movements was rapid and complete. The fort, the garrison, the artillery, the military stores, all fell into the hands of the English. Nearly five hundred European troops were among the prisoners.

The Nabob had feared and hated the English, even while he was still able to oppose to them their French rivals. The French were now vanquished; and he began to regard the English with still greater fear and still greater hatred. His weak and unprincipled mind oscillated between servility and insolence. One day he sent a large sum to Calcutta, as part of the compensation due for the wrongs which he had committed. The next day he sent a present of jewels to Bussy, exhorting that distinguished officer to hasten to protect Bengal "against Clive, the daring in war, on whom," says his Highness, "may all bad fortune attend." He ordered his army to march against the English. He countermanded his orders. He tore Clive's letters. He then sent answers in the most florid language of compliment. He ordered Watts out of his presence, and threatened to impale him. He again sent for Watts, and begged pardon for the insult. In the meantime, his wretched maladministration, his folly, his dissolute manners, and his love of the lowest company, had disgusted all classes of his subjects, soldiers, traders, civil functionaries, the proud and ostentatious Mohammedans, the timid, supple, parsimonious Hindoos. A formidable confederacy was formed against him, in which were included Roydullub, the minister of finance, Meer Jaffier, the principal commander of the troops, and Jugget Seit, the richest banker in India. The plot was confided to the

English agents, and a communication was opened between the malcontents at Moorshedabad and the committee at Calcutta.

In the committee there was much hesitation; but Clive's voice was given in favor of the conspirators, and his vigor and firmness bore down all opposition. It was determined that the English should lend their powerful assistance to depose Surajah Dowlah, and to place Meer Jaffier on the throne of Bengal. In return, Meer Jaffier promised ample compensation to the Company and its servants, and a liberal donative to the army, the navy, and the committee. The odious vices of Surajah Dowlah, the wrongs which the English had suffered at his hands, the dangers to which our trade must have been exposed had he continued to reign, appear to us fully to justify the resolution of deposing him. But nothing can justify the dissimulation which Clive stooped to practice. He wrote to Surajah Dowlah in terms so affectionate that they for a time lulled that weak prince into perfect security. The same courier who carried this "soothing letter," as Clive calls it, to the Nabob, carried to Mr. Watts a letter in the following terms: "Tell Meer Jaffier to fear nothing. I will join him with five thousand men who never turned their backs. Assure him I will march night and day to his assistance, and stand by him as long as I have a man left."

It was impossible that a plot which had so many ramifications should long remain entirely concealed. Enough reached the ears of the Nabob to arouse his suspicions. But he was soon quieted by the fictions and artifices which the inventive genius of Omichund produced with miraculous readiness. All was going well; the plot was nearly ripe; when Clive learned that Omichund was likely to play false. The artful Bengalee had been promised a liberal compensation for all that he had lost at Calcutta. But this would not satisfy him. His services had been great. He held the thread of the whole intrigue. By one word breathed in the ear of Surajah Dowlah, he could undo all that he had done. The lives of Watts, of Meer Jaffier, of all the conspirators, were at his mercy; and he determined to take advantage of his situation and to make his own terms. He demanded three hundred thousand pounds sterling as the price of his secrecy and of his assistance. The committee, incensed by the treachery, and appalled by the danger, knew not what course to take. But Clive was more than Omichund's match in Omichund's own arts. The man, he said, was a villain. Any artifice which would defeat such knavery was justifiable. The best course would be to promise what was asked. Omichund would soon be at their mercy; and then they might punish him by withholding from him, not only the bribe which he now demanded, but also the compensation which all the other sufferers of Calcutta were to receive.

His advice was taken. But how was the wary and sagacious Hindoo to be deceived? He had demanded that an article touching his claims should be inserted in the treaty between Meer Jaffier and the English, and he would not be satisfied unless he saw it with his own eyes. Clive had an expedient ready. Two treaties were drawn up, one on white paper, the other on red, the former real, the latter fictitious. In the former Omichund's name was not mentioned; the latter, which was to be shown to him, contained a stipulation in his favor.

But another difficulty arose. Admiral Watson had scruples against signing the red treaty. Omichund's vigilance and acuteness were such that the absence of so important a name would probably awaken suspicions. But Clive was not a man to do anything by halves. We almost blush to write it. He forged Admiral Watson's name.

All was now ready for action. Mr. Watts fled secretly from Moorshedabad. Clive put his troops in motion, and wrote to the Nabob in a tone very different from that of his previous letters. He set forth all the wrongs which the British had suffered, offered to submit the points in dispute to the arbitration of Meer Jaffier, and concluded by announcing that, as the rains were about to set in, he and his men would do themselves the honor of waiting on his Highness for an answer.

Surajah Dowlah instantly assembled his whole force, and marched to encounter the English. It had been agreed that Meer Jaffier should separate himself from the Nabob, and carry over his division to Clive. But, as the decisive moment approached, the fears of the conspirator overpowered his ambition. Clive had advanced to Cossimbuzar; the Nabob lay with a mighty power a few miles off at Plassey; and still Meer Jaffier delayed to fulfil his engagements, and returned evasive answers to the earnest remonstrances of the English general.

Clive was in a painfully anxious situation. He could place no confidence in the sincerity or in the courage of his confederate: and whatever confidence he might place in his own military talents, and in the valor and discipline of his troops, it was no light thing to engage an army twenty times as numerous as his own. Before him lay a river over which it was easy to advance, but over which, if things went ill, not one of his little band would ever return. On this occasion, for the first and for the last time, his dauntless spirit, during a few hours, shrank from the fearful responsibility of making a decision. He called a council of war. The majority pronounced against fighting; and Clive declared his concurrence with the majority. Long afterwards, he said that he had never called but one council of war, and that, if he had taken the advice of that council, the British would never have been masters of Bengal. But scarcely had the meeting broke up when he was himself again. He retired alone under the shade of some trees, and passed near an hour there in thought. He came back determined to put everything to the hazard, and gave orders that all should be in readiness for passing the river on the morrow.

The river was passed; and, at the close of a toilsome day's march, the army, long after sunset, took up its quarters in a grove of mango trees near Plassey, within a mile of the enemy. Clive was unable to sleep; he heard through the whole night the sound of drums and cymbals from the vast camp of the Nabob. It is not strange that even his stout heart should now and then have sunk, when he reflected against what odds, and for what a prize, he was in a few hours to contend.

Nor was the rest of Surajah Dowlah more peaceful. His mind, at once weak and stormy, was distracted by wild and horrible apprehensions. Appalled by the greatness and nearness of the crisis, distrusting his captains, dreading every one who approached him, dreading to be left alone, he sat gloomily in his tent, haunted, a Greek poet would have said, by the furies [1] of those who had cursed him with their last breath in the Black Hole.

The day broke, the day which was to decide the fate of India. At sunrise, the army of the Nabob,[2] pouring through many openings from the camp, began to move towards the grove where the English lay. Forty thousand infantry, armed with firelocks, pikes, swords, bows, and arrows, covered the plain. They were accompanied by fifty pieces of ordnance of the largest size, each tugged by a long team of white oxen, and each pushed on from behind by an elephant. Some smaller guns, under the direction of a few French auxiliaries, were perhaps more formidable. The cavalry were fifteen thousand, drawn, not from the effeminate population of Bengal, but from the bolder race which inhabits the northern provinces; and the practised eye of Clive could perceive that the men and the horses were more powerful than those of the Carnatic. The force which he had to oppose to this great multitude consisted of only three thousand men. But of these nearly a thousand were English; and all were led by English officers, and trained in the English discipline. Conspicuous in the ranks of the little army were the men of the Thirty-Ninth Regiment, which still bears on its colors, amidst many honorable additions won under Wellington in Spain and Gascony, the name of Plassey, and the proud motto, *Primus in Indis.*

The battle commenced with a cannonade in which the artillery of the Nabob did scarcely any execution while the few field-pieces of the English produced great effect. Several of the most distinguished officers in Surajah Dowlah's service fell. Disorder began to spread through his ranks. His own terror increased every moment. One of the conspirators urged on him the expediency of retreating. The insidious advice, agreeing as it did with what his own terrors suggested, was readily received. He ordered his army to fall back, and this order decided his fate. Clive snatched the moment, and ordered his troops to advance. The confused and dispirited multitude gave way before the onset of disciplined valor. No mob attacked by regular soldiers was ever more completely routed. The little band of Frenchmen, who alone ventured to confront the English, were swept down the stream of fugitives. In an hour the forces of Surajah Dowlah were dispersed, never to reassemble. Only five hundred of the vanquished were slain. But their camp, their guns, their baggage, innumerable wagons, innumerable cattle, remained in the power of the conquerors. With the loss of twenty-two soldiers killed and fifty wounded, Clive had scattered an army of nearly sixty thousand men, and subdued an empire larger and more populous than Great Britain.[1]

Meer Jaffier had given no assistance to the English during the action. But as soon as he saw that the fate of the day was decided, he drew off his division of the army, and, when the battle was over, sent his congratulations to his ally. The next morning he repaired to the English quarters, not a little uneasy as to the reception which awaited him there. He gave evident signs of alarm when a guard was drawn out to receive him with the honors due to his rank. But his apprehensions were speedily removed. Clive came forward to meet him, embraced him, saluted him as Nabob of the three great provinces of Bengal, Bahar, and Orissa, listened graciously to his apologies, and advised him to march without delay to Moorshedabad.

Surajah Dowlah had fled from the field of battle with all the speed with which a fleet camel could carry him, and arrived at Moorshedabad in little more than twenty-four hours. There he called his councillors round him. The wisest advised him to put himself into the hands of the English, from whom he had nothing worse to fear than deposition and confinement. But he attributed this suggestion to treachery. Others urged him to try the chance of war again. He approved the advice, and issued orders accordingly. But he wanted spirit to adhere even during one day to a manly resolution. He learned that Meer Jaffier had arrived; and his terrors became insupportable. Disguised in a mean dress, with a casket of jewels in his hand, he let himself down at night from a window of his palace, and, accompanied by only two attendants, embarked on the river for Patna.

In a few days Clive arrived at Moorshedabad, escorted by two hundred English soldiers and three hundred sepoys. For his residence had been assigned a palace which was surrounded by a garden so spacious that all the troops who accompanied him could conveniently encamp within it. The ceremony of the installation of Meer Jaffier was instantly performed. Clive led the new Nabob to the seat of honor, placed him on it, presented to him, after the immemorial fashion of the East, an offering of gold, and then, turning to the natives who filled the hall, congratulated them on the good fortune which had freed them from a tyrant. He was compelled on this occasion to use the services of an interpreter; for it is remarkable that, long as he resided in India, intimately acquainted as he was with Indian politics and with the Indian character, and adored as he was by his Indian soldiery, he never learned to express himself with facility in any Indian language. He is said indeed to have been sometimes under the necessity of employing, in his intercourse with natives of India, the smattering of Portuguese which he had acquired, when a lad, in Brazil.

The new sovereign was now called upon to fulfil the engagements into which he had entered with his allies. A conference was held at the house of Jugget Seit, the great banker, for the purpose of making the necessary arrangements. Omichund came thither, fully believing himself to stand high in the favor of Clive, who, with dissimulation surpassing even the dissimulation of Bengal, had up to that day treated him with undiminished kindness. The white treaty was produced and read. Clive then turned to Mr. Scrafton, one of the servants of the Company, and said in English, "It is now time to undeceive Omichund." "Omichund," said Mr. Scrafton in Hindostanee, "the red treaty is a trick. You are to have nothing." Omichund fell back insensible into the arms of his attendants. He revived; but his mind was irreparably ruined. Clive, who, though little troubled by scruples of conscience in his dealings with Indian politicians, was not inhuman, seems to have been touched. He saw Omichund a few days later, spoke to him kindly, advised him to make a pilgrimage to one of the great temples of India, in the hope that change of scene might restore his health, and was even disposed, notwithstanding all that had passed, again to employ his talents in the public service. But from the moment of that sudden shock, the unhappy man sank gradually into idiocy. He who had formerly been distinguished by the strength of his understanding and the simplicity of his habits, now squandered the remains of his fortune on childish trinkets, and loved to exhibit himself dressed in rich garments, and hung with precious stones. In this abject state he languished a few months, and then died.

We should not think it necessary to offer any remarks for the purpose of directing the judgment of our readers, with respect to this transaction, had not Sir John Malcolm undertaken to defend it in all its parts. He regrets, indeed, that it was necessary to employ means so liable to abuse as forgery; but he will not admit that any blame attaches to those who deceived the deceiver. He thinks that the English were not bound to keep faith with one who kept no faith with them, and that, if they had fulfilled their engagements with the wily Bengalee, so signal an example of successful treason would have produced a crowd of imitators. Now, we will not discuss this point on any rigid principles of morality. Indeed, it is quite unnecessary to do so; for, looking at the question as a question of expediency in the lowest sense of the word, and using no arguments but such as Machiavelli [1] might have employed in his conferences with Borgia,[2] we are convinced that Clive was altogether in the wrong, and that he committed, not merely a crime, but a blunder. That honesty is the best policy, is a maxim which we firmly believe to be generally correct, even with respect to the temporal interests of individuals; but with respect to societies, the rule is subject to still fewer exceptions, and that for this reason, that the life of societies is longer than the life of individuals. It is possible to mention men who have owed great worldly prosperity to breaches of private faith; but we doubt whether it be possible to mention a state which has on the whole been a gainer by a breach of public faith. The entire history of British India is an illustration of the great truth, that it is not prudent to oppose perfidy to perfidy, and that the most efficient weapon with which men can encounter falsehood is truth. During a long course of years, the English rulers in India, surrounded by allies and enemies whom no engagement could bind, have generally acted with sincerity and uprightness; and the event has proved that sincerity and uprightness are wisdom. English valor and English intelligence have done less to extend and to preserve our Oriental empire than English veracity. All that we could have gained by imitating the doublings, the evasions, the fictions, the perjuries which have been employed against us is as nothing, when compared with what we have gained by being the one power in India on whose word reliance can be placed. No oath which superstition can devise, no hostage however precious, inspires a hundredth part of the confidence which is produced by the "yea, yea," and "nay, nay," of a British envoy. No fastness, however strong by art or nature, gives to its inmates a security like that enjoyed by the chief who, passing through the territories of powerful and deadly enemies, is armed with the British guarantee. The mightiest princes of the East can scarcely, by the offer of enormous usury, draw forth any portion of the wealth which is concealed under the hearths of their subjects. The British Government offers little more than four per cent.; and avarice hastens to bring forth tens of millions of rupees from its most secret repositories. A hostile monarch may promise mountains of gold to our sepoys, on condition that they will desert the standard of the Company. The Company promises only a moderate pension after a long service. But every sepoy knows that the promise of the Company will be kept: he knows that if he lives a hundred years his rice and salt are as secure as the salary of the Governor-General: and he knows that there is not another state in India which would not, in spite of the most solemn vows, leave him to die of hunger in a ditch as soon as he had ceased to be useful. The greatest advantage which a government can possess is to be the one trustworthy government in the midst of governments which nobody can trust. This advantage we enjoy in Asia. Had we acted during the last two generations on the principles which Sir John Malcolm appears to have considered as sound, had we, as often as we had to deal with people like Omichund, retaliated by lying and forging, and breaking faith, after their fashion, it is our firm belief that no courage or capacity could have upheld our empire.

Sir John Malcolm admits that Clive's breach of faith could be justified only by the strongest necessity. As we think that breach of faith not only unnecessary, but most inexpedient, we need hardly say that we altogether condemn it.

Omichund was not the only victim of the revolution. Surajah Dowlah was taken a few days after his flight, and was brought before Meer Jaffier. There he flung himself on the ground in convulsions of fear, and with tears and loud cries implored the mercy which he had never shown. Meer Jaffier hesitated; but his son Meeran, a youth of seventeen, who in feebleness of brain and savageness of nature greatly resembled the wretched captive, was implacable. Surajah Dowlah was led into a secret chamber, to which in a short time the ministers of death were sent. In this act the English bore no part; and Meer Jaffier understood so much of their feelings, that he thought it necessary to apologize to them for having avenged them on their most malignant enemy.

The shower of wealth [1] now fell copiously on the Company and its servants. A sum of eight hundred thousand pounds sterling, in coined silver, was sent down the river from Moorshedabad to Fort William. The fleet which conveyed this treasure consisted of more than a hundred boats, and performed its triumphal voyage with flags flying and music playing. Calcutta, which a few months before had been desolate, was now more prosperous than ever. Trade revived; and the signs of affluence appeared in every English house. As to Clive, there was no limit to his acquisitions but his own moderation. The treasury of Bengal was thrown open to him. There were piled up, after the usage of Indian princes, immense masses of coin, among which might not seldom be detected the florins [2] and byzants [3] with which, before any European ship [4] had turned the Cape of Good Hope, the Venetians purchased the stuffs and spices of the East. Clive walked between heaps of gold and silver, crowned with rubies and diamonds, and was at liberty to help himself. He accepted between two and three hundred thousand pounds.

The pecuniary transactions between Meer Jaffier and Clive were sixteen years later condemned by the public voice, and severely criticised in Parliament. They are vehemently defended by Sir John Malcolm. The accusers of the victorious general represented his gains as the wages of corruption, or as plunder extorted at the point of the sword from a helpless ally. The biographer,[1] on the other hand, considers these great acquisitions as free gifts, honorable alike to the donor and to the receiver, and compares them to the rewards bestowed by foreign powers on Marlborough, on Nelson, and on Wellington. It had always, he says, been customary in the East to give and receive presents; and there was, as yet, no act of Parliament positively prohibiting English functionaries in India from profiting by this Asiatic usage. This reasoning, we own, does not quite satisfy us. We do not suspect Clive of selling the interests of his employers or his country; but we cannot acquit him of having done what, if not in itself evil, was yet of evil example. Nothing is more clear than that a general ought to be the servant of his own government, and of no other. It follows that whatever rewards he receives for his services ought to be given either by his own government, or with the full knowledge and approbation of his own government. This rule ought to be strictly maintained even with respect to the merest bauble, with respect to a cross, a medal, or a yard of colored ribbon. But how can any government be well served, if those who command its forces are at liberty, without its permission, without its privity, to accept princely fortunes from its allies? It is idle to say that there was then no Act of Parliament prohibiting the practice of taking presents from Asiatic sovereigns. It is not on the Act which was passed at a later period for the purpose of preventing any such taking of presents, but on grounds which were valid before the Act was passed, on grounds of common law and common sense, that we arraign the conduct of Clive. There is no Act that we know of, prohibiting the Secretary of State for Foreign Affairs from being in the pay of continental powers, but it is not the less true that a Secretary who should receive a secret pension from France would grossly violate his duty, and would deserve severe punishment. Sir John Malcolm compares the conduct of Clive with that of the Duke of Wellington. Suppose,—and we beg pardon for putting such a supposition even for the sake of argument,—that the Duke of Wellington had, after the campaign of 1815, and while he commanded the army of occupation in France, privately accepted two hundred thousand pounds from Louis the Eighteenth, as a mark of gratitude for the great services which his Grace had rendered to the House of Bourbon; what would be thought of such a transaction? Yet the statute-book no more forbids the taking of presents in Europe now than it forbade the taking of presents in Asia then.

At the same time, it must be admitted that in Clive's case, there were many extenuating circumstances. He considered himself as the general, not of the Crown, but of the Company. The Company had, by implication at least, authorized its agents to enrich themselves by means of the liberality of the native princes, and by other means still more objectionable. It was hardly to be expected that the servant should entertain stricter notions of his duty than were entertained by his masters. Though Clive did not distinctly acquaint his employers with what had taken place and request their sanction, he did not, on the other hand, by studied concealment, show that he was conscious of having done wrong. On the contrary, he avowed with the greatest openness that the Nabob's bounty had raised him to affluence. Lastly, though we think that he ought not in such a way to have taken anything, we must admit that he deserves praise for having taken so little. He accepted twenty lacs of rupees. It would have cost him only a word to make the twenty forty. It was a very easy exercise of virtue to declaim in England against Clive's rapacity; but not one in a hundred of his accusers would have shown so much self-command in the treasury of Moorshedabad.

Meer Jaffier could be upheld on the throne only by the hand which had placed him upon it. He was not, indeed, a mere boy; nor had he been so unfortunate as to be born in the purple. He was not, therefore, quite so imbecile or quite so depraved as his predecessor had been. But he had none of the talents or virtues which his post required; and his son and heir, Meeran, was another Surajah Dowlah. The recent revolution had unsettled the minds of men. Many chiefs were in open insurrection against the new Nabob. The viceroy of the rich and powerful province of Oude,[1] who, like the other viceroys of the Mogul, was now in truth an independent sovereign, menaced Bengal with invasion. Nothing but the talents and authority of Clive could support the tottering government. While things were in this state, a ship arrived with despatches which had been written at the India House before the news of the battle of Plassey had reached London. The Directors had determined to place the English settlements in Bengal under a government constituted in the most cumbrous and absurd manner; and, to make the matter worse, no place in the arrangement was assigned to Clive. The persons who were selected to form this new government, greatly to their honor, took on themselves the responsibility of disobeying these preposterous orders, and invited Clive to exercise the supreme authority. He consented; and it soon appeared that the servants of the Company had only anticipated the wishes of their employers. The Directors, on receiving news of Clive's brilliant success, instantly appointed him governor of their possessions in Bengal, with the highest marks of gratitude and esteem. His power was now boundless, and far surpassed even that which Dupleix had attained in the south of India. Meer Jaffier regarded him with slavish awe. On one occasion, the Nabob spoke with severity to a native chief of high rank, whose followers had been engaged in a brawl with some of the Company's sepoys. "Are you yet to learn," he said, "who that Colonel Clive is, and in what station God has placed him?" The chief, who, as a famous jester and an old friend of Meer Jaffier, could venture to take liberties, answered, "I affront the Colonel! I, who never get up in the morning without making three low bows to his jackass!" This was hardly an exaggeration. Europeans and natives were alike at Clive's feet. The English regarded him as the only man who could force Meer Jaffier to keep his engagements with them. Meer Jaffier regarded him as the only man who could protect the new dynasty against turbulent subjects and encroaching neighbors.

It is but justice to say that Clive used his power ably and vigorously for the advantage of his country. He sent forth an expedition against the tract lying to the north of the Carnatic.[1] In this tract the French still had the ascendency; and it was important to dislodge them. The conduct of the enterprise was intrusted to an officer of the name of Forde, who was then little known, but in whom the keen eye of the governor had detected military talents of a high order. The success of the expedition was rapid and splendid.

While a considerable part of the army of Bengal was thus engaged at a distance, a new and formidable danger menaced the western frontier. The Great Mogul was a prisoner at Delhi in the hands of a subject. His eldest son, named Shah Alum, destined to be, during many years, the sport of adverse fortune, and to be a tool in the hands, first of the Mahrattas, and then of the English, had fled from the palace of his father. His birth was still revered in India. Some powerful princes, the Nabob of Oude in particular, were inclined to favor him. Shah Alum found it easy to draw to his standard great numbers of the military adventurers with whom every part of the country swarmed. An army of forty thousand men, of various races and religions, Mahrattas, Rohillas, Jauts, and Afghans, was speedily assembled round him; and he formed the design of overthrowing the upstart whom the English had elevated to a throne, and of establishing his own authority throughout Bengal, Orissa, and Bahar.

Meer Jaffier's terror was extreme; and the only expedient which occurred to him was to purchase, by the payment of a large sum of money, an accommodation with Shah Alum. This expedient had been repeatedly employed by those who, before him, had ruled the rich and unwarlike provinces near the mouth of the Ganges. But Clive treated the suggestion with a scorn worthy of his strong sense and dauntless courage. "If you do this," he wrote, "you will have the Nabob of Oude, the Mahrattas, and many more, come from all parts of the confines of your country, who will bully you out of money till you have none left in your treasury. I beg your Excellency will rely on the fidelity of the English, and of those troops which are attached to you." He wrote in a similar strain to the governor of Patna, a brave native soldier whom he highly esteemed. "Come to no terms; defend your city to the last. Rest assured that the English are stanch and firm friends, and that they never desert a cause in which they have once taken a part."

He kept his word. Shah Alum had invested Patna, and was on the point of proceeding to storm, when he learned that the Colonel was advancing by forced marches. The whole army which was approaching consisted only of four hundred and fifty Europeans and two thousand five hundred sepoys. But Clive and his Englishmen were now objects of dread over all the East. As soon as his advanced guard appeared, the besiegers fled before him. A few French adventurers who were about the person of the prince advised him to try the chance of battle; but in vain. In a few days this great army, which had been regarded with so much uneasiness by the court of Moorshedabad, melted away before the mere terror of the British name.

The conqueror returned in triumph to Fort William. The joy of Meer Jaffier was as unbounded as his fears had been, and led him to bestow on his preserver a princely token of gratitude. The quit-rent [1] which the East India Company were bound to pay to the Nabob for the extensive lands held by them to the south of Calcutta amounted to near thirty thousand pounds sterling a year. The whole of this splendid estate, sufficient to support with dignity the highest rank of the British peerage, was now conferred on Clive for life.

This present we think Clive justified in accepting. It was a present which, from its very nature, could be no secret. In fact, the Company itself was his tenant, and by its acquiescence, signified its approbation of Meer Jaffier's grant.

But the gratitude of Meer Jaffier did not last long. He had for some time felt that the powerful ally who had set him up might pull him down, and had been looking round for support against the formidable strength by which he had himself been hitherto supported. He knew that it would be impossible to find among the natives of India any force which would look the Colonel's little army in the face. The French power in Bengal was extinct. But the fame of the Dutch had anciently been great in the Eastern seas; and it was not yet distinctly known in Asia how much the power of Holland had declined in Europe. Secret communications passed between the court of Moorshedabad and the Dutch factory at Chinsurah; and urgent letters were sent from Chinsurah, exhorting the government of Batavia [1] to fit out an expedition which might balance the power of the English in Bengal. The authorities of Batavia, eager to extend the influence of their country, and still more eager to obtain for themselves a share of the wealth which had recently raised so many English adventurers to opulence, equipped a powerful armament. Seven large ships from Java arrived unexpectedly in the Hoogley. The military force on board amounted to fifteen hundred men, of whom about one-half were Europeans. The enterprise was well timed. Clive had sent such large detachments to oppose the French in the Carnatic that his army was now inferior in number to that of the Dutch. He knew that Meer Jaffier secretly favored the invaders. He knew that he took on himself a serious responsibility if he attacked the forces of a friendly power; that the English ministers could not wish to see a war with Holland added to that in which they were already engaged with France; that they might disavow his acts; that they might punish him. He had recently remitted a great part of his fortune to Europe, through the Dutch East India Company; and he had therefore a strong interest in avoiding any quarrel. But he was satisfied that, if he suffered the Batavian armament to pass up the river and to join the garrison of Chinsurah, Meer Jaffier would throw himself into the arms of these new allies, and that the English ascendency in Bengal would be exposed to most serious danger. He took his resolution with characteristic boldness, and was most ably seconded by his officers, particularly by Colonel Forde, to whom the most important part of the operations was intrusted. The Dutch attempted to force a passage. The English encountered them both by land and water. On both elements the enemy had a great superiority of force. On both they were signally defeated. Their ships were taken. Their troops were put to a total rout. Almost all the European soldiers, who constituted the main strength of the invading army, were killed or taken. The conquerors sat down before Chinsurah; and the chiefs of that settlement, now thoroughly humbled, consented to the terms which Clive dictated. They engaged to build no fortifications, and to raise no troops beyond a small force necessary for the police of their factories; and it was distinctly provided that any violation of these covenants should be punished with instant expulsion from Bengal.

Three months after this great victory, Clive sailed for England. At home, honors and rewards awaited him, not indeed equal to his claims or to his ambition, but still such as, when his age, his rank in the army, and his original place in society are considered, must be pronounced rare and splendid. He was raised to the Irish peerage,[1] and encouraged to expect an English title. George the Third, who had just ascended the throne, received him with great distinction. The ministers paid him marked attention; and Pitt,[2] whose influence in the House of Commons and in the country was unbounded, was eager to mark his regard for one whose exploits had contributed so much to the lustre of that memorable period.[3] The great orator had already in Parliament described Clive as a heaven-born general, as a man who, bred to the labor of the desk, had displayed a military genius which might excite the admiration of the King of Prussia.[4] There were then no reporters [5] in the gallery; but these words, emphatically spoken by the first statesman of the age, had passed from mouth to mouth, had been transmitted to Clive in Bengal, and had greatly delighted and flattered him. Indeed, since the death of Wolfe, Clive was the only English general of whom his countrymen had much reason to be proud. The Duke of Cumberland had been generally unfortunate; and his single victory,[6] having been gained over his countrymen and used with merciless severity, had been more fatal to his popularity than his many defeats. Conway,[1] versed in the learning of his profession, and personally courageous, wanted vigor and capacity. Granby,[2] honest, generous, and as brave as a lion, had neither science nor genius. Sackville,[3] inferior in knowledge and abilities to none of his contemporaries, had incurred, unjustly as we believe, the imputation most fatal to the character of a soldier. It was under the command of a foreign general [4] that the British had triumphed at Minden and Warburg. The people, therefore, as was natural, greeted with pride and delight a captain of their own, whose native courage and self-taught skill had placed him on a level with the great tacticians of Germany.

The wealth of Clive was such as enabled him to vie with the first grandees of England. There remains proof that he had remitted more than a hundred and eighty thousand pounds through the Dutch East India Company, and more than forty thousand pounds through the English Company. The amount which he had sent home through private houses was also considerable. He had invested great sums in jewels, then a very common mode of remittance from India. His purchases of diamonds at Madras alone amounted to twenty-five thousand pounds. Besides a great mass of ready money, he had his Indian estate, valued by himself at twenty-seven thousand a year. His whole annual income, in the opinion of Sir John Malcolm, who is desirous to state it as low as possible, exceeded forty thousand pounds; and incomes of forty thousand pounds at the time of the accession of George the Third were at least as rare as incomes of a hundred thousand pounds now. We may safely affirm that no Englishman who started with nothing has ever, in any line of life, created such a fortune at the early age of thirty-four.

It would be unjust not to add that Clive made a creditable use of his riches. As soon as the battle of Plassey had laid the foundation of his fortune, he sent ten thousand pounds to his sisters, bestowed as much more on other poor friends and relations, ordered his agent to pay eight hundred a year to his parents, and to insist that they should keep a carriage, and settled five hundred a year on his old commander Lawrence, whose means were very slender. The whole sum which Clive expended in this manner may be calculated at fifty thousand pounds.

He now set himself to cultivate Parliamentary interest. His purchases of land seem to have been made in great measure with that view, and after the general election of 1761, he found himself in the House of Commons, at the head of a body of dependents whose support must have been important to any administration. In English politics, however, he did not take a prominent part. His first attachments, as we have seen, were to Mr. Fox; at a later period he was attracted by the genius and success of Mr. Pitt; but finally he connected himself in the closest manner with George Grenville. Early in the session of 1764, when the illegal and impolitic persecution of that worthless demagogue Wilkes[1] had strongly excited the public mind, the town was amused by an anecdote, which we have seen in some unpublished memoirs of Horace Walpole. Old Mr. Richard Clive, who since his son's elevation had been introduced into society for which his former habits had not well fitted him, presented himself at the levee. The King asked him where Lord Clive was. "He will be in town very soon," said the old gentleman, loud enough to be heard by the whole circle, "and then your Majesty will have another vote."

But in truth all Clive's views were directed towards the country in which he had so eminently distinguished himself as a soldier and a statesman; and it was by considerations relating to India that his conduct as a public man in England was regulated. The power of the Company, though an anomaly, is in our time, we are firmly persuaded, a beneficial anomaly. In the time of Clive, it was not merely an anomaly, but a nuisance. There was no Board of Control.[1] The Directors were for the most part mere traders, ignorant of general politics, ignorant of the peculiarities of the empire which had strangely become subject to them. The Court of Proprietors, wherever it chose to interfere, was able to have its way. That court was more numerous, as well as more powerful, than at present; for then every share of five hundred pounds conferred a vote. The meetings were large, stormy, even riotous, the debates indecently virulent. All the turbulence of a Westminster election, all the trickery and corruption of a Grampound election, disgraced the proceedings of this assembly on questions of the most solemn importance. Fictitious votes were manufactured on a gigantic scale. Clive himself laid out a hundred thousand pounds in the purchase of stock, which he then divided among nominal proprietors on whom he could depend, and whom he brought down in his train to every discussion and every ballot. Others did the same, though not to quite so enormous an extent.

The interest taken by the public of England in Indian questions was then far greater than at present, and the reason is obvious. At present a writer enters the service young; he climbs slowly; he is fortunate if, at forty-five, he can return to his country with an annuity of a thousand a year, and with savings amounting to thirty thousand pounds. A great quantity of wealth is made by English functionaries in India; but no single functionary makes a very large fortune, and what is made is slowly, hardly, and honestly earned. Only four or five high political offices are reserved for public men from England. The residencies, the secretaryships, the seats in the boards of revenue and in the Sudder courts are all filled by men who have given the best years of life to the service of the Company; nor can any talents however splendid or any connections however powerful obtain those lucrative posts for any person who has not entered by the regular door, and mounted by the regular gradations. Seventy years ago, less money was brought home from the East than in our time. But it was divided among a very much smaller number of persons, and immense sums were often accumulated in a few months. Any Englishman, whatever his age might be, might hope to be one of the lucky emigrants. If he made a good speech in Leadenhall Street,[1] or published a clever pamphlet in defence of the chairman, he might be sent out in the Company's service, and might return in three or four years as rich as Pigot or as Clive. Thus the India House was a lottery-office, which invited everybody to take a chance, and held out ducal fortunes as the prizes destined for the lucky few. As soon as it was known that there was a part of the world where a lieutenant-colonel had one morning received as a present an estate as large as that of the Earl of Bath or the Marquess of Rockingham, and where it seemed that such a trifle as ten or twenty thousand pounds was to be had by any British functionary for the asking, society began to exhibit all the symptoms of the South Sea year,[2] a feverish excitement, an ungovernable impatience to be rich, a contempt for slow, sure, and moderate gains.

At the head of the preponderating party in the India House, had long stood a powerful, able, and ambitious director of the name of Sulivan. He had conceived a strong jealousy of Clive, and remembered with bitterness the audacity with which the late governor of Bengal had repeatedly set at naught the authority of the distant Directors of the Company. An apparent reconciliation took place after Clive's arrival; but enmity remained deeply rooted in the hearts of both. The whole body of Directors was then chosen annually. At the election of 1763, Clive attempted to break down the power of the dominant faction. The contest was carried on with a violence which he describes as tremendous. Sulivan was victorious, and hastened to take his revenge. The grant of rent which Clive had received from Meer Jaffier was, in the opinion of the best English lawyers, valid. It had been made by exactly the same authority from which the Company had received their chief possessions in Bengal, and the Company had long acquiesced in it. The Directors, however, most unjustly determined to confiscate it, and Clive was forced to file a bill in Chancery against them.

But a great and sudden turn in affairs was at hand. Every ship from Bengal had for some time brought alarming tidings. The internal misgovernment of the province had reached such a point that it could go no further. What, indeed, was to be expected from a body of public servants exposed to temptation such as that, as Clive once said,[1] flesh and blood could not bear it, armed with irresistible power, and responsible only to the corrupt, turbulent, distracted, ill-informed Company, situated at such a distance that the average interval between the sending of a despatch and the receipt of an answer was above a year and a half? Accordingly, during the five years which followed the departure of Clive from Bengal, the misgovernment of the English was carried to a point such as seems hardly compatible with the very existence of society. The Roman proconsul,[2] who, in a year or two, squeezed out of a province the means of rearing marble palaces and baths on the shores of Campania, of drinking from amber, of feasting on singing birds, of exhibiting armies of gladiators and flocks of camelopards; the Spanish viceroy,[1] who, leaving behind him the curses of Mexico or Lima, entered Madrid with a long train of gilded coaches, and of sumpter-horses trapped and shod with silver, were now outdone. Cruelty, indeed, properly so called, was not among the vices of the servants of the Company. But cruelty itself could hardly have produced greater evils than sprang from their unprincipled eagerness to be rich. They pulled down their creature, Meer Jaffier. They set up in his place another Nabob, named Meer Cossim. But Meer Cossim had talents and a will; and, though sufficiently inclined to oppress his subjects himself, he could not bear to see them ground to the dust by oppressions which yielded him no profit, nay, which destroyed his revenue in its very source. The English accordingly pulled down Meer Cossim, and set up Meer Jaffier again; and Meer Cossim, after revenging himself by a massacre surpassing in atrocity that of the Black Hole, fled to the dominions of the Nabob of Oude. At every one of these revolutions, the new prince divided among his foreign masters whatever could be scraped together from the treasury of his fallen predecessor. The immense population of his dominions was given up as a prey to those who had made him a sovereign, and who could unmake him. The servants of the Company obtained, not for their employers, but for themselves, a monopoly of almost the whole internal trade. They forced the natives to buy dear and to sell cheap. They insulted with impunity the tribunals, the police, and the fiscal authorities of the country. They covered with their protection a set of native dependents who ranged through the provinces, spreading desolation and terror wherever they appeared. Every servant of a British factor was armed with all the power of his master; and his master was armed with all the power of the Company. Enormous fortunes were thus rapidly accumulated at Calcutta, while thirty millions of human beings were reduced to the extremity of wretchedness. They had been accustomed to live under tyranny, but never under tyranny like this. They found the little finger of the Company thicker than the loins [1] of Surajah Dowlah. Under their old masters they had at least one resource: when the evil became insupportable, the people rose and pulled down the government. But the English government was not to be so shaken off. That government, oppressive as the most oppressive form of barbarian despotism, was strong with all the strength of civilization. It resembled the government of evil Genii, rather than the government of human tyrants. Even despair could not inspire the soft Bengalee with courage to confront men of English breed, the hereditary nobility of mankind, whose skill and valor had so often triumphed in spite of tenfold odds. The unhappy race never attempted resistance. Sometimes they submitted in patient misery. Sometimes they fled from the white man, as their fathers had been used to fly from the Mahratta; and the palanquin of the English traveller was often carried through silent villages and towns, which the report of his approach had made desolate.

The foreign lords of Bengal were naturally objects of hatred to all the neighboring powers; and to all the haughty race presented a dauntless front. The English armies, everywhere outnumbered, were everywhere victorious. A succession of commanders, formed in the school of Clive, still maintained the fame of their country. "It must be acknowledged," says the Mussulman historian[1] of those times, "that this nation's presence of mind, firmness of temper, and undaunted bravery, are past all question. They join the most resolute courage to the most cautious prudence; nor have they their equals in the art of ranging themselves in battle array and fighting in order. If to so many military qualifications they knew how to join the arts of government, if they exerted as much ingenuity and solicitude in relieving the people of God, as they do in whatever concerns their military affairs, no nation in the world would be preferable to them, or worthier of command. But the people under their dominion groan everywhere, and are reduced to poverty and distress. Oh God! come to the assistance of thine afflicted servants, and deliver them from the oppressions which they suffer."

It was impossible, however, that even the military establishment should long continue exempt from the vices which pervaded every other part of the government. Rapacity, luxury, and the spirit of insubordination, spread from the civil service to the officers of the army, and from the officers to the soldiers. The evil continued to grow till every mess-room became the seat of conspiracy and cabal, and till the sepoys [1] could be kept in order only by wholesale executions.

At length the state of things in Bengal began to excite uneasiness at home. A succession of revolutions; a disorganized administration; the natives pillaged, yet the Company not enriched; every fleet bringing back fortunate adventurers who were able to purchase manors and to build stately dwellings, yet bringing back also alarming accounts of the financial prospects of the government; war on the frontiers; disaffection in the army; the national character disgraced by excesses resembling those of Verres and Pizarro; [2] such was the spectacle which dismayed those who were conversant with Indian affairs. The general cry was that Clive, and Clive alone, could save the empire which he had founded.

This feeling manifested itself in the strongest manner at a very full General Court of Proprietors. Men of all parties, forgetting their feuds and trembling for their dividends, exclaimed that Clive was the man whom the crisis required, that the oppressive proceedings which had been adopted respecting his estate ought to be dropped, and that he ought to be entreated to return to India.

Clive rose. As to his estate, he said, he would make such propositions to the Directors, as would, he trusted, lead to an amicable settlement. But there was a still greater difficulty. It was proper to tell them that he never would undertake the government of

Bengal while his enemy Sulivan was Chairman of the Company. The tumult was violent. Sulivan could scarcely obtain a hearing. An overwhelming majority of the assembly was on Clive's side. Sulivan wished to try the result of a ballot. But, according to the by-laws of the Company, there can be no ballot except on a requisition signed by nine proprietors; and, though hundreds were present, nine persons could not be found to set their hands to such a requisition.

Clive was in consequence nominated Governor and Commander-in-chief of the British possessions in Bengal. But he adhered to his declaration, and refused to enter on his office till the event of the next election of directors should be known. The contest was obstinate; but Clive triumphed. Sulivan, lately absolute master of the India House, was within a vote of losing his own seat; and both the chairman and the deputy-chairman were friends of the new governor.

Such were the circumstances under which Lord Clive sailed for the third and last time to India. In May, 1765, he reached Calcutta; and he found the whole machine of government even more fearfully disorganized than he had anticipated. Meer Jaffier, who had some time before lost his eldest son, Meeran, had died while Clive was on his voyage out. The English functionaries at Calcutta had already received from home strict orders not to accept presents from the native princes. But, eager for gain, and unaccustomed to respect the commands of their distant, ignorant, and negligent masters, they again set up the throne of

Bengal to sale. About one hundred and forty thousand pounds sterling were distributed among nine of the most powerful servants of the Company; and, in consideration of this bribe, an infant son of the deceased Nabob was placed on the seat of his father. The news of the ignominious bargain met Clive on his arrival. In a private letter, written, immediately after his landing, to an intimate friend, he poured out his feelings in language which, proceeding from a man so daring, so resolute, and so little given to theatrical display of sentiment, seems to us singularly touching. "Alas!" he says, "how is the English name sunk! I could not avoid paying the tribute of a few tears to the departed and lost fame of the British nation—irrecoverably so, I fear. However, I do declare by that great Being who is the searcher of all hearts, and to whom we must be accountable if there be a hereafter, that I am come out with a mind superior to all corruption, and that I am determined to destroy these great and growing evils, or perish in the attempt."

The Council met, and Clive stated to them his full determination to make a thorough reform, and to use for that purpose the whole of the ample authority, civil and military, which had been confided to him. Johnstone, one of the boldest and worst men in the assembly, made some show of opposition. Clive interrupted him, and haughtily demanded whether he meant to question the power of the new government. Johnstone was cowed, and disclaimed any such intention. All the faces round the board grew long and pale, and not another syllable of dissent was uttered.

Clive redeemed his pledge. He remained in India about a year and a half; and in that short time effected one of the most extensive, difficult, and salutary reforms that ever was accomplished by any statesman. This was the part of his life on which he afterwards looked back with the most pride. He had it in his power to triple his already splendid fortune; to connive at abuses while pretending to remove them; to conciliate the good-will of all the English in Bengal, by giving up to their rapacity a helpless and timid race, who knew not where lay the island which sent forth their oppressors, and whose complaints had little chance of being heard across fifteen thousand miles of ocean. He knew that, if he applied himself in earnest to the work of reformation, he should raise every bad passion in arms against him. He knew how unscrupulous, how implacable, would be the hatred of those ravenous adventurers who, having counted on accumulating in a few months fortunes sufficient to support peerages, should find all their hopes frustrated. But he had chosen the good part; and he called up all the force of his mind for a battle far harder than that of Plassey. At first success seemed hopeless; but soon all obstacles began to bend before that iron courage and that vehement will. The receiving of presents from the natives was rigidly prohibited. The private trade of the servants of the Company was put down. The whole settlement seemed to be set, as one man, against these measures. But the inexorable governor declared that, if he could not find support at Fort William, he would procure it elsewhere, and sent for some civil servants from Madras to assist him in carrying on the administration. The most factious of his opponents he turned out of their offices. The rest submitted to what was inevitable; and in a very short time all resistance was quelled.

But Clive was far too wise a man not to see that the recent abuses were partly to be ascribed to a cause which could not fail to produce similar abuses as soon as the pressure of his strong hand was withdrawn. The Company had followed a mistaken policy with respect to the remuneration of its servants. The salaries were too low to afford even those indulgences which are necessary to the health and comfort of Europeans in a tropical climate. To lay by a rupee from such scanty pay was impossible. It could not be supposed that men of even average abilities would consent to pass the best years of life in exile, under a burning sun, for no other consideration than these stinted wages. It had accordingly been understood, from a very early period, that the Company's agents were at liberty to enrich themselves by their private trade. This practice had been seriously injurious to the commercial interests of the corporation. That very intelligent observer, Sir Thomas Roe, in the reign of James the First, strongly urged the Directors to apply a remedy to the abuse. "Absolutely prohibit the private trade," said he; "for your business will be better done. I know this is harsh. Men profess they come not for bare wages. But you will take away this plea if you give great wages to their content; and then you know what you part from."

In spite of this excellent advice, the Company adhered to the old system, paid low salaries, and connived at the indirect gains of the agents. The pay of a member of Council was only three hundred pounds a year. Yet it was notorious that such a functionary could not live in India for less than ten times that sum; and it could not be expected that he would be content to live even handsomely in India without laying up something against the time of his return to England. This system, before the conquest of Bengal, might affect the amount of the dividends payable to the proprietors, but could do little harm in any other way. But the Company was now a ruling body. Its servants might still be called factors, junior merchants, senior merchants. But they were in truth proconsuls, proprætors, procurators of extensive regions. They had immense power. Their regular pay was universally admitted to be insufficient. They were, by the ancient usage of the service, and by the implied permission of their employers, warranted in enriching themselves by indirect means; and this had been the origin of the frightful oppression and corruption which had desolated Bengal. Clive saw clearly that it was absurd to give men power, and to require them to live in penury. He justly concluded that no reform could be effectual which should not be coupled with a plan for liberally remunerating the civil servants of the Company. The Directors, he knew, were not disposed to sanction any increase of the salaries out of their own treasury. The only course which remained open to the governor was one which exposed him to much misrepresentation, but which we think him fully justified in adopting. He appropriated to the support of the service the monopoly of salt, which has formed, down to our time, a principal head of Indian revenue; and he divided the proceeds according to a scale which seems to have been not unreasonably fixed. He was in consequence accused by his enemies, and has been accused by historians,[1] of disobeying his instructions, of violating his promises, of authorizing that very abuse which it was his special mission to destroy, namely, the trade of the Company's servants. But every discerning and impartial judge will admit that there was really nothing in common between the system which he set up and that which he was sent to destroy. The monopoly of salt had been a source of revenue to the governments of India before Clive was born. It continued to be so long after his death. The civil servants were clearly entitled to a maintenance out of the revenue; and all that Clive did was to charge a particular portion of the revenue with their maintenance. He thus, while he put an end to the practices by which gigantic fortunes had been rapidly accumulated, gave to every British functionary employed in the East the means of slowly, but surely, acquiring a competence. Yet, such is the injustice of mankind, that none of those acts which are the real stains of his life has drawn on him so much obloquy as this measure, which was in truth a reform necessary to the success of all his other reforms.

He had quelled the opposition of the civil service; that of the army was more formidable. Some of the retrenchments which had been ordered by the Directors affected the interests of the military service; and a storm arose, such as even Cæsar would not willingly have faced. It was no light thing to encounter the resistance of those who held the power of the sword, in a country governed only by the sword. Two hundred English officers engaged in a conspiracy against the government, and determined to resign their commissions on the same day, not doubting that Clive would grant any terms rather than see the army, on which alone the British empire in the East rested, left without commanders. They little knew the unconquerable spirit with which they had to deal. Clive had still a few officers round his person on whom he could rely. He sent to Fort St. George for a fresh supply. He gave commissions even to mercantile agents who were disposed to support him at this crisis; and he sent orders that every officer who resigned should be instantly brought up to Calcutta. The conspirators found that they had miscalculated. The governor was inexorable. The troops were steady. The sepoys, over whom Clive had always possessed extraordinary influence, stood by him with unshaken fidelity. The leaders in the plot were arrested, tried, and cashiered.[1] The rest, humbled and dispirited, begged to be permitted to withdraw their resignations. Many of them declared their repentance even with tears. The younger offenders Clive treated with lenity. To the ringleaders he was inflexibly severe; but his severity was pure from all taint of private malevolence. While he sternly upheld the just authority of his office, he passed by personal insults and injuries with magnanimous disdain. One of the conspirators [1] was accused of having planned the assassination of the governor; but Clive would not listen to the charge. "The officers," he said, "are Englishmen, not assassins."

While he reformed the civil service and established his authority over the army, he was equally successful in his foreign policy. His landing on Indian ground was the signal for immediate peace. The Nabob of Oude, with a large army, lay at that time on the frontier of Bahar. He had been joined by many Afghans and Mahrattas, and there was no small reason to expect a general coalition of all the native powers against the English. But the name of Clive quelled in an instant all opposition. The enemy implored peace in the humblest language, and submitted to such terms as the new governor chose to dictate.

At the same time, the government of Bengal was placed on a new footing. The power of the English in that province had hitherto been altogether undefined. It was unknown to the ancient constitution of the empire, and it had been ascertained by no compact. It resembled the power which, in the last decrepitude of the Western Empire, was exercised over Italy by the great chiefs of foreign mercenaries, the Ricimers and the Odoacers,[1] who put up and pulled down at their pleasure a succession of insignificant princes, dignified with the names of Cæsar and Augustus. But as in Italy, so in India, the warlike strangers at length found it expedient to give to a domination which had been established by arms the sanction of law and ancient prescription. Theodoric [2] thought it politic to obtain from the distant court of Byzantium a commission appointing him ruler of Italy; and Clive, in the same manner, applied to the Court of Delhi for a formal grant of the powers of which he already possessed the reality. The Mogul was absolutely helpless; and, though he murmured, had reason to be well pleased that the English were disposed to give solid rupees, which he never could have extorted from them, in exchange for a few Persian characters which cost him nothing. A bargain was speedily struck; and the titular sovereign of Hindostan issued a warrant, empowering the Company to collect and administer the revenues of Bengal, Orissa, and Bahar.

There was still a Nabob, who stood to the British authorities in the same relation in which the last drivelling Chilperics [3] and Childerics of the Merovingian line stood to their able and vigorous Mayors of the Palace, to Charles Martel and to Pepin. At one time Clive had almost made up his mind to discard this phantom altogether: but he afterwards thought that it might be convenient still to use the name of the Nabob, particularly in dealings with other European nations. The

French, the Dutch, and the Danes, would, he conceived, submit far more readily to the authority of the native Prince, whom they had always been accustomed to respect, than to that of a rival trading corporation. This policy may, at that time, have been judicious. But the pretence was soon found to be too flimsy to impose on anybody; and it was altogether laid aside. The heir of Meer Jaffier still resides at Mooreshedabad, the ancient capital of his house, still bears the title of Nabob, is still accosted by the English as "Your Highness," and is still suffered to retain a portion of the regal state which surrounded his ancestors. A pension of a hundred and sixty thousand pounds a year is annually paid to him by the government. His carriage is surrounded by guards, and preceded by attendants with silver maces. His person and his dwelling are exempted from the ordinary authority of the ministers of justice. But he has not the smallest share of political power, and is, in fact, only a noble and wealthy subject of the Company.

It would have been easy for Clive, during his second administration in Bengal, to accumulate riches such as no subject in Europe possessed. He might, indeed, without subjecting the rich inhabitants of the province to any pressure beyond that to which their mildest rulers had accustomed them, have received presents to the amount of three hundred thousand pounds a year. The neighboring princes would gladly have paid any price for his favor. But he appears to have strictly adhered to the rules which he had laid down for the guidance of others. The Rajah of Benares offered him diamonds of great value. The Nabob of Oude pressed him to accept a large sum of money, and a casket of costly jewels. Clive courteously but peremptorily refused: and it should be observed that he made no merit of his refusal, and that the facts did not come to light till after his death. He kept an exact account of his salary, of his share of the profits accruing from the trade in salt, and of those presents which, according to the fashion of the East, it would be churlish to refuse. Out of the sum arising from these resources he defrayed the expenses of his situation. The surplus he divided among a few attached friends who had accompanied him to India. He always boasted, and, as far as we can judge, he boasted with truth, that his last administration diminished instead of increasing his fortune.

One large sum indeed he accepted. Meer Jaffier had left him by will above sixty thousand pounds sterling in specie and jewels: and the rules which had been recently laid down extended only to presents from the living, and did not affect legacies from the dead. Clive took the money, but not for himself. He made the whole over to the Company, in trust for officers and soldiers invalided in their service. The fund which still bears his name, owes its origin to this princely donation.

After a stay of eighteen months, the state of his health made it necessary for him to return to Europe. At the close of January, 1767, he quitted for the last time the country on whose destinies he had exercised so mighty an influence.

His second return from Bengal was not, like his first, greeted by the acclamations of his countrymen. Numerous causes were already at work which embittered the remaining years of his life, and hurried him to an untimely grave. His old enemies at the India House were still powerful and active; and they had been reinforced by a large band of allies, whose violence far exceeded their own. The whole crew of pilferers and oppressors from whom he had rescued Bengal persecuted him with the implacable rancor which belongs to such abject natures. Many of them even invested their property in India stock, merely that they might be better able to annoy the man whose firmness had set bounds to their rapacity. Lying newspapers were set up for no purpose but to abuse him; and the temper of the public mind was then such, that these arts, which, under ordinary circumstances would have been ineffectual against truth and merit, produced an extraordinary impression.

The great events which had taken place in India had called into existence a new class of Englishmen, to whom their countrymen gave the name of Nabobs. These persons had generally sprung from families neither ancient nor opulent; they had generally been sent at an early age to the East; and they had there acquired large fortunes, which they had brought back to their native land. It was natural that, not having had much opportunity of mixing with the best society, they should exhibit some of the awkwardness and some of the pomposity of upstarts. It was natural that, during their sojourn in Asia, they should have acquired some tastes and habits surprising, if not disgusting, to persons who had never quitted Europe. It was natural that, having enjoyed great consideration in the East, they should not be disposed to sink into obscurity at home; and as they had money, and had not birth or high connection, it was natural that they should display a little obtrusively the single advantage which they possessed. Wherever they settled there was a kind of feud between them and the old nobility and gentry, similar to that which raged in France between the farmer-general[1] and the marquess. This enmity to the aristocracy long continued to distinguish the servants of the Company. More than twenty years after the time of which we are now speaking, Burke pronounced that among the Jacobins might be reckoned "the East Indians almost to a man, who cannot bear to find that their present importance does not bear a proportion to their wealth."

The Nabobs soon became a most unpopular class of men. Some of them had in the East displayed eminent talents, and rendered great services to the state; but at home their talents were not shown to advantage, and their services were little known. That they had sprung from obscurity, that they had acquired great wealth, that they exhibited it insolently, that they spent it extravagantly, that they raised the price of everything in their neighborhood, from fresh eggs to rotten boroughs, that their liveries outshone those of dukes, that their coaches were finer than that of the Lord Mayor, that the examples of their large and ill-governed households corrupted half the servants in the country, that some of them, with all their magnificence, could not catch the tone of good society, but, in spite of the stud and the crowd of menials, of the plate and the Dresden china, of the venison and the Burgundy, were still low men; these were things which excited, both in the class from which they had sprung and in the class into which they attempted to force themselves, the bitter aversion which is the effect of mingled envy and contempt. But when it was also rumored that the fortune which enabled its possessor to eclipse the Lord Lieutenant on the race-ground, or to carry the county against the head of a house as old as Domesday Book,[1] had been accumulated by violating public faith, by deposing legitimate princes, by reducing whole provinces to beggary, all the higher and better as well as all the low and evil parts of human nature were stirred against the wretch who had obtained by guilt and dishonor the riches which he now lavished with arrogant and inelegant profusion. The unfortunate Nabob seemed to be made up of those foibles against which comedy has pointed the most merciless ridicule, and of those crimes which have thrown the deepest gloom over tragedy, of Turcaret[2] and Nero, of Monsieur Jourdain[3] and Richard the Third. A tempest of execration and derision, such as can be compared only to that outbreak of public feeling against the Puritans which took place at the time of the Restoration, burst on the servants of the Company. The humane man was horror-struck at the way in which they had got their money, the thrifty man at the way in which they spent it. The dilettante [1] sneered at their want of taste. The maccaroni [2] black-balled them as vulgar fellows. Writers the most unlike in sentiment and style, Methodists and libertines, philosophers and buffoons, were for once on the same side. It is hardly too much to say that, during a space of about thirty years, the whole lighter literature of England was colored by the feelings which we have described. Foote [3] brought on the stage an Anglo-Indian chief, dissolute, ungenerous, and tyrannical, ashamed of the humble friends of his youth, hating the aristocracy, yet childishly eager to be numbered among them, squandering his wealth on pandars and flatterers, tricking out his chairmen [4] with the most costly hot-house flowers, and astounding the ignorant with jargon about rupees, lacs, and jaghires.[5] Mackenzie,[6] with more delicate humor, depicted a plain country family raised by the Indian acquisitions of one of its members to sudden opulence, and exciting derision by an awkward mimicry of the manners of the great. Cowper [7] in that lofty expostulation which glows with the very spirit of the Hebrew poets, placed the oppression of India foremost in the list of those national crimes for which God had punished England with years of disastrous war, with discomfiture in her own seas, and with the loss of her transatlantic empire. If any of our readers will take the trouble to search in the dusty recesses of circulating libraries for some novel published sixty years ago, the chance is that the villain or sub-villain of the story will prove to be a savage old Nabob, with an immense fortune, a tawny complexion, a bad liver, and a worse heart.

Such, as far as we can now judge, was the feeling of the country respecting Nabobs in general. And Clive was eminently the Nabob, the ablest, the most celebrated, the highest in rank, the highest in fortune, of all the fraternity. His wealth was exhibited in a manner which could not fail to excite odium. He lived with great magnificence in Berkeley Square. He reared one palace in Shropshire and another at Claremont. His parliamentary influence might vie with that of the greatest families. But in all this splendor and power envy found something to sneer at. On some of his relations wealth and dignity seem to have sat as awkwardly as on Mackenzie's Margery Mushroom. Nor was he himself, with all his great qualities, free from those weaknesses which the satirists of that age represented as characteristic of his whole class. In the field, indeed, his habits were remarkably simple. He was constantly on horseback, was never seen but in his uniform, never wore silk, never entered a palanquin, and was content with the plainest fare. But when he was no longer at the head of an army, he laid aside his Spartan temperance[1] for the ostentatious luxury of a Sybarite. Though his person was ungraceful, and though his harsh features were redeemed from vulgar ugliness only by their stern, dauntless, and commanding expression, he was fond of rich and gay clothing, and replenished his wardrobe with absurd profusion. Sir John Malcolm gives us a letter worthy of Sir Matthew Mite,[1] in which Clive orders "two hundred shirts, the best and finest that can be got for love or money." A few follies of this description, grossly exaggerated by report, produced an unfavorable impression on the public mind. But this was not the worst. Black stories, of which the greater part were pure inventions, were circulated respecting his conduct in the East. He had to bear the whole odium, not only of those bad acts to which he had once or twice stooped, but of all the bad acts of all the English in India, of bad acts committed when he was absent, nay, of bad acts which he had manfully opposed and severely punished. The very abuses against which he had waged an honest, resolute, and successful war, were laid to his account. He was, in fact, regarded as the personification of all the vices and weaknesses which the public, with or without reason, ascribed to the English adventurers in Asia. We have ourselves heard old men, who knew nothing of his history, but who still retained the prejudices conceived in their youth, talk of him as an incarnate fiend. Johnson always held this language. Brown, whom Clive employed to lay out his pleasure grounds, was amazed to see in the house of his noble employer a chest which had once been filled with gold from the treasury of Moorshedabad, and could not understand how the conscience of the criminal could suffer him to sleep with such an object so near to his bedchamber. The peasantry of Surrey looked with mysterious horror on the stately house which was rising at Claremont, and whispered that the great wicked lord had ordered the walls to be made so thick in order to keep out the devil, who would one day carry him away bodily. Among the gaping clowns who drank in this frightful story was a worthless ugly lad of the name of Hunt, since widely known as William Huntington, S. S.;[1] and the superstition which was strangely mingled with the knavery of that remarkable impostor seems to have derived no small nutriment from the tales which he heard of the life and character of Clive.

In the meantime, the impulse which Clive had given to the administration of Bengal was constantly becoming fainter and fainter. His policy was to a great extent abandoned; the abuses which he had suppressed began to revive; and at length the evils which a bad government had engendered were aggravated by one of those fearful visitations which the best government cannot avert. In the summer of 1770, the rains failed; the earth was parched up; the tanks were empty; the rivers shrank within their beds; and a famine, such as is known only in countries where every household depends for support on its own little patch of cultivation, filled the whole valley of the Ganges with misery and death. Tender and delicate women, whose veils had never been lifted before the public gaze, came forth from the inner chambers in which Eastern jealousy had kept watch over their beauty, threw themselves on the earth before the passers-by and, with loud wailings, implored a handful of rice for their children. The Hoogley every day rolled down thousands of corpses close to the porticos and gardens of the English conquerors. The very streets of Calcutta were blocked up by the dying and the dead. The lean and feeble survivors had not energy enough to bear the bodies of their kindred to the funeral pile or the holy river, or even to scare away the jackals and vultures, that fed on human remains in the face of day. The extent of the mortality was never ascertained; but it was popularly reckoned by millions. This melancholy intelligence added to the excitement which already prevailed in England on Indian subjects. The proprietors of East India stock were uneasy about their dividends. All men of common humanity were touched by the calamities of our unhappy subjects; and indignation soon began to mingle itself with pity. It was rumored that the Company's servants had created the famine by engrossing all the rice of the country; that they had sold grain for eight, ten, twelve times the price at which they had bought it; that one English functionary who, the year before, was not worth a hundred guineas, had, during that season of misery, remitted sixty thousand pounds to London. These charges we believe to have been unfounded. That servants of the Company had ventured, since Clive's departure, to deal in rice, is probable. That, if they dealt in rice, they must have gained by the scarcity, is certain. But there is no reason for thinking that they either produced or aggravated an evil which physical causes sufficiently explain. The outcry which was raised against them on this occasion was, we suspect, as absurd as the imputations which, in times of dearth at home, were once thrown by statesmen and judges, and are still thrown by two or three old women, on the corn-factors. It was, however, so loud and so general that it appears to have imposed even on an intellect raised so high above vulgar prejudices as that of Adam Smith.[1] What was still more extraordinary, these unhappy events greatly increased the unpopularity of Lord Clive. He had been some years in England when the famine took place. None of his acts had the smallest tendency to produce such a calamity. If the servants of the Company had traded in rice, they had done so in direct contravention of the rule which he had laid down, and, while in power, had resolutely enforced. But, in the eyes of his countrymen, he was, as we have said, the Nabob, the Anglo-Indian character personified; and, while he was building and planting in Surrey, he was held responsible for all the effects of a dry season in Bengal.

Parliament had hitherto bestowed very little attention on our Eastern possessions. Since the death of George the Second, a rapid succession of weak administrations, each of which was in turn flattered and betrayed by the Court, had held the semblance of power. Intrigues in the palace, riots in the capital, and insurrectionary movements in the American colonies, had left the advisers of the crown little leisure to study Indian politics. When they did interfere, their interference was feeble and irresolute. Lord Chatham indeed, during the short period of his ascendency in the councils of George the Third, had meditated a bold attack on the Company. But his plans were rendered abortive by the strange malady [1] which about that time began to overcloud his splendid genius.

At length, in 1772, it was generally felt that Parliament could no longer neglect the affairs of India. The Government was stronger than any which had held power since the breach between Mr. Pitt and the great Whig connection in 1761. No pressing question of domestic or European policy required the attention of public men. There was a short and delusive lull between two tempests. The excitement produced by the Middlesex election [2] was over; the discontents of America did not yet threaten civil war; the financial difficulties of the Company brought on a crisis; the Ministers were forced to take up the subject; and the whole storm, which had long been gathering, now broke at once on the head of Clive.

His situation was indeed singularly unfortunate. He was hated throughout the country, hated at the India House, hated, above all, by those wealthy and powerful servants of the Company, whose rapacity and tyranny he had withstood. He had to bear the double odium of his bad and of his good actions, of every Indian abuse and of every Indian reform. The state of the political world was such that he could count on the support of no powerful connection. The party to which he had belonged, that of George Grenville, had been hostile to the Government, and yet had never cordially united with the other sections of the Opposition, with the little band which still followed the fortunes of Lord Chatham, or with the large and respectable body of which Lord Rockingham was the acknowledged leader. George Grenville was now dead; his followers were scattered; and Clive, unconnected with any of the powerful factions which divided the Parliament, could reckon only on the votes of those members who were returned by himself. His enemies, particularly those who were the enemies of his virtues, were unscrupulous, ferocious, implacable. Their malevolence aimed at nothing less than the utter ruin of his fame and fortune. They wished to see him expelled from Parliament, to see his spurs chopped off,[1] to see his estate confiscated; and it may be doubted whether even such a result as this would have quenched their thirst for revenge.

Clive's parliamentary tactics resembled his military tactics. Deserted, surrounded, outnumbered, and with everything at stake, he did not even deign to stand on the defensive, but pushed boldly forward to the attack. At an early stage of the discussions on Indian affairs he rose, and in a long and elaborate speech vindicated himself from a large part of the accusations which had been brought against him. He is said to have produced a great impression on his audience. Lord Chatham, who, now the ghost of his former self, loved to haunt the scene of his glory, was that night under the gallery of the House of Commons, and declared that he had never heard a finer speech. It was subsequently printed under Clive's direction, and, when the fullest allowance has been made for the assistance which he may have obtained from literary friends, proves him to have possessed, not merely strong sense and manly spirit, but talents both for disquisition and declamation which assiduous culture might have improved into the highest excellence. He confined his defence on this occasion to the measures of his last administration, and succeeded so far that his enemies thenceforth thought it expedient to direct their attacks chiefly against the earlier part of his life.

The earlier part of his life unfortunately presented some assailable points to their hostility. A committee was chosen by ballot to inquire into the affairs of India; and by this committee the whole history of that great revolution which threw down Surajah Dowlah and raised Meer Jaffier was sifted with malignant care. Clive was subjected to the most unsparing examination and cross-examination, and afterwards bitterly complained that he, the Baron of Plassey, had been treated like a sheep-stealer. The boldness and ingenuousness of his replies would alone suffice to show how alien from his nature were the frauds to which, in the course of his Eastern negotiations, he had sometimes descended. He avowed the arts which he had employed to deceive Omichund, and resolutely said that he was not ashamed of them, and that, in the same circumstances, he would again act in the same manner. He admitted that he had received immense sums from Meer Jaffier; but he denied that, in doing so, he had violated any obligation of morality or honor. He laid claim, on the contrary, and not without some reason, to the praise of eminent disinterestedness. He described in vivid language the situation in which his victory had placed him; a great prince dependent on his pleasure; an opulent city afraid of being given up to plunder; wealthy bankers bidding against each other for his smiles; vaults piled with gold and jewels thrown open to him alone. "By God, Mr. Chairman," he exclaimed, "at this moment I stand astonished at my own moderation."

The inquiry was so extensive that the Houses rose [1] before it had been completed. It was continued in the following session. When at length the committee had concluded its labors, enlightened and impartial men had little difficulty in making up their minds as to the result. It was clear that Clive had been guilty of some acts which it is impossible to vindicate without attacking the authority of all the most sacred laws which regulate the intercourse of individuals and of states. But it was equally clear that he had displayed great talents, and even great virtues; that he had rendered eminent services both to his country and to the people of India; and that it was in truth not for his dealings with Meer Jaffier, nor for the fraud which he had practised on Omichund, but for his determined resistance to avarice and tyranny, that he was now called in question.

Ordinary criminal justice knows nothing of set-off. The greatest desert cannot be pleaded in answer to a charge of the slightest transgression. If a man has sold beer on Sunday morning, it is no defence that he has saved the life of a fellow-creature at the risk of his own. If he has harnessed a Newfoundland dog to his little child's carriage, it is no defence that he was wounded at Waterloo. But it is not in this way that we ought to deal with men who, raised far above ordinary restraints, and tried by far more than ordinary temptations, are entitled to a more than ordinary measure of indulgence. Such men should be judged by their contemporaries as they will be judged by posterity. Their bad actions ought not, indeed, to be called good: but their good and bad actions ought to be fairly weighed; and if on the whole the good preponderate, the sentence ought to be one, not merely of acquittal, but of approbation. Not a single great ruler in history can be absolved by a judge who fixes his eye inexorably on one or two unjustifiable acts. Bruce [1] the deliverer of Scotland, Maurice the deliverer of Germany, William the deliverer of Holland, his great descendant the deliverer of England, Murray the good regent, Cosmo the father of his country, Henry the Fourth of France, Peter the Great of Russia, how would the best of them pass such a scrutiny? History takes wider views; and the best tribunal for great political cases is the tribunal which anticipates the verdict of history.

Reasonable and moderate men of all parties felt this in Clive's case. They could not pronounce him blameless; but they were not disposed to abandon him to that low-minded and rancorous pack who had run him down and were eager to worry him to death. Lord North, though not very friendly to him, was not disposed to go to extremities against him. While the inquiry was still in progress, Clive, who had some years before been created a Knight of the Bath, was installed with great pomp in Henry the Seventh's Chapel.[1] He was soon after appointed Lord Lieutenant of Shropshire. When he kissed hands, George the Third, who had always been partial to him, admitted him to a private audience, talked to him half an hour on Indian politics, and was visibly affected when the persecuted general spoke of his services and of the way in which they had been requited.

At length the charges came in a definite form before the House of Commons. Burgoyne,[2] chairman of the committee, a man of wit, fashion, and honor, an agreeable dramatic writer, an officer whose courage was never questioned, and whose skill was at that time highly esteemed, appeared as the accuser. The members of the administration took different sides; for in that age all questions were open questions, except such as were brought forward by the Government, or such as implied some censure on the Government. Thurlow, the Attorney General, was among the assailants. Wedderburne, the Solicitor General, strongly attached to Clive, defended his friend with extraordinary force of argument and language. It is a curious circumstance that, some years later, Thurlow was the most conspicuous champion of Warren Hastings, while Wedderburne was among the most unrelenting persecutors of that great though not faultless statesman. Clive spoke in his own defence, at less length and with less art than in the preceding year, but with much energy and pathos. He recounted his great actions and his wrongs: and, after bidding his hearers remember that they were about to decide not only on his honor but their own, he retired from the House.

The Commons resolved that acquisitions made by the arms of the State belong to the State alone, and that it is illegal in the servants of the State to appropriate such acquisitions to themselves. They resolved that this wholesome rule appeared to have been systematically violated by the English functionaries in Bengal. On a subsequent day they went a step farther, and resolved that Clive had, by means of the power which he possessed as commander of the British forces in India, obtained large sums from Meer Jaffier. Here the Commons stopped. They had voted the major and minor of Burgoyne's syllogism; but they shrank from drawing the logical conclusion. When it was moved that Lord Clive had abused his powers, and set an evil example to the servants of the public, the previous question [1] was put and carried. At length, long after the sun had risen on an animated debate, Wedderburne moved that Lord Clive had at the same time rendered great and meritorious services to his country; and this motion passed without a division.

The result of this memorable inquiry appears to us, on the whole, honorable to the justice, moderation, and discernment of the Commons. They had, indeed, no great temptation to do wrong. They would have been very bad judges of an accusation brought against Jenkinson or against Wilkes. But the question respecting Clive was not a party question; and the House accordingly acted with the good sense and good feeling which may always be expected from an assembly of English gentlemen, not blinded by faction.

The equitable and temperate proceedings of the British Parliament were set off to the greatest advantage by a foil. The wretched government of Louis the Fifteenth had murdered, directly or indirectly, almost every Frenchman who had served his country with distinction in the East. Labourdonnais was flung into the Bastile, and, after years of suffering, left it only to die. Dupleix, stripped of his immense fortune, and broken-hearted by humiliating attendance in antechambers, sank into an obscure grave. Lally was dragged to the common place of execution with a gag between his lips. The Commons of England, on the other hand, treated their living captain with that discriminating justice which is seldom shown except to the dead. They laid down sound general principles; they delicately pointed out where he had deviated from those principles; and they tempered the gentle censure with liberal eulogy. The contrast struck Voltaire, always partial to England, and always eager to expose the abuses of the Parliaments of France. Indeed he seems, at this time, to have meditated a history of the conquest of Bengal. He mentioned his design to Dr. Moore when that amusing writer visited him at

Ferney. Wedderburne took great interest in the matter, and pressed Clive to furnish materials. Had the plan been carried into execution, we have no doubt that Voltaire would have produced a book containing much lively and picturesque narrative, many just and humane sentiments poignantly expressed, many grotesque blunders, many sneers at the Mosaic chronology, much scandal about the Catholic missionaries, and much sublime theophilanthropy, stolen from the New Testament, and put into the mouths of virtuous and philosophical Brahmins.

Clive was now secure in the enjoyment of his fortune and his honors. He was surrounded by attached friends and relations; and he had not yet passed the season of vigorous bodily and mental exertion. But clouds had long been gathering over his mind, and now settled on it in thick darkness. From early youth he had been subject to fits of that strange melancholy "which rejoiceth exceedingly [1] and is glad when it can find the grave." While still a writer at Madras, he had twice attempted to destroy himself. Business and prosperity had produced a salutary effect on his spirits. In India, while he was occupied by great affairs, in England, while wealth and rank had still the charm of novelty, he had borne up against his constitutional misery; but he had now nothing to do, and nothing to wish for. His active spirit in an inactive situation drooped and withered like a plant in an uncongenial air. The malignity with which his enemies had pursued him, the indignity with which he had been treated by the committee, the censure, lenient as it was, which the House of Commons had pronounced, the knowledge that he was regarded by a large portion of his countrymen as a cruel and perfidious tyrant, all concurred to irritate and depress him. In the meantime his temper was tried by acute physical suffering. During his long residence in tropical climates, he had contracted several painful distempers. In order to obtain ease he called in the help of opium; and he was gradually enslaved by this treacherous ally. To the last, however, his genius occasionally flashed through the gloom. It was said that he would sometimes, after sitting silent and torpid for hours, rouse himself to the discussion of some great question, would display in full vigor all the talents of the soldier and statesman, and would then sink back into his melancholy repose.

The disputes with America had now become so serious that an appeal to the sword seemed inevitable; and the Ministers were desirous to avail themselves of the services of Clive. Had he still been what he was when he raised the siege of Patna, and annihilated the Dutch army and navy at the mouth of the Ganges, it is not improbable that the resistance of the Colonists would have been put down, and that the inevitable separation would have been deferred for a few years. But it was too late. His strong mind was fast sinking under many kinds of suffering. On the twenty-second of November, 1774, he died by his own hand. He had just completed his forty-ninth year.

In the awful close of so much prosperity and glory, the vulgar saw only a confirmation of all their prejudices; and some men of real piety and genius so far forgot the maxims both of religion and of philosophy as confidently to ascribe the mournful event to the just vengeance of God, and to the horrors of an evil conscience. It is with very different feelings that we contemplate the spectacle of a great mind ruined by the weariness of satiety, by the pangs of wounded honor, by fatal diseases, and more fatal remedies.

Clive committed great faults; and we have not attempted to disguise them. But his faults, when weighed against his merits, and viewed in connection with his temptations, do not appear to us to deprive him of his right to an honorable place in the estimation of posterity.

From his first visit to India dates the renown of the English arms in the East. Till he appeared, his countrymen were despised as mere pedlers, while the French were revered as people formed for victory and command. His courage and capacity dissolved the charm. With the defence of Arcot commences that long series of Oriental triumphs which closes with the fall of Ghizni.[1] Nor must we forget that he was only twenty-five years old when he approved himself ripe for military command. This is a rare if not a singular distinction. It is true that Alexander, Condé, and Charles the Twelfth [2] won great battles at a still earlier age; but those princes were surrounded by veteran generals of distinguished skill, to whose suggestions must be attributed the victories of the Granicus, of Rocroi, and of Narva. Clive, an inexperienced youth, had yet more experience than any of those who served under him. He had to form himself, to form his officers, and to form his army. The only man, as far as we recollect, who at an equally early age ever gave equal proof of talents for war, was Napoleon Bonaparte.

From Clive's second visit to India dates the political ascendency of the English in that country. His dexterity and resolution realized, in the course of a few months, more than all the gorgeous visions which had floated before the imagination of Dupleix. Such an extent of cultivated territory, such an amount of revenue, such a multitude of subjects, was never added to the dominion of Rome by the most successful proconsul. Nor were such wealthy spoils ever borne under arches of triumph, down the Sacred Way,[1] and through the crowded Forum, to the threshold of Tarpeian Jove. The fame of those who subdued Antiochus and Tigranes[2] grows dim when compared with the splendor of the exploits which the young English adventurer achieved at the head of an army not equal in numbers to one-half of a Roman legion.

From Clive's third visit to India dates the purity of the administration of our Eastern empire. When he landed in Calcutta in 1765, Bengal was regarded as a place to which Englishmen were sent only to get rich, by any means, in the shortest possible time. He first made dauntless and unsparing war on that gigantic system of oppression, extortion, and corruption. In that war he manfully put to hazard his ease, his fame, and his splendid fortune. The same sense of justice which forbids us to conceal or extenuate the faults of his earlier days compels us to admit that those faults were nobly repaired. If the reproach of the Company and of its servants has been taken away, if in India the yoke of foreign masters, elsewhere the heaviest of all yokes, has been found lighter than that of any native dynasty, if to that gang of public robbers, which formerly spread terror through the whole plain of Bengal, has succeeded a body of functionaries not more highly distinguished by ability and diligence than by integrity, disinterestedness, and public spirit, if we now see such men as Munroe, Elphinstone, and Metcalfe,[1] after leading victorious armies, after making and deposing kings, return, proud of their honorable poverty, from a land which once held out to every greedy factor the hope of boundless wealth, the praise is in no small measure due to Clive. His name stands high on the roll of conquerors. But it is found in a better list, in the list of those who have done and suffered much for the happiness of mankind. To the warrior, history will assign a place in the same rank with Lucullus and Trajan.[2] Nor will she deny to the reformer a share of that veneration with which France cherishes the memory of Turgot,[3] and with which the latest generations of Hindoos will contemplate the statue of Lord William Bentinck.[4]

WARREN HASTINGS

WARREN HASTINGS

We are inclined to think that we shall best meet the wishes of our readers, if, instead of minutely examining this book,[1] we attempt to give, in a way necessarily hasty and imperfect, our own view of the life and character of Mr. Hastings. Our feeling towards him is not exactly that of the House of Commons which impeached him in 1787; neither is it that of the House of Commons which uncovered [2] and stood up to receive him in 1813. He had great qualities, and he rendered great services to the state. But to represent him as a man of stainless virtue is to make him ridiculous; and from a regard for his memory, if from no other feeling, his friends would have done well to lend no countenance to such adulation. We believe that, if he were now living, he would have sufficient judgment and sufficient greatness of mind to wish to be shown as he was. He must have known that there were dark spots on his fame. He might also have felt with pride that the splendor of his fame would bear many spots. He would have wished posterity to have a likeness of him, though an unfavorable likeness, rather than a daub at once insipid and unnatural, resembling neither him nor anybody else. "Paint me as I am," said Oliver Cromwell, while sitting to young Lely. "If you leave out the scars and wrinkles,

I will not pay you a shilling." Even in such a trifle, the great Protector showed both his good sense and his magnanimity. He did not wish all that was characteristic in his countenance to be lost, in the vain attempt to give him the regular features and smooth blooming cheeks of the curl-pated minions of James the First. He was content that his face should go forth marked with all the blemishes which had been put on it by time, by war, by sleepless nights, by anxiety, perhaps by remorse; but with valor, policy, authority, and public care written in all its princely lines. If men truly great knew their own interest, it is thus that they would wish their minds to be portrayed.

Warren Hastings sprang from an ancient and illustrious race. It has been affirmed that his pedigree can be traced back to the great Danish sea-king,[1] whose sails were long the terror of both coasts of the Bristol Channel, and who, after many fierce and doubtful struggles, yielded at last to the valor and genius of Alfred. But the undoubted splendor of the line of Hastings needs no illustration from fable. One branch of that line wore, in the fourteenth century, the coronet of Pembroke. From another branch sprang the renowned Chamberlain,[2] the faithful adherent of the White Rose,[3] whose fate has furnished so striking a theme both to poets and to historians. His family received from the Tudors the earldom of Huntingdon, which, after long dispossession, was regained in our time by a series of events scarcely paralleled in romance.

The lords of the manor of Daylesford, in Worcestershire, claimed to be considered as the heads of this distinguished family. The main stock, indeed, prospered less than some of the younger shoots. But the Daylesford family, though not ennobled, was wealthy and highly considered, till, about two hundred years ago, it was overwhelmed by the great ruin of the civil war. The Hastings of that time was a zealous cavalier. He raised money on his lands, sent his plate to the mint at Oxford,[1] joined the royal army, and, after spending half his property in the cause of King Charles, was glad to ransom himself by making over most of the remaining half to speaker Lenthal. The old seat at Daylesford still remained in the family; but it could no longer be kept up; and in the following generation it was sold to a merchant of London.

Before this transfer took place, the last Hastings of Daylesford had presented his second son to the rectory of the parish in which the ancient residence of the family stood. The living [2] was of little value; and the situation of the poor clergyman, after the sale of the estate, was deplorable. He was constantly engaged in lawsuits about his tithes [3] with the new lord of the manor, and was at length utterly ruined. His eldest son, Howard, a well-conducted young man, obtained a place in the Customs. The second son, Pynaston, an idle worthless boy, married before he was sixteen, lost his wife in two years, and died in the West Indies, leaving to the care of his unfortunate father a little orphan, destined to strange and memorable vicissitudes of fortune.

Warren, the son of Pynaston, was born on the sixth of December, 1732. His mother died a few days later, and he was left dependent on his distressed grandfather. The child was early sent to the village school, where he learned his letters on the same bench with the sons of the peasantry; nor did anything in his garb or fare indicate that his life was to take a widely different course from that of the young rustics with whom he studied and played. But no cloud could overcast the dawn of so much genius and so much ambition. The very ploughmen observed, and long remembered, how kindly little Warren took to his book. The daily sight of the lands which his ancestors had possessed, and which had passed into the hands of strangers, filled his young brain with wild fancies and projects. He loved to hear stories of the wealth and greatness of his progenitors, of their splendid housekeeping, their loyalty, and their valor. On one bright summer day, the boy, then just seven years old, lay on the bank of the rivulet which flows through the old domain of his house to join the Isis. There, as threescore and ten years later he told the tale, rose in his mind a scheme which, through all the turns of his eventful career, was never abandoned. He would recover the estate which had belonged to his fathers. He would be Hastings of Daylesford. This purpose, formed in infancy and poverty, grew stronger as his intellect expanded and as his fortune rose. He pursued his plan with that calm but indomitable force of will which was the most striking peculiarity of his character. When, under a tropical sun, he ruled fifty millions of

Asiatics, his hopes, amidst all the cares of war, finance, and legislation, still pointed to Daylesford. And when his long public life, so singularly chequered with good and evil, with glory and obloquy, had at length closed for ever, it was to Daylesford that he retired to die.

When he was eight years old, his uncle Howard determined to take charge of him, and to give him a liberal education. The boy went up to London, and was sent to a school at Newington, where he was well taught but ill fed. He always attributed the smallness of his stature to the hard and scanty fare of this seminary. At ten he was removed to Westminster school,[1] then flourishing under the care of Dr. Nichols. Vinny Bourne, as his pupils affectionately called him, was one of the masters. Churchill, Colman, Lloyd, Cumberland, Cowper,[2] were among the students. With Cowper Hastings formed a friendship which neither the lapse of time, nor a wide dissimilarity of opinions and pursuits, could wholly dissolve. It does not appear that they ever met after they had grown to manhood. But forty years later, when the voices of many great orators were crying for vengeance on the oppressor of India, the shy and secluded poet could image to himself Hastings the Governor-General only as the Hastings with whom he had rowed on the Thames and played in the cloister, and refused to believe that so good-tempered a fellow could have done anything very wrong. His own life had been spent in praying, musing, and rhyming among the water-lilies of the Ouse. He had preserved in no common measure the innocence of childhood. His spirit had indeed been severely tried,[1] but not by temptations which impelled him to any gross violations of the rules of social morality. He had never been attacked by combinations of powerful and deadly enemies. He had never been compelled to make a choice between innocence and greatness,[2] between crime and ruin. Firmly as he held in theory the doctrine of human depravity, his habits were such that he was unable to conceive how far from the path of right even kind and noble natures may be hurried by the rage of conflict and the lust of dominion.

Hastings had another associate at Westminster of whom we shall have occasion to make frequent mention, Elijah Impey. We know little about their school days. But, we think, we may safely venture to guess that, whenever Hastings wished to play any trick more than usually naughty, he hired Impey with a tart or a ball to act as fag in the worst part of the prank.

Warren was distinguished among his comrades as an excellent swimmer, boatman, and scholar. At fourteen he was first in the examination for the foundation. His name in gilded letters on the walls of the dormitory still attests his victory over many older competitors. He stayed two years longer at the school, and was looking forward to a studentship at Christ Church, when an event happened which changed the whole course of his life. Howard Hastings died, bequeathing his nephew to the care of a friend and distant relation, named Chiswick. This gentleman, though he did not absolutely refuse the charge, was desirous to rid himself of it as soon as possible. Dr. Nichols made strong remonstrances against the cruelty of interrupting the studies of a youth who seemed likely to be one of the first scholars of the age. He even offered to bear the expense of sending his favorite pupil to Oxford. But Mr. Chiswick was inflexible. He thought the years which had already been wasted on hexameters [1] and pentameters quite sufficient. He had it in his power to obtain for the lad a writership [2] in the service of the East India Company.[3] Whether the young adventurer, when once shipped off, made a fortune, or died of a liver complaint, he equally ceased to be a burden to anybody. Warren was accordingly removed from Westminster school, and placed for a few months at a commercial academy, to study arithmetic and book-keeping. In January, 1750, a few days after he had completed his seventeenth year, he sailed for Bengal, and arrived at his destination in the October following.

He was immediately placed at a desk in the Secretary's office at Calcutta, and labored there during two years. Fort William was then a purely commercial settlement. In the south of India the encroaching policy of Dupleix [4] had transformed the servants of the English company, against their will, into diplomatists and generals. The war of the succession was raging in the Carnatic; [5] and the tide had been suddenly turned against the French by the genius of young Robert Clive. But in Bengal [6] the European settlers, at peace with the natives and with each other, were wholly occupied with ledgers and bills of lading.

After two years passed in keeping accounts at Calcutta, Hastings was sent up the country to Cossimbazar, a town which lies on the Hoogley,[1] about a mile from Moorshedabad, and which then bore to Moorshedabad a relation, if we may compare small things with great, such as the city of London bears to Westminster. Moorshedabad was the abode of the prince [2] who, by an authority ostensibly derived from the Mogul,[3] but really independent, ruled the three great provinces of Bengal, Orissa, and Bahar. At Moorshedabad were the court, the harem, and the public offices. Cossimbazar was a port and a place of trade, renowned for the quantity and excellence of the silks which were sold in its marts, and constantly receiving and sending forth fleets of richly laden barges. At this important point, the Company had established a small factory subordinate to that of Fort William. Here, during several years, Hastings was employed in making bargains for stuffs with native brokers. While he was thus engaged, Surajah Dowlah succeeded to the government, and declared war against the English. The defenceless settlement of Cossimbazar, lying close to the tyrant's capital, was instantly seized. Hastings was sent a prisoner to Moorshedabad, but, in consequence of the humane intervention of the servants of the Dutch Company, was treated with indulgence. Meanwhile the Nabob marched on Calcutta; the governor and the commandant fled; the town and citadel were taken, and most of the English prisoners perished in the Black Hole.[4]

In these events originated the greatness of Warren Hastings. The fugitive governor and his companions had taken refuge on the dreary islet of Fulda, near the mouth of the Hoogley. They were naturally desirous to obtain full information respecting the proceedings of the Nabob; and no person seemed so likely to furnish it as Hastings, who was a prisoner at large in the immediate neighborhood of the court. He thus became a diplomatic agent, and soon established a high character for ability and resolution. The treason [1] which at a later period was fatal to Surajah Dowlah was already in progress; and Hastings was admitted to the deliberations of the conspirators. But the time for striking had not arrived. It was necessary to postpone the execution of the design; and Hastings, who was now in extreme peril, fled to Fulda.

Soon after his arrival at Fulda, the expedition from Madras, commanded by Clive,[2] appeared in the Hoogley. Warren, young, intrepid, and excited probably by the example of the Commander of the Forces, who, having like himself been a mercantile agent of the Company, had been turned by public calamities into a soldier, determined to serve in the ranks. During the early operations of the war he carried a musket. But the quick eye of Clive soon perceived that the head of the young volunteer would be more useful than his arm. When, after the battle of Plassey, Meer Jaffier was proclaimed Nabob of Bengal, Hastings was appointed to reside at the court of the new prince as agent for the Company.

He remained at Moorshedabad till the year 1761, when he became a member of Council, and was consequently forced to reside at Calcutta. This was during the interval between Clive's first and second administration, an interval which has left on the fame of the East India Company a stain, not wholly effaced by many years of just and humane government. Mr. Vansittart, the Governor, was at the head of a new and anomalous empire. On the one side was a band of English functionaries, daring, intelligent, eager to be rich. On the other side was a great native population, helpless, timid, accustomed to crouch under oppression. To keep the stronger race from preying on the weaker, was an undertaking which tasked to the utmost the talents and energy of Clive. Vansittart, with fair intentions, was a feeble and inefficient ruler. The master caste, as was natural, broke loose from all restraint; and then was seen what we believe to be the most frightful of all spectacles, the strength of civilization without its mercy. To all other despotism there is a check, imperfect indeed, and liable to gross abuse, but still sufficient to preserve society from the last extreme of misery. A time comes when the evils of submission are obviously greater than those of resistance, when fear itself begets a sort of courage, when a convulsive burst of popular rage and despair warns tyrants not to presume too far on the patience of mankind. But against misgovernment such as then afflicted Bengal it was impossible to struggle. The superior intelligence and energy of the dominant class made their power irresistible. A war of Bengalees against Englishmen was like a war of sheep against wolves, of men against demons. The only protection which the conquered could find was in the moderation, the clemency, the enlarged policy of the conquerors. That protection, at a later period, they found. But at first English power came among them unaccompanied by English morality. There was an interval between the time at which they became our subjects, and the time at which we began to reflect that we were bound to discharge towards them the duties of rulers. During that interval the business of a servant of the Company was simply to wring out of the natives a hundred or two hundred thousand pounds as speedily as possible, that he might return home before his constitution had suffered from the heat, to marry a peer's daughter, to buy rotten boroughs [1] in Cornwall, and to give balls in St. James's Square. Of the conduct of Hastings at this time little is known; but the little that is known, and the circumstance that little is known, must be considered as honorable to him. He could not protect the natives: all that he could do was to abstain from plundering and oppressing them; and this he appears to have done. It is certain that at this time he continued poor; and it is equally certain that by cruelty and dishonesty he might easily have become rich. It is certain that he was never charged with having borne a share in the worst abuses which then prevailed; and it is almost equally certain that, if he had borne a share in those abuses, the able and bitter enemies who afterwards persecuted him would not have failed to discover and to proclaim his guilt. The keen, severe, and even malevolent scrutiny to which his whole public life was subjected, a scrutiny unparalleled, as we believe, in the history of mankind, is in one respect advantageous to his reputation. It brought many lamentable blemishes to light; but it entitles him to be considered pure from every blemish which has not been brought to light.

The truth is that the temptations to which so many English functionaries yielded in the time of Mr. Vansittart were not temptations addressed to the ruling passions of Warren Hastings. He was not squeamish in pecuniary transactions; but he was neither sordid nor rapacious. He was far too enlightened a man to look on a great empire merely as a buccaneer would look on a galleon. Had his heart been much worse than it was, his understanding would have preserved him from that extremity of baseness. He was an unscrupulous, perhaps an unprincipled, statesman; but still he was a statesman, and not a freebooter.

In 1764 Hastings returned to England. He had realized only a very moderate fortune; and that moderate fortune was soon reduced to nothing, partly by his praiseworthy liberality, and partly by his mismanagement. Towards his relations he appears to have acted very generously. The greater part of his savings he left in Bengal, hoping probably to obtain the high usury of India. But high usury and bad security generally go together; and Hastings lost both interest and principal.

He remained four years in England. Of his life at this time very little is known. But it has been asserted, and is highly probable, that liberal studies and the society of men of letters occupied a great part of his time. It is to be remembered to his honor that, in days when the languages of the East were regarded by other servants of the Company merely as the means of communicating with weavers and money-changers, his enlarged and accomplished mind sought in Asiatic learning for new forms of intellectual enjoyment, and for new views of government and society. Perhaps, like most persons who have paid much attention to departments of knowledge which lie out of the common track, he was inclined to overrate the value of his favorite studies. He conceived that the cultivation of Persian literature might with advantage be made a part of the liberal education of an English gentleman; and he drew up a plan with that view. It is said that the University of Oxford, in which Oriental learning had never, since the revival of letters, been wholly neglected, was to be the seat of the institution which he contemplated. An endowment was expected from the munificence of the Company: and professors thoroughly competent to interpret Hafiz and Ferdusi were to be engaged in the East. Hastings called on Johnson, with the hope, as it should seem, of interesting in this project a man who enjoyed the highest literary reputation, and who was particularly connected with Oxford. The interview appears to have left on Johnson's mind a most favorable impression of the talents and attainments of his visitor. Long after, when Hastings was ruling the immense population of British India, the old philosopher wrote to him, and referred in the most courtly terms, though with great dignity, to their short but agreeable intercourse.

Hastings soon began to look again towards India. He had little to attach him to England; and his pecuniary embarrassments were great. He solicited his old masters the Directors for employment. They acceded to his request, with high compliments both to his abilities and to his integrity, and appointed him a Member of Council at Madras. It would be unjust not to mention that, though forced to borrow money for his outfit, he did not withdraw any portion of the sum which he had appropriated to the relief of his distressed relations. In the spring of 1769 he embarked on board of the Duke of Grafton, and commenced a voyage distinguished by incidents which might furnish matter for a novel.

Among the passengers in the Duke of Grafton was a German of the name of Imhoff. He called himself a Baron; but he was in distressed circumstances, and was going out to Madras as a portrait-painter, in the hope of picking up some of the pagodas [1] which were then lightly got and as lightly spent by the English in India. The Baron was accompanied by his wife, a native, we have somewhere read, of Archangel. This young woman who, born under the Arctic circle, was destined to play the part of a Queen under the tropic of Cancer, had an agreeable person, a cultivated mind, and manners in the highest degree engaging. She despised her husband heartily, and, as the story which we have to tell sufficiently proves, not without reason. She was interested by the conversation and flattered by the attentions of Hastings. The situation was indeed perilous. No place is so propitious to the formation either of close friendships or of deadly enmities as an Indiaman.[1] There are very few people who do not find a voyage which lasts several months insupportably dull. Anything is welcome which may break that long monotony, a sail, a shark, an albatross, a man overboard. Most passengers find some resource in eating twice as many meals as on land. But the great devices for killing the time are quarrelling and flirting. The facilities for both these exciting pursuits are great. The inmates of the ship are thrown together far more than in any country-seat or boarding-house. None can escape from the rest except by imprisoning himself in a cell in which he can hardly turn. All food, all exercise, is taken in company. Ceremony is to a great extent banished. It is every day in the power of a mischievous person to inflict innumerable annoyances. It is every day in the power of an amiable person to confer little services. It not seldom happens that serious distress and danger call forth, in genuine beauty and deformity, heroic virtues and abject vices which, in the ordinary intercourse of good society, might remain during many years unknown even to intimate associates. Under such circumstances met Warren Hastings and the Baroness Imhoff, two persons whose accomplishments would have attracted notice in any court of Europe. The gentleman had no domestic ties. The lady was tied to a husband for whom she had no regard, and who had no regard for his own honor. An attachment sprang up, which was soon strengthened by events such as could hardly have occurred on land. Hastings fell ill. The Baroness nursed him with womanly tenderness, gave him his medicines with her own hand, and even sat up in his cabin while he slept. Long before the Duke of Grafton reached Madras, Hastings was in love. But his love was of a most characteristic description. Like his hatred, like his ambition, like all his passions, it was strong, but not impetuous. It was calm, deep, earnest, patient of delay, unconquerable by time. Imhoff was called into council by his wife and his wife's lover. It was arranged that the Baroness should institute a suit for a divorce in the courts of Franconia, that the Baron should afford every facility to the proceeding, and that, during the years which might elapse before the sentence should be pronounced, they should continue to live together. It was also agreed that Hastings should bestow some very substantial marks of gratitude on the complaisant husband, and should, when the marriage was dissolved, make the lady his wife, and adopt the children whom she had already borne to Imhoff.

At Madras, Hastings found the trade of the Company in a very disorganized state. His own tastes would have led him rather to political than to commercial pursuits: but he knew that the favor of his employers depended chiefly on their dividends, and that their dividends depended chiefly on the investment. He therefore, with great judgment, determined to apply his vigorous mind for a time to this department of business, which had been much neglected, since the servants of the Company had ceased to be clerks, and had become warriors and negotiators.

In a very few months he effected an important reform. The Directors notified to him their high approbation, and were so much pleased with his conduct that they determined to place him at the head of the government of Bengal. Early in 1772 he quitted Fort St. George for his new post. The Imhoffs, who were still man and wife, accompanied him, and lived at Calcutta on the same plan which they had already followed during more than two years.

When Hastings took his seat at the head of the council board, Bengal was still governed according to the system which Clive [1] had devised, a system which was, perhaps, skilfully contrived for the purpose of facilitating and concealing a great revolution, but which, when that revolution was complete and irrevocable, could produce nothing but inconvenience. There were two governments,[2] the real and the ostensible. The supreme power belonged to the Company, and was in truth the most despotic power that can be conceived. The only restraint on the English masters of the country was that which their own justice and humanity imposed on them. There was no constitutional check on their will, and resistance to them was utterly hopeless.

But, though thus absolute in reality, the English had not yet assumed the style of sovereignty. They held their territories as vassals of the throne of Delhi; they raised their revenues as collectors appointed by the imperial commission: their public seal was inscribed with the imperial titles; and their mint struck only the imperial coin.

There was still a nabob of Bengal, who stood to the English rulers of his country in the same relation in which Augustulus stood to Odoacer,[1] or the last Merovingians to Charles Martel and Pepin. He lived at Moorshedabad, surrounded by princely magnificence. He was approached with outward marks of reverence, and his name was used in public instruments. But in the government of the country he had less real share than the youngest writer or cadet [2] in the Company's service.

The English council which represented the Company at Calcutta was constituted on a very different plan from that which has since been adopted. At present the Governor is, as to all executive measures, absolute. He can declare war, conclude peace, appoint public functionaries or remove them, in opposition to the unanimous sense of those who sit with him in council. They are, indeed, entitled to know all that is done, to discuss all that is done, to advise, to remonstrate, to send protests to England. But it is with the Governor that the supreme power resides, and on him that the whole responsibility rests. This system, which was introduced by Mr. Pitt and Mr. Dundas in spite of the strenuous opposition of Mr. Burke, we conceive to be on the whole the best that was ever devised for the government of a country where no materials can be found for a representative constitution. In the time of Hastings the Governor had only one vote in council, and, in case of an equal division, a casting vote. It therefore happened not unfrequently that he was overruled on the gravest questions; and it was possible that he might be wholly excluded, for years together, from the real direction of public affairs.

The English functionaries at Fort William had as yet paid little or no attention to the internal government of Bengal. The only branch of politics about which they much busied themselves was negotiation with the native princes. The police, the administration of justice, the details of the collection of revenue, were almost entirely neglected. We may remark that the phraseology of the Company's servants still bears the traces of this state of things. To this day they always use the word "political" as synonymous with "diplomatic." We could name a gentleman still living, who was described by the highest authority as an invaluable public servant, eminently fit to be at the head of the internal administration of a whole presidency, but unfortunately quite ignorant of all political business.

The internal government of Bengal the English rulers delegated to a great native minister, who was stationed at Moorshedabad. All military affairs, and, with the exception of what pertains to mere ceremonial, all foreign affairs, were withdrawn from his control; but the other departments of the administration were entirely confided to him. His own stipend amounted to near a hundred thousand pounds sterling a year. The personal allowance of the nabob, amounting to more than three hundred thousand pounds a year, passed through the minister's hands, and was, to a great extent, at his disposal. The collection of the revenue, the administration of justice, the maintenance of order, were left to this high functionary; and for the exercise of his immense power he was responsible to none but the British masters of the country.

A situation so important, lucrative, and splendid, was naturally an object of ambition to the ablest and most powerful natives. Clive had found it difficult to decide between conflicting pretensions. Two candidates stood out prominently from the crowd, each of them the representative of a race and of a religion.

One of these was Mahommed Reza Khan, a Mussulman of Persian extraction, able, active, religious after the fashion of his people, and highly esteemed by them. In England he might perhaps have been regarded as a corrupt and greedy politician. But, tried by the lower standard of Indian morality, he might be considered as a man of integrity and honor.

His competitor was a Hindoo Brahmin whose name has, by a terrible and melancholy event, been inseparably associated with that of Warren Hastings, the Maharajah Nuncomar. This man had played an important part in all the revolutions which, since the time of

Surajah Dowlah, had taken place in Bengal. To the consideration which in that country belongs to high and pure caste, he added the weight which is derived from wealth, talents, and experience. Of his moral character it is difficult to give a notion to those who are acquainted with human nature only as it appears in our island. What the Italian is to the Englishman, what the Hindoo is to the Italian, what the Bengalee [1] is to other Hindoos, that was Nuncomar to other Bengalees. The physical organization of the Bengalee is feeble even to effeminacy. He lives in a constant vapor bath. His pursuits are sedentary, his limbs delicate, his movements languid. During many ages he has been trampled upon by men of bolder and more hardy breeds. Courage, independence, veracity, are qualities to which his constitution and his situation are equally unfavorable. His mind bears a singular analogy to his body. It is weak even to helplessness for purposes of manly resistance; but its suppleness and its tact move the children of sterner climates to admiration not unmingled with contempt. All those arts which are the natural defence of the weak are more familiar to this subtle race than to the Ionian of the time of Juvenal, or to the Jew of the dark ages. What the horns are to the buffalo, what the paw is to the tiger, what the sting is to the bee, what beauty, according to the old Greek song, is to woman, deceit is to the Bengalee. Large promises, smooth excuses, elaborate tissues of circumstantial falsehood, chicanery, perjury, forgery, are the weapons, offensive and defensive, of the people of the Lower Ganges. All those millions do not furnish one sepoy to the armies of the Company. But as usurers, as money-changers, as sharp legal practitioners, no class of human beings can bear a comparison with them. With all his softness, the Bengalee is by no means placable in his enmities or prone to pity. The pertinacity with which he adheres to his purposes yields only to the immediate pressure of fear. Nor does he lack a certain kind of courage which is often wanting to his masters. To inevitable evils he is sometimes found to oppose a passive fortitude, such as the Stoics attributed to their ideal sage. A European warrior, who rushes on a battery of cannon with a loud hurrah, will sometimes shriek under the surgeon's knife, and fall into an agony of despair at the sentence of death. But the Bengalee, who would see his country overrun, his house laid in ashes, his children murdered or dishonored, without having the spirit to strike one blow, has yet been known to endure torture with the firmness of Mucius, and to mount the scaffold with the steady step and even pulse of Algernon Sidney.

In Nuncomar, the national character was strongly and with exaggeration personified. The Company's servants had repeatedly detected him in the most criminal intrigues. On one occasion he brought a false charge against another Hindoo, and tried to substantiate it by producing forged documents. On another occasion it was discovered that, while professing the strongest attachment to the English, he was engaged in several conspiracies against them, and in particular that he was the medium of a correspondence between the court of Delhi and the French authorities in the Carnatic. For these and similar practices he had been long detained in confinement. But his talents and influence had not only procured his liberation, but had obtained for him a certain degree of consideration even among the British rulers of his country.

Clive was extremely unwilling to place a Mussulman at the head of the administration of Bengal. On the other hand, he could not bring himself to confer immense power on a man to whom every sort of villany had repeatedly been brought home. Therefore, though the nabob, over whom Nuncomar had by intrigue acquired great influence, begged that the artful Hindoo might be intrusted with the government, Clive, after some hesitation, decided honestly and wisely in favor of Mahommed Reza Khan. When Hastings became Governor, Mahommed Reza Khan had held power seven years. An infant son of Meer Jaffier was now nabob; and the guardianship of the young prince's person had been confided to the minister.

Nuncomar, stimulated at once by cupidity and malice, had been constantly attempting to hurt the reputation of his successful rival. This was not difficult. The revenues of Bengal, under the administration established by Clive, did not yield such a surplus as had been anticipated by the Company; for, at that time, the most absurd notions were entertained in England respecting the wealth of India. Palaces of porphyry, hung with the richest brocade, heaps of pearls and diamonds, vaults from which pagodas and gold mohurs were measured out by the bushel, filled the imagination even of men of business. Nobody seemed to be aware of what nevertheless was most undoubtedly the truth, that India was a poorer country than countries which in Europe are reckoned poor, than Ireland, for example, or than Portugal. It was confidently believed by Lords of the Treasury and members for the city that Bengal would not only defray its own charges, but would afford an increased dividend to the proprietors of India stock, and large relief to the English finances. These absurd expectations were disappointed; and the Directors, naturally enough, chose to attribute the disappointment rather to the mismanagement of Mahommed Reza Khan than to their own ignorance of the country intrusted to their care. They were confirmed in their error by the agents of Nuncomar; for Nuncomar had agents even in Leadenhall Street.[1] Soon after Hastings reached Calcutta, he received a letter addressed by the Court of Directors, not to the council generally, but to himself in particular. He was directed to remove Mahommed Reza Khan, to arrest him, together with all his family and all his partisans, and to institute a strict inquiry into the whole administration of the province. It was added that the Governor would do well to avail himself of the assistance of Nuncomar in the investigation. The vices of Nuncomar were acknowledged. But even from his vices, it was said, much advantage might at such a conjuncture be derived; and, though he could not safely be trusted, it might still be proper to encourage him by hopes of reward.

The Governor bore no good will to Nuncomar. Many years before, they had known each other at Moorshedabad; and then a quarrel had arisen between them which all the authority of their superiors could hardly compose. Widely as they differed in most points, they resembled each other in this, that both were men of unforgiving natures. To Mahommed Reza Khan, on the other hand, Hastings had no feelings of hostility. Nevertheless he proceeded to execute the instructions of the Company with an alacrity which he never showed, except when instructions were in perfect conformity with his own views. He had, wisely as we think, determined to get rid of the system of double government in Bengal. The orders of the Directors furnished him with the means of effecting his purpose, and dispensed him from the necessity of discussing the matter with his Council. He took his measures with his usual vigor and dexterity. At midnight, the palace of Mahommed Reza Khan at Moorshedabad was surrounded by a battalion of sepoys. The minister was roused from his slumbers and informed that he was a prisoner. With the Mussulman gravity, he bent his head and submitted himself to the will of God. He fell not alone. A chief named Schitab Roy had been intrusted with the government of Bahar. His valor and his attachment to the English had more than once been signally proved. On that memorable day on which the people of Patna saw from their walls the whole army of the Mogul scattered by the little band of Captain Knox, the voice of the British conquerors assigned the palm of gallantry to the brave Asiatic. "I never," said Knox, when he introduced Schitab Roy, covered with blood and dust, to the English functionaries assembled in the factory, "I never saw a native fight so before." Schitab Roy was involved in the ruin of Mahommed Reza Khan, was removed from office, and was placed under arrest. The members of the Council received no intimation of these measures till the prisoners were on their road to Calcutta.

The inquiry into the conduct of the minister was postponed on different pretences. He was detained in an easy confinement during many months. In the meantime, the great revolution which Hastings had planned was carried into effect. The office of minister was abolished. The internal administration was transferred to the servants of the Company. A system, a very imperfect system, it is true, of civil and criminal justice, under English superintendence, was established. The nabob was no longer to have even an ostensible share in the government; but he was still to receive a considerable annual allowance, and to be surrounded with the state of sovereignty. As he was an infant, it was necessary to provide guardians for his person and property. His person was intrusted to a lady of his father's harem, known by the name of the Munny Begum. The office of treasurer of the household was bestowed on a son of Nuncomar, named Goordas. Nuncomar's services were wanted; yet he could not safely be trusted with power; and Hastings thought it a masterstroke of policy to reward the able and unprincipled parent by promoting the inoffensive child.

The revolution completed, the double government dissolved, the Company installed in the full sovereignty of Bengal, Hastings had no motive to treat the late ministers with rigor. Their trial had been put off on various pleas till the new organization was complete. They were then brought before a committee, over which the Governor presided. Schitab Roy was speedily acquitted with honor. A formal apology was made to him for the restraint to which he had been subjected. All the Eastern marks of respect were bestowed on him. He was clothed in a robe of state, presented with jewels and with a richly harnessed elephant, and sent back to his government at Patna. But his health had suffered from confinement; his high spirit had been cruelly wounded; and soon after his liberation he died of a broken heart.

The innocence of Mahommed Reza Khan was not so clearly established. But the Governor was not disposed to deal harshly. After a long hearing, in which Nuncomar appeared as the accuser, and displayed both the art and the inveterate rancor which distinguished him, Hastings pronounced that the charges had not been made out, and ordered the fallen minister to be set at liberty.

Nuncomar had purposed to destroy the Mussulman administration, and to rise on its ruin. Both his malevolence and his cupidity had been disappointed. Hastings had made him a tool, had used him for the purpose of accomplishing the transfer of the government from Moorshedabad to Calcutta, from native to European hands. The rivals, the enemy, so long envied, so implacably persecuted, had been dismissed unhurt. The situation so long and ardently desired had been abolished. It was natural that the Governor should be from that time an object of the most intense hatred to the vindictive Brahmin. As yet, however, it was necessary to suppress such feelings. The time was coming when that long animosity was to end in a desperate and deadly struggle.

In the meantime, Hastings was compelled to turn his attention to foreign affairs. The object of his diplomacy was at this time simply to get money. The finances of his government were in an embarrassed state; and this embarrassment he was determined to relieve by some means, fair or foul. The principle which directed all his dealings with his neighbors is fully expressed by the old motto of one of the great predatory families of Teviotdale, "Thou shalt want ere I want." He seems to have laid it down, as a fundamental proposition which could not be disputed, that, when he had not as many lacs of rupees as the public service required, he was to take them from anybody who had. One thing, indeed, is to be said in excuse for him. The pressure applied to him by his employers at home, was such as only the highest virtue could have withstood, such as left him no choice except to commit great wrongs, or to resign his high post, and with that post all his hopes of fortune and distinction. The Directors, it is true, never enjoined or applauded any crime. Far from it. Whoever examines their letters written at that time will find there many just and humane sentiments, many excellent precepts, in short, an admirable code of political ethics. But every exhortation is modified or nullified by a demand for money. "Govern leniently, and send more money; practise strict justice and moderation towards neighboring powers, and send more money;" this is in truth the sum of almost all the instructions that Hastings ever received from home. Now these instructions, being interpreted, mean simply, "Be the father and the oppressor of the people; be just and unjust, moderate and rapacious." The Directors dealt with India, as the church, in the good old times, dealt with a heretic. They delivered the victim over to the executioners, with an earnest request that all possible tenderness might be shown. We by no means accuse or suspect those who framed these despatches of hypocrisy. It is probable that, writing fifteen thousand miles from the place where their orders were to be carried into effect, they never perceived the gross inconsistency of which they were guilty. But the inconsistency was at once manifest to their vicegerent at Calcutta, who, with an empty treasury, with an unpaid army, with his own salary often in arrear, with deficient crops, with government tenants daily running away, was called upon to remit home another half million without fail. Hastings saw that it was absolutely necessary for him to disregard either the moral discourses or the pecuniary requisitions of his employers. Being forced to disobey them in something, he had to consider what kind of disobedience they would most readily pardon; and he correctly judged that the safest course would be to neglect the sermons and to find the rupees.[1]

A mind so fertile as his, and so little restrained by conscientious scruples, speedily discovered several modes of relieving the financial embarrassments of the government. The allowance of the Nabob of Bengal was reduced at a stroke from three hundred and twenty thousand pounds a year to half that sum. The Company had bound itself to pay near three hundred thousand pounds a year to the Great Mogul,[2] as a mark of homage for the provinces which he had intrusted to their care; and they had ceded to him the districts of Corah and Allahabad. On the plea that the Mogul was not really independent, but merely a tool in the hands of others, Hastings determined to retract these concessions. He accordingly declared that the English would pay no more tribute, and sent troops to occupy Allahabad and Corah. The situation of these places was such, that there would be little advantage and great expense in retaining them. Hastings, who wanted money and not territory, determined to sell them. A purchaser was not wanting. The rich province of Oude[3] had, in the general dissolution of the Mogul Empire, fallen to the share of the great Mussulman house by which it is still governed. About twenty years ago, this house, by the permission of the British government, assumed the royal title; but, in the time of Warren Hastings, such an assumption would have been considered by the Mahommedans of India as a monstrous impiety. The Prince of Oude, though he held the power, did not venture to use the style of sovereignty. To the appellation of Nabob [1] or Viceroy, he added that of Vizier of the monarchy of Hindostan, just as in the last century the Electors of Saxony and Brandenburg, though independent of the Emperor, and often in arms against him, were proud to style themselves his Grand Chamberlain and Grand Marshal. Sujah Dowlah, then Nabob Vizier, was on excellent terms with the English. He had a large treasure. Allahabad and Corah were so situated that they might be of use to him and could be of none to the Company. The buyer and seller soon came to an understanding; and the provinces which had been torn from the Mogul were made over to the government of Oude for about half a million sterling.

But there was another matter still more important to be settled by the Vizier and the Governor. The fate of a brave people was to be decided. It was decided in a manner which has left a lasting stain on the fame of Hastings and of England.

The people of Central Asia had always been to the inhabitants of India what the warriors of the German forests were to the subjects of the decaying monarchy of Rome. The dark, slender, and timid Hindoo shrank from a conflict with the strong muscle and resolute spirit of the fair race, which dwelt beyond their passes. There is reason to believe that, at a period anterior to the dawn of regular history, the people who spoke the rich and flexible Sanscrit came from regions lying far beyond the Hyphasis and the Hystaspes, and imposed their yoke on the children of the soil. It is certain that, during the last ten centuries, a succession of invaders descended from the west on Hindostan; nor was the course of conquest ever turned back towards the setting sun, till that memorable campaign in which the cross of Saint George[1] was planted on the walls of Ghizni.

The Emperors of Hindostan themselves came from the other side of the great mountain ridge; and it had always been their practice to recruit their army from the hardy and valiant race from which their own illustrious house sprang. Among the military adventurers who were allured to the Mogul standards from the neighborhood of Cabul and Candahar, were conspicuous several gallant bands, known by the name of the Rohillas.[2] Their services had been rewarded with large tracts of land, fiefs of the spear, if we may use an expression drawn from an analogous state of things, in that fertile plain through which the Ramgunga flows from the snowy heights of Kumaon to join the Ganges. In the general confusion which followed the death of Aurungzebe, the warlike colony became virtually independent. The Rohillas were distinguished from the other inhabitants of India by a peculiarly fair complexion. They were more honorably distinguished by courage in war, and by skill in the arts of peace. While anarchy raged from Lahore to Cape Comorin, their little territory enjoyed the blessings of repose under the guardianship of valor. Agriculture and commerce flourished among them; nor were they negligent of rhetoric and poetry. Many persons now living have heard aged men talk with regret of the golden days when the Afghan princes ruled in the vale of Rohilcund.

Sujah Dowlah had set his heart on adding this rich district to his own principality. Right or show of right, he had absolutely none. His claim was in no respect better founded than that of Catherine to Poland,[1] or that of the Bonaparte family to Spain. The Rohillas held their country by exactly the same title by which he held his, and had governed their country far better than his had ever been governed. Nor were they a people whom it was perfectly safe to attack. Their land was indeed an open plain destitute of natural defences; but their veins were full of the high blood of Afghanistan. As soldiers, they had not the steadiness which is seldom found except in company with strict discipline; but their impetuous valor had been proved on many fields of battle. It was said that their chiefs, when united by common peril, could bring eighty thousand men into the field. Sujah Dowlah had himself seen them fight, and wisely shrank from a conflict with them. There was in India one army, and only one, against which even those proud Caucasian tribes could not stand. It had been abundantly proved that neither tenfold odds, nor the martial ardor of the boldest Asiatic nations, could avail aught against English science and resolution. Was it possible to induce the Governor of Bengal to let out to hire the irresistible energies of the imperial people, the skill against which the ablest chiefs of Hindostan were helpless as infants, the discipline which had so often triumphed over the frantic struggles of fanaticism and despair, the unconquerable British courage which is never so sedate and stubborn as towards the close of a doubtful and murderous day?

This was what the Nabob Vizier asked, and what Hastings granted. A bargain was soon struck. Each of the negotiators had what the other wanted. Hastings was in need of funds to carry on the government of Bengal, and to send remittances to London; and Sujah Dowlah had an ample revenue. Sujah Dowlah was bent on subjugating the Rohillas; and Hastings had at his disposal the only force by which the Rohillas could be subjugated. It was agreed that an English army should be lent to the Nabob Vizier, and that, for the loan, he should pay four hundred thousand pounds sterling, besides defraying all the charge of the troops while employed in his service.

"I really cannot see," says Mr. Gleig, "upon what grounds, either of political or moral justice, this proposition deserves to be stigmatized as infamous." If we understand the meaning of words, it is infamous to commit a wicked action for hire, and it is wicked to engage in war without provocation. In this particular war, scarcely one aggravating circumstance was wanting. The object of the Rohilla war was this, to deprive a large population, who had never done us the least harm, of a good government, and to place them, against their will, under an execrably bad one. Nay, even this is not all. England now descended far below the level even of those petty German princes who, about the same time, sold us troops to fight the Americans. The hussar-mongers of Hesse and Anspach had at least the assurance that the expeditions on which their soldiers were to be employed would be conducted in conformity with the humane rules of civilized warfare. Was the Rohilla war likely to be so conducted? Did the Governor stipulate that it should be so conducted? He well knew what Indian warfare was. He well knew that the power which he covenanted to put into Sujah Dowlah's hands would, in all probability, be atrociously abused; and he required no guarantee, no promise that it should not be so abused. He did not even reserve to himself the right of withdrawing his aid in case of abuse, however gross. We are almost ashamed to notice Major Scott's absurd plea, that Hastings was justified in letting out English troops to slaughter the Rohillas, because the Rohillas were not of Indian race, but a colony from a distant country. What were the English themselves? Was it for them to proclaim a crusade for the expulsion of all intruders from the countries watered by the Ganges? Did it lie in their mouths to contend that a foreign settler who establishes an empire in India is a *caput lupinum?* What would they have said if any other power had, on such a ground, attacked Madras or Calcutta without the slightest provocation? Such a defence was wanting to make the infamy of the transaction complete. The atrocity of the crime, and the hypocrisy of the apology, are worthy of each other.

One of the three brigades of which the Bengal army consisted was sent under Colonel Champion to join Sujah Dowlah's forces. The Rohillas expostulated, entreated, offered a large ransom, but in vain. They then resolved to defend themselves to the last. A bloody battle was fought. "The enemy," says Colonel Champion, "gave proof of a good share of military knowledge; and it is impossible to describe a more obstinate firmness of resolution than they displayed." The dastardly sovereign of Oude fled from the field. The English were left unsupported; but their fire and their charge were irresistible. It was not, however, till the most distinguished chiefs had fallen, fighting bravely at the head of their troops, that the Rohilla ranks gave way. Then the Nabob Vizier and his rabble made their appearance, and hastened to plunder the camp of the valiant enemies, whom they had never dared to look in the face. The soldiers of the Company, trained in an exact discipline, kept unbroken order, while the tents were pillaged by these worthless allies. But many voices were heard to exclaim, "We have had all the fighting, and those rogues are to have all the profit."

Then the horrors of Indian war were let loose on the fair valleys and cities of Rohilcund. The whole country was in a blaze. More than a hundred thousand people fled from their homes to pestilential jungles, preferring famine, and fever, and the haunts of tigers, to the tyranny of him, to whom an English and a Christain government had, for shameful lucre, sold their substance, and their blood, and the honor of their wives and daughters. Colonel Champion remonstrated with the Nabob Vizier, and sent strong representations to Fort William; but the Governor had made no conditions as to the mode in which the war was to be carried on. He had troubled himself about nothing but his forty lacs; and, though he might disapprove of Sujah Dowlah's wanton barbarity, he did not think himself entitled to interfere, except by offering advice. This delicacy excites the admiration of the biographer. "Mr. Hastings," he says, "could not himself dictate to the Nabob, nor permit the commander of the Company's troops to dictate how the war was to be carried on." No, to be sure. Mr. Hastings had only to put down by main force the brave struggles of innocent men fighting for their liberty. Their military resistance crushed, his duties ended; and he had then only to fold his arms and look on, while their villages were burned, their children butchered, and their women violated. Will Mr. Gleig seriously maintain this opinion? Is any rule more plain than this, that whoever voluntarily gives to another irresistible power over human beings is bound to take order that such power shall not be barbarously abused? But we beg pardon of our readers for arguing a point so clear.

We hasten to the end of this sad and disgraceful story. The war ceased. The finest population in India was subjected to a greedy, cowardly, cruel tyrant. Commerce and agriculture languished. The rich province which had tempted the cupidity of Sujah Dowlah became the most miserable part even of his miserable dominions. Yet is the injured nation not extinct. At long intervals gleams of its ancient spirit have flashed forth; and even at this day, valor, and self-respect, and a chivalrous feeling rare among Asiatics, and a bitter remembrance of the great crime of England, distinguish that noble Afghan race. To this day they are regarded as the best of all sepoys at the cold steel; and it was very recently remarked, by one who had enjoyed great opportunities of observation, that the only natives of India to whom the word "gentleman" can with perfect propriety be applied, are to be found among the Rohillas.

Whatever we may think of the morality of Hastings, it cannot be denied that the financial results of his policy did honor to his talents. In less than two years after he assumed the government, he had, without imposing any additional burdens on the people subject to his authority, added about four hundred and fifty thousand pounds to the annual income of the Company, besides procuring about a million in ready money. He had also relieved the finances of Bengal from military expenditure, amounting to near a quarter of a million a year, and had thrown that charge on the Nabob of Oude. There can be no doubt that this was a result which, if it had been obtained by honest means, would have entitled him to the warmest gratitude of his country, and which, by whatever means obtained, proved that he possessed great talents for administration.

In the meantime, Parliament had been engaged in long and grave discussions on Asiatic affairs. The ministry of Lord North, in the session of 1773, introduced a measure which made a considerable change in the constitution of the Indian government. This law, known by the name of the Regulating Act, provided that the presidency of Bengal should exercise a control over the other possessions of the Company; that the chief of that presidency should be styled Governor-General; that he should be assisted by four Councillors; and that a supreme court of judicature, consisting of a chief justice and three inferior judges, should be established at Calcutta. This court was made independent of the Governor-General and Council, and was intrusted with a civil and criminal jurisdiction of immense and, at the same time, of undefined extent.

The Governor-General and Councillors were named in the act, and were to hold their situations for five years. Hastings was to be the first Governor-General. One of the four new Councillors, Mr. Barwell, an experienced servant of the Company, was then in India. The other three, General Clavering, Mr. Monson, and Mr. Francis, were sent out from England.

The ablest of the new Councillors was, beyond all doubt, Philip Francis. His acknowledged compositions prove that he possessed considerable eloquence and information. Several years passed in the public offices had formed him to habits of business. His enemies have never denied that he had a fearless and manly spirit; and his friends, we are afraid, must acknowledge that his estimate of himself was extravagantly high, that his temper was irritable, that his deportment was often rude and petulant, and that his hatred was of intense bitterness and long duration.

It is scarcely possible to mention this eminent man without adverting for a moment to the question which his name at once suggests to every mind. Was he the author of the *Letters of Junius?*[1] Our own firm belief is that he was. The evidence is, we think, such as would support a verdict in a civil, nay, in a criminal proceeding. The handwriting of Junius is the very peculiar handwriting of Francis, slightly disguised. As to the position, pursuits, and connections of Junius, the following are the most important facts which can be considered as clearly proved: first, that he was acquainted with the technical forms of the secretary of state's office; secondly, that he was intimately acquainted with the business of the war-office; thirdly, that he, during the year 1770, attended debates in the House of Lords, and took notes of speeches, particularly of the speeches of Lord Chatham;[2] fourthly, that he bitterly resented the appointment of Mr. Chamier to the place of deputy secretary-at-war; fifthly, that he was bound by some strong tie to the first Lord Holland. Now, Francis passed some years in the secretary of state's office. He was subsequently chief clerk of the war-office. He repeatedly mentioned that he had himself in 1770, heard speeches of Lord Chatham; and some of these speeches were actually printed from his notes. He resigned his clerkship at the war-office from resentment at the appointment of Mr. Chamier. It was by Lord Holland that he was first introduced into the public service. Now, here are five marks, all of which ought to be found in Junius. They are all five found in Francis. We do not believe that more than two of them can be found in any other person whatever. If this argument does not settle the question, there is an end of all reasoning on circumstantial evidence.

The internal evidence seems to us to point the same way. The style of Francis bears a strong resemblance to that of Junius; nor are we disposed to admit, what is generally taken for granted, that the acknowledged compositions of Francis are very decidedly inferior to the anonymous letters. The argument from inferiority, at all events, is one which may be urged with at least equal force against every claimant that has ever been mentioned, with the single exception of Burke; and it would be a waste of time to prove that Burke was not Junius. And what conclusion, after all, can be drawn from mere inferiority? Every writer must produce his best work; and the interval between his best work and his second best work may be very wide indeed. Nobody will say that the best letters of Junius are more decidedly superior to the acknowledged works of Francis than three or four of Corneille's tragedies to the rest, than three or four of Ben Jonson's comedies to the rest, than the *Pilgrim's Progress* to the other works of Bunyan, than *Don Quixote* to the other works of Cervantes. Nay, it is certain that Junius, whoever he may have been, was a most unequal writer. To go no further than the letters which bear the signature of Junius; the letter to the King, and the letters to Horne Tooke, have little in common, except the asperity; and asperity was an ingredient seldom wanting either in the writings or in the speeches of Francis.

Indeed one of the strongest reasons for believing that Francis was Junius is the moral resemblance between the two men. It is not difficult, from the letters which, under various signatures, are known to have been written by Junius, and from his dealings with Woodfall [1] and others, to form a tolerably correct notion of his character. He was clearly a man not destitute of real patriotism and magnanimity, a man whose vices were not of a sordid kind. But he must also have been a man in the highest degree arrogant and insolent, a man prone to malevolence, and prone to the error of mistaking his malevolence for public virtue. "Doest thou well to be angry?" was the question asked in old time of the Hebrew prophet. And he answered, "I do well." This was evidently the temper of Junius; and to this cause we attribute the savage cruelty which disgraces several of his letters. No man is so merciless as he who, under a strong self-delusion, confounds his antipathies with his duties. It may be added that Junius, though allied with the democratic party by common enmities, was the very opposite of a democratic politician. While attacking individuals with a ferocity which perpetually violated all the laws of literary warfare, he regarded the most defective parts of old institutions with a respect amounting to pedantry, pleaded the cause of Old Sarum [1] with fervor, and contemptuously told the capitalists of Manchester and Leeds that, if they wanted votes, they might buy land and become freeholders of Lancashire and Yorkshire. All this, we believe, might stand, with scarcely any change, for a character of Philip Francis.

It is not strange that the great anonymous writer should have been willing at that time to leave the country which had been so powerfully stirred by his eloquence. Everything had gone against him. That party which he clearly preferred to every other, the party of George Grenville, had been scattered by the death of its chief; and Lord Suffolk had led the greater part of it over to the ministerial benches. The ferment produced by the Middlesex election had gone down. Every faction must have been alike an object of aversion to Junius. His opinions on domestic affairs separated him from the ministry; his opinions on colonial affairs from the opposition. Under such circumstances, he had thrown down his pen in misanthropical despair. His farewell letter to Woodfall bears date the nineteenth of January 1773. In that letter, he declared that he must be an idiot to write again; that he had meant well by the cause and the public; that both were given up; that there were not ten men who would act steadily together on any question. "But it is all alike, he added, "vile and contemptible. You have never flinched that I know of; and I shall always rejoice to hear of your prosperity." These were the last words of Junius. In a year from that time, Philip Francis was on his voyage to Bengal.

With the three new Councillors came out the judges of the Supreme Court. The chief justice was Sir Elijah Impey.[1] He was an old acquaintance of Hastings; and it is probable that the Governor-General, if he had searched through all the Inns of Court, could not have found an equally serviceable tool. But the members of Council were by no means in an obsequious mood. Hastings greatly disliked the new form of government, and had no very high opinion of his coadjutors. They had heard of this, and were disposed to be suspicious and punctilious. When men are in such a frame of mind, any trifle is sufficient to give occasion for dispute. The members of Council expected a salute of twenty-one guns [2] from the batteries of Fort William. Hastings allowed them only seventeen. They landed in ill-humor. The first civilities were exchanged with cold reserve. On the morrow commenced that long quarrel which, after distracting British India, was renewed in England, and in which all the most eminent statesmen and orators of the age took active part on one or the other side.

Hastings was supported by Barwell. They had not always been friends. But the arrival of the new members of Council from England naturally had the effect of uniting the old servants of the Company. Clavering, Monson, and Francis formed the majority. They instantly wrested the government out of the hands of Hastings, condemned, certainly not without justice, his late dealings with the Nabob Vizier, recalled the English agent from Oude, and sent thither a creature of their own, ordered the brigade which had conquered the unhappy Rohillas to return to the Company's territories, and instituted a severe inquiry into the conduct of the war. Next, in spite of the Governor-General's remonstrances, they proceeded to exercise, in the most indiscreet manner, their new authority over the subordinate presidencies; threw all the affairs of Bombay into confusion; and interfered, with an incredible union of rashness and feebleness, in the intestine disputes of the Mahratta government.[1] At the same time, they fell on the internal administration of Bengal, and attacked the whole fiscal and judicial system, a system which was undoubtedly defective, but which it was very improbable that gentlemen fresh from England would be competent to amend. The effect of their reforms was that all protection to life and property was withdrawn, and that gangs of robbers plundered and slaughtered with impunity in the very suburbs of Calcutta. Hastings continued to live in the Government-house, and to draw the salary of Governor-General. He continued even to take the lead at the council-board in the transaction of ordinary business; for his opponents could not but feel that he knew much of which they were ignorant, and that he decided, both surely and speedily, many questions which to them would have been hopelessly puzzling. But the higher powers of government and the most valuable patronage had been taken from him.

The natives soon found this out. They considered him as a fallen man; and they acted after their kind. Some of our readers may have seen, in India, a cloud of crows pecking a sick vulture to death, no bad type of what happens in that country, as often as fortune deserts one who has been great and dreaded. In an instant, all the sycophants who had lately been ready to lie for him, to forge for him, to pander for him, to poison for him, hasten to purchase the favor of his victorious enemies by accusing him. An Indian government has only to let it be understood that it wishes a particular man to be ruined; and, in twenty-four hours, it will be furnished with grave charges, supported by depositions so full and circumstantial that any person unaccustomed to Asiatic mendacity would regard them as decisive. It is well if the signature of the destined victim is not counterfeited at the foot of some illegal compact, and if some treasonable paper is not slipped into a hiding-place in his house. Hastings was now regarded as helpless. The power to make or mar the fortune of every man in Bengal had passed, as it seemed, into the hands of the new Councillors. Immediately charges against the Governor-General began to pour in. They were eagerly welcomed by the majority, who, to do them justice, were men of too much honor knowingly to countenance false accusations, but who were not sufficiently acquainted with the East to be aware that, in that part of the world, a very little encouragement from power will call forth, in a week, more Oateses,[1] and Bedloes, and Dangerfields, than Westminster Hall sees in a century.

It would have been strange indeed if, at such a juncture, Nuncomar had remained quiet. That bad man was stimulated at once by malignity, by avarice, and by ambition. Now was the time to be avenged on his old enemy, to wreak a grudge of seventeen years, to establish himself in the favor of the majority of the Council, to become the greatest native in Bengal. From the time of the arrival of the new Councillors, he had paid the most marked court to them, and had in consequence been excluded, with all indignity, from the Government-house. He now put into the hands of Francis, with great ceremony, a paper containing several charges of the most serious description. By this document Hastings was accused of putting offices up for sale, and of receiving bribes for suffering offenders to escape. In particular, it was alleged that Mahommed Reza Khan had been dismissed with impunity, in consideration of a great sum paid to the Governor-General.

Francis read the paper in Council. A violent altercation followed. Hastings complained in bitter terms of the way in which he was treated, spoke with contempt of Nuncomar and of Nuncomar's accusation, and denied the right of the Council to sit in judgment on the Governor. At the next meeting of the Board, another communication from Nuncomar was produced.

He requested that he might be permitted to attend the Council, and that he might be heard in support of his assertions. Another tempestuous debate took place. The Governor-General maintained that the council-room was not a proper place for such an investigation; that from persons who were heated by daily conflict with him he could not expect the fairness of judges; and that he could not, without betraying the dignity of his post, submit to be confronted with such a man as Nuncomar. The majority, however, resolved to go into the charges. Hastings rose, declared the sitting at an end, and left the room, followed by Barwell. The other members kept their seats, voted themselves a council, put Clavering in the chair, and ordered Nuncomar to be called in. Nuncomar not only adhered to the original charges, but, after the fashion of the East, produced a large supplement. He stated that Hastings had received a great sum for appointing Rajah Goordas treasurer of the Nabob's household, and for committing the care of his Highness's person to the Munny Begum.[1] He put in a letter purporting to bear the seal of the Munny Begum, for the purpose of establishing the truth of his story. The seal, whether forged, as Hastings affirmed, or genuine, as we are rather inclined to believe, proved nothing. Nuncomar, as everybody knows who knows India, had only to tell the Munny Begum that such a letter would give pleasure to the majority of the Council, in order to procure her attestation. The majority, however, voted that the charge was made out; that Hastings had corruptly received between thirty and forty thousand pounds; and that he ought to be compelled to refund.

The general feeling among the English in Bengal was strongly in favor of the Governor-General. In talents for business, in knowledge of the country, in general courtesy of demeanor, he was decidedly superior to his persecutors. The servants of the Company were naturally disposed to side with the most distinguished member of their own body against a clerk from the war-office, who, profoundly ignorant of the native languages and of the native character, took on himself to regulate every department of the administration. Hastings, however, in spite of the general sympathy of his countrymen, was in a most painful situation. There was still an appeal to higher authority in England. If that authority took part with his enemies, nothing was left to him but to throw up his office. He accordingly placed his resignation in the hands of his agent in London, Colonel Macleane. But Macleane was instructed not to produce the resignation unless it should be fully ascertained that the feeling at the India House was adverse to the Governor-General.

The triumph of Nuncomar seemed to be complete. He held a daily levee, to which his countrymen resorted in crowds, and to which, on one occasion, the majority of the Council condescended to repair. His house was an office for the purpose of receiving charges against the Governor-General. It was said that, partly by threats, and partly by wheedling, the villainous Brahmin had induced many of the wealthiest men of the province to send in complaints. But he was playing a perilous game. It was not safe to drive to despair a man of such resources and such determination as Hastings. Nuncomar, with all his acuteness, did not understand the nature of the institutions under which he lived. He saw that he had with him the majority of the body which made treaties, gave places, raised taxes. The separation between political and judicial functions was a thing of which he had no conception. It had probably never occurred to him that there was in Bengal an authority perfectly independent of the Council, an authority which could protect one whom the Council wished to destroy, and send to the gibbet one whom the Council wished to protect. Yet such was the fact. The Supreme Court was, within the sphere of its own duties, altogether independent of the Government. Hastings, with his usual sagacity, had seen how much advantage he might derive from possessing himself of this stronghold; and he had acted accordingly. The Judges, especially the Chief Justice, were hostile to the majority of the Council. The time had now come for putting this formidable machinery into action.

On a sudden, Calcutta was astounded by the news that Nuncomar had been taken up on a charge of felony, committed, and thrown into the common gaol. The crime imputed to him was that six years before he had forged a bond. The ostensible prosecutor was a native. But it was then, and still is, the opinion of everybody, idiots and biographers excepted, that Hastings was the real mover in the business.

The rage of the majority rose to the highest point. They protested against the proceedings of the Supreme Court, and sent several urgent messages to the Judges, demanding that Nuncomar should be admitted to bail. The Judges returned haughty and resolute answers. All that the Council could do was to heap honors and emoluments on the family of Nuncomar; and this they did. In the meantime the assizes commenced; a true bill was found; and Nuncomar was brought before Sir Elijah Impey and a jury composed of Englishmen. A great quantity of contradictory swearing, and the necessity of having every word of the evidence interpreted, protracted the trial to a most unusual length. At last a verdict of guilty was returned, and the Chief Justice pronounced sentence of death on the prisoner.

That Impey ought to have respited Nuncomar we hold to be perfectly clear. Whether the whole proceeding was not illegal, is a question. But it is certain that, whatever may have been, according to technical rules of construction, the effect of the statute under which the trial took place, it was most unjust to hang a Hindoo for forgery. The law which made forgery capital in England was passed without the smallest reference to the state of society in India. It was unknown to the natives of India. It had never been put in execution among them, certainly not for want of delinquents. It was in the highest degree shocking to all their notions. They were not accustomed to the distinction which many circumstances, peculiar to our own state of society, have led us to make between forgery and other kinds of cheating. The counterfeiting of a seal was, in their estimation, a common act of swindling; nor had it ever crossed their minds that it was to be punished as severely as gang-robbery or assassination. A just judge would, beyond all doubt, have reserved the case for the consideration of the sovereign. But Impey would not hear of mercy or delay.

The excitement among all classes was great. Francis and Francis's few English adherents described the Governor-General and the Chief Justice as the worst of murderers. Clavering, it was said, swore that, even at the foot of the gallows, Nuncomar should be rescued. The bulk of the European society, though strongly attached to the Governor-General, could not but feel compassion for a man who with all his crimes, had so long filled so large a space in their sight, who had been great and powerful before the British empire in India began to exist, and to whom, in the old times, governors and members of council, then mere commercial factors, had paid court for protection. The feeling of the Hindoos was infinitely stronger. They were, indeed, not a people to strike one blow for their countryman. But his sentence filled them with sorrow and dismay. Tried even by their low standard of morality, he was a bad man. But, bad as he was, he was the head of their race and religion, a Brahmin of the Brahmins.[1] He had inherited the purest and highest caste. He had practised with the greatest punctuality all those ceremonies to which the superstitious Bengalees ascribe far more importance than to the correct discharge of the social duties. They felt, therefore, as a devout Catholic in the dark ages would have felt, at seeing a prelate of the highest dignity sent to the gallows by a secular tribunal. According to their old national laws, a Brahmin could not be put to death for any crime whatever. And the crime for which Nuncomar was about to die was regarded by them in much the same light in which the selling of an unsound horse, for a sound price, is regarded by a Yorkshire jockey.

The Mussulmans alone appear to have seen with exultation the fate of the powerful Hindoo, who had attempted to rise by means of the ruin of Mahommed Reza Khan. The Mahommedan historian [1] of those times takes delight in aggravating the charge. He assures us that in Nuncomar's house a casket was found containing counterfeits of the seals of all the richest men of the province. We have never fallen in with any other authority for this story, which in itself is by no means improbable.

The day drew near; and Nuncomar prepared himself to die with that quiet fortitude with which the Bengalee, so effeminately timid in personal conflict, often encounters calamities for which there is no remedy. The sheriff, with the humanity which is seldom wanting in an English gentleman, visited the prisoner on the eve of the execution, and assured him that no indulgence, consistent with the law, should be refused to him. Nuncomar expressed his gratitude with great politeness and unaltered composure. Not a muscle of his face moved. Not a sigh broke from him. He put his finger to his forehead, and calmly said that fate would have its way, and that there was no resisting the pleasure of God. He sent his compliments to Francis, Clavering, and Monson, and charged them to protect Rajah Goordas, who was about to become the head of the Brahmins of Bengal. The sheriff withdrew, greatly agitated by what had passed, and Nuncomar sat composedly down to write notes and examine accounts.

The next morning, before the sun was in his power, an immense concourse assembled round the place where the gallows had been set up. Grief and horror were on every face; yet to the last the multitude could hardly believe that the English really purposed to take the life of the great Brahmin. At length the mournful procession came through the crowd. Nuncomar sat up in his palanquin, and looked round him with unaltered serenity. He had just parted from those who were most nearly connected with him. Their cries and contortions had appalled the European ministers of justice, but had not produced the smallest effect on the iron stoicism of the prisoner. The only anxiety which he expressed was that men of his own priestly caste might be in attendance to take charge of his corpse. He again desired to be remembered to his friends in the Council, mounted the scaffold with firmness, and gave the signal to the executioner. The moment that the drop fell, a howl of sorrow and despair rose from the innumerable spectators. Hundreds turned away their faces from the polluting sight, fled with loud wailings toward the Hoogley, and plunged into its holy waters, as if to purify themselves from the guilt of having looked on such a crime. These feelings were not confined to Calcutta. The whole province was greatly excited; and the population of Decca, in particular, gave strong signs of grief and dismay.

Of Impey's [1] conduct it is impossible to speak too severely. We have already said that, in our opinion, he acted unjustly in refusing to respite Nuncomar. No rational man can doubt that he took this course in order to gratify the Governor-General. If we had ever had any doubts on that point, they would have been dispelled by a letter which Mr. Gleig has published. Hastings, three or four years later, described Impey as the man "to whose support he was at one time indebted for the safety of his fortune, honor, and reputation." These strong words can refer only to the case of Nuncomar; and they must mean that Impey hanged Nuncomar in order to support Hastings. It is, therefore, our deliberate opinion that Impey, sitting as a judge, put a man unjustly to death in order to serve a political purpose.

But we look on the conduct of Hastings in a somewhat different light. He was struggling for fortune, honor, liberty, all that makes life valuable. He was beset by rancorous and unprincipled enemies. From his colleagues he could expect no justice. He cannot be blamed for wishing to crush his accusers. He was indeed bound to use only legitimate means for that end. But it was not strange that he should have thought any means legitimate which were pronounced legitimate by the sages of the law, by men whose peculiar duty it was to deal justly between adversaries, and whose education might be supposed to have peculiarly qualified them for the discharge of that duty. Nobody demands from a party the unbending equity of a judge. The reason that judges are appointed is, that even a good man cannot be trusted to decide a cause in which he is himself concerned. Not a day passes on which an honest prosecutor does not ask for what none but a dishonest tribunal would grant. It is too much to expect that any man, when his dearest interests are at stake, and his strongest passions excited, will, as against himself, be more just than the sworn dispensers of justice. To take an analogous case from the history of our own island: suppose that Lord Stafford, when in the Tower on suspicion of being concerned in the Popish plot, had been apprised that Titus Oates had done something which might, by a questionable construction, be brought under the head of felony. Should we severely blame Lord Stafford, in the supposed case, for causing a prosecution to be instituted, for furnishing funds, for using all his influence to intercept the mercy of the Crown? We think not. If a judge, indeed, from favor to the Catholic lords, were to strain the law in order to hang Oates, such a judge would richly deserve impeachment. But it does not appear to us that the Catholic lord, by bringing the case before the judge for decision, would materially overstep the limits of a just self-defence.

While, therefore, we have not the least doubt that this memorable execution is to be attributed to Hastings, we doubt whether it can with justice be reckoned among his crimes. That his conduct was dictated by a profound policy is evident. He was in a minority in Council. It was possible that he might long be in a minority. He knew the native character well. He knew in what abundance accusations are certain to flow in against the most innocent inhabitant of India who is under the frown of power. There was not in the whole black population of Bengal a place-holder, a place-hunter, a government tenant, who did not think that he might better himself by sending up a deposition against the Governor-General. Under these circumstances, the persecuted statesman resolved to teach the whole crew of accusers and witnesses that, though in a minority at the council-board, he was still to be feared. The lesson which he gave them was indeed a lesson not to be forgotten. The head of the combination which had been formed against him, the richest, the most powerful, the most artful of the Hindoos, distinguished by the favor of those who then held the government, fenced round by the superstitious reverence of millions, was hanged in broad day before many thousands of people. Everything that could make the warning impressive, dignity in the sufferer, solemnity in the proceeding, was found in this case. The helpless rage and vain struggles of the Council made the triumph more signal. From that moment the conviction of every native was that it was safer to take the part of Hastings in a minority than that of Francis in a majority, and that he who was so venturous as to join in running down the Governor-General might chance, in the phrase of the Eastern poet, to find a tiger, while beating the jungle for a deer. The voices of a thousand informers were silenced in an instant. From that time, whatever difficulties Hastings might have to encounter, he was never molested by accusations from natives of India.

It is a remarkable circumstance that one of the letters of Hastings to Dr. Johnson bears date a very few hours after the death of Nuncomar. While the whole settlement was in commotion, while a mighty and ancient priesthood were weeping over the remains of their chief, the conqueror in that deadly grapple sat down, with characteristic self-possession, to write about the *Tour to the Hebrides*, *Jones's Persian Grammar*,[1] and the history, traditions, arts, and natural productions of India.

In the meantime, intelligence of the Rohilla war, and of the first disputes between Hastings and his colleagues, had reached London. The Directors took part with the majority, and sent out a letter filled with severe reflections on the conduct of Hastings. They condemned, in strong but just terms, the iniquity of undertaking offensive wars merely for the sake of pecuniary advantage. But they entirely forgot that, if Hastings had by illicit means obtained pecuniary advantages, he had done so, not for his own benefit, but in order to meet their demands. To enjoin honesty, and to insist on having what could not be honestly got, was then the constant practice of the Company. As Lady Macbeth says of her husband, they "would not play false, and yet would wrongly win."

The Regulating Act, by which Hastings had been appointed Governor-General for five years, empowered the Crown to remove him on an address from the Company. Lord North [1] was desirous to procure such an address. The three members of Council who had been sent out from England were men of his own choice. General Clavering, in particular, was supported by a large parliamentary connection, such as no cabinet could be inclined to disoblige. The wish of the minister was to displace Hastings, and to put Clavering at the head of the government. In the Court of Directors parties were very nearly balanced. Eleven voted against Hastings; ten for him. The Court of Proprietors was then convened. The great sale-room presented a singular appearance. Letters had been sent by the Secretary of the Treasury, exhorting all the supporters of government who held India stock to be in attendance. Lord Sandwich marshalled the friends of the administration with his usual dexterity and alertness. Fifty peers and privy councillors, seldom seen so far eastward, were counted in the crowd. The debate lasted till midnight. The opponents of Hastings had a small superiority on the division; but a ballot was demanded; and the result was that the Governor-General triumphed by a majority of above a hundred votes over the combined efforts of the Directors and the Cabinet. The ministers were greatly exasperated by this defeat. Even Lord North lost his temper, no ordinary occurrence with him, and threatened to convoke Parliament before Christmas, and to bring in a bill for depriving the Company of all political power, and for restricting it to its old business of trading in silks and teas.

Colonel Macleane, who through all this conflict had zealously supported the cause of Hastings, now thought that his employer was in imminent danger of being turned out, branded with parliamentary censure, perhaps prosecuted. The opinion of the crown lawyers had already been taken respecting some parts of the Governor-General's conduct. It seemed to be high time to think of securing an honorable retreat. Under these circumstances, Macleane thought himself justified in producing the resignation with which he had been entrusted. The instrument was not in very accurate form; but the Directors were too eager to be scrupulous. They accepted the resignation, fixed on Mr. Wheler, one of their own body, to succeed Hastings, and sent out orders that General Clavering, as senior member of Council, should exercise the functions of Governor-General till Mr. Wheler should arrive.

But, while these things were passing in England, a great change had taken place in Bengal. Monson was no more. Only four members of the government were left. Clavering and Francis were on one side, Barwell and the Governor-General on the other; and the Governor-General had the casting vote. Hastings, who had been during two years destitute of all power and patronage, became at once absolute. He instantly proceeded to retaliate on his adversaries. Their measures were reversed: their creatures were displaced. A new valuation of the lands of Bengal, for the purpose of taxation, was ordered: and it was provided that the whole inquiry should be conducted by the Governor-General, and that all the letters relating to it should run in his name. He began, at the same time, to revolve vast plans of conquest and dominion, plans which he lived to see realized, though not by himself. His project was to form subsidiary alliances with the native princes, particularly with those of Oude and Berar, and thus to make Britain the paramount power in India. While he was meditating these great designs, arrived the intelligence that he had ceased to be Governor-General, that his resignation had been accepted, that Wheler was coming out immediately, and that, till Wheler arrived, the chair was to be filled by Clavering.

Had Hastings still been in a minority, he would probably have retired without a struggle; but he was now the real master of British India, and he was not disposed to quit his high place. He asserted that he had never given any instructions which could warrant the steps taken at home. What his instructions had been, he owned he had forgotten. If he had kept a copy of them he had mislaid it. But he was certain that he had repeatedly declared to the Directors that he would not resign. He could not see how the court, possessed of that declaration from himself, could receive his resignation from the doubtful hands of an agent. If the resignation were invalid, all the proceedings which were founded on that resignation were null, and Hastings was still Governor-General.

He afterwards affirmed that, though his agents had not acted in conformity with his instructions, he would nevertheless have held himself bound by their acts, if Clavering had not attempted to seize the supreme power by violence. Whether this assertion were or were not true, it cannot be doubted that the imprudence of Clavering gave Hastings an advantage. The General sent for the keys of the fort and of the treasury, took possession of the records, and held a council at which Francis attended. Hastings took the chair in another apartment, and Barwell sat with him. Each of the two parties had a plausible show of right. There was no authority entitled to their obedience within fifteen thousand miles. It seemed that there remained no way of settling the dispute except an appeal to arms; and from such an appeal Hastings, confident of his influence over his countrymen in India, was not inclined to shrink. He directed the officers of the garrison at Fort William and of all the neighboring stations to obey no orders but his. At the same time, with admirable judgment, he offered to submit the case to the Supreme Court, and to abide by its decision. By making this proposition he risked nothing; yet it was a proposition which his opponents could hardly reject. Nobody could be treated as a criminal for obeying what the judges should solemnly pronounce to be the lawful government. The boldest man would shrink from taking arms in defence of what the judges should pronounce to be usurpation. Clavering and Francis, after some delay, unwillingly consented to abide by the award of the court. The court pronounced that the resignation was invalid, and that therefore Hastings was still Governor-General under the Regulating Act; and the defeated members of the Council, finding that the sense of the whole settlement was against them, acquiesced in the decision.

About this time arrived the news that, after a suit which had lasted several years, the Franconian courts had decreed a divorce between Imhoff and his wife. The Baron left Calcutta, carrying with him the means of buying an estate in Saxony. The lady became Mrs. Hastings. The event was celebrated by great festivities; and all the most conspicuous persons at Calcutta, without distinction of parties, were invited to the Government-house. Clavering, as the Mohammedan chronicler tells the story, was sick in mind and body, and excused himself from joining the splendid assembly. But Hastings, whom, as it should seem, success in ambition and in love had put into high good-humor, would take no denial. He went himself to the General's house, and at length brought his vanquished rival in triumph to the gay circle which surrounded the bride. The exertion was too much for a frame broken by mortification as well as by disease. Clavering died a few days later.

Wheler, who came out expecting to be Governor-

General, and was forced to content himself with a seat at the council-board, generally voted with Francis. But the Governor-General, with Barwell's help and his own casting vote, was still the master. Some change took place at this time in the feeling both of the Court of Directors and of the Ministers of the Crown. All designs against Hastings were dropped; and, when his original term of five years expired, he was quietly reappointed. The truth is, that the fearful dangers to which the public interests in every quarter were now exposed, made both Lord North and the Company unwilling to part with a Governor whose talents, experience, and resolution, enmity itself was compelled to acknowledge.

The crisis was indeed formidable. The great and victorious empire, on the throne of which George the Third had taken his seat eighteen years before, with brighter hopes than had attended the accession of any of the long line of English sovereigns, had, by the most senseless misgovernment, been brought to the verge of ruin. In America millions of Englishmen were at war with the country from which their blood, their language, their religion, and their institutions were derived, and to which, but a short time before, they had been as strongly attached as the inhabitants of Norfolk and Leicestershire. The great powers of Europe, humbled to the dust by the vigor and genius which had guided the councils of George the Second, now rejoiced in the prospect of a signal revenge. The time was approaching when our island, while struggling to keep down the United States of America, and pressed with a still nearer danger by the too just discontents of Ireland, was to be assailed by France, Spain, and Holland, and to be threatened by the armed neutrality of the Baltic; when even our maritime supremacy was to be in jeopardy; when hostile fleets were to command the Straits of Calpe and the Mexican Sea; when the British flag was to be scarcely able to protect the British Channel. Great as were the faults of Hastings, it was happy for our country that at that conjuncture, the most terrible through which she has ever passed, he was the ruler of her Indian dominions.

An attack by sea on Bengal was little to be apprehended. The danger was that the European enemies of England might form an alliance with some native power, might furnish that power with troops, arms, and ammunition, and might thus assail our possessions on the side of the land. It was chiefly from the Mahrattas that Hastings anticipated danger. The original seat of that singular people was the wild range of hills which runs along the western coast of India. In the reign of Aurungzebe the inhabitants of those regions, led by the great Sevajee, began to descend on the possessions of their wealthier and less warlike neighbors. The energy, ferocity, and cunning of the Mahrattas, soon made them the most conspicuous among the new powers which were generated by the corruption of the decaying monarchy. At first they were only robbers. They soon rose to the dignity of conquerors. Half the provinces of the empire were turned into Mahratta principalities. Freebooters, sprung from low castes, and accustomed to menial employments, became mighty Rajahs. The Bonslas, at the head of a band of plunderers, occupied the vast region of Berar. The Guicowar, which is, being interpreted, the Herdsmen, founded that dynasty which still reigns in Guzerat. The houses of Scindia and Holkar waxed great in Malwa. One adventurous captain made his nest on the impregnable rock of Gooti. Another became the lord of the thousand villages which are scattered among the green rice-fields of Tanjore.

That was the time, throughout India, of double government. The form and the power were everywhere separated. The Mussulman nabobs who had become sovereign princes, the Vizier in Oude, and the Nizam at Hyderabad, still called themselves the viceroys of the house of Tamerlane. In the same manner the Mahratta states, though really independent of each other, pretended to be members of one empire. They all acknowledged, by words and ceremonies, the supremacy of the heir of Sevajee, a *roi fainéant* who chewed bang and toyed with dancing girls in a state prison at Sattara, and of his Peshwa or mayor of the palace,[1] a great hereditary magistrate, who kept a court with kingly state at Poonah, and whose authority was obeyed in the spacious provinces of Aurungabad and Bejapoor.

Some months before war was declared in Europe the government of Bengal was alarmed by the news that a French adventurer, who passed for a man of quality, had arrived at Poonah. It was said that he had been received there with great distinction, that he had delivered to the Peshwa letters and presents from Lewis the Sixteenth, and that a treaty, hostile to England, had been concluded between France and the Mahrattas.[1]

Hastings immediately resolved to strike the first blow. The title of the Peshwa was not undisputed. A portion of the Mahratta nation was favorable to a pretender. The Governor-General determined to espouse this pretender's interest, to move an army across the peninsular of India, and to form a close alliance with the chief of the house of Bonsla, who ruled Berar, and who, in power and dignity, was inferior to none of the Mahratta princes.

The army had marched, and the negotiations with Berar were in progress, when a letter from the English consul at Cairo brought the news that war had been proclaimed both in London and Paris. All the measures which the crisis required were adopted by Hastings without a moment's delay. The French factories in Bengal were seized. Orders were sent to Madras that Pondicherry should instantly be occupied. Near Calcutta, works were thrown up which were thought to render the approach of a hostile force impossible. A maritime establishment was formed for the defence of the river. Nine new battalions of sepoys were raised, and a corps of native artillery was formed out of the hardy Lascars of the Bay of Bengal. Having made these arrangements, the Governor-General with calm confidence pronounced his presidency secure from all attack, unless the Mahrattas should march against it in conjunction with the French.

The expedition which Hastings had sent westward was not so speedily or completely successful as most of his undertakings. The commanding officer procrastinated. The authorities at Bombay blundered. But the Governor-General persevered. A new commander repaired the errors of his predecessor. Several brilliant actions spread the military renown of the English through regions where no European flag had ever been seen. It is probable that, if a new and more formidable danger had not compelled Hastings to change his whole policy, his plans respecting the Mahratta empire would have been carried into complete effect.

The authorities in England had wisely sent out to Bengal, as commander of the forces and member of the Council, one of the most distinguished soldiers of that time. Sir Eyre Coote had, many years before, been conspicuous among the founders of the British empire in the East. At the council of war which preceded the battle of Plassey, he earnestly recommended, in opposition to the majority, that daring course which, after some hesitation, was adopted, and which was crowned with such splendid success. He subsequently commanded in the south of India against the brave and unfortunate Lally,[1] gained the decisive battle of Wandewash over the French and their native allies, took Pondicherry, and made the English power supreme in the Carnatic. Since those great exploits near twenty years had elapsed. Coote had no longer the bodily activity which he had shown in earlier days; nor was the vigor of his mind altogether unimpaired. He was capricious and fretful, and required much coaxing to keep him in good-humor. It must, we fear, be added that the love of money had grown upon him, and that he thought more about his allowances, and less about his duties, than might have been expected from so eminent a member of so noble a profession. Still he was perhaps the ablest officer that was then to be found in the British army. Among the native soldiers his name was great and his influence unrivalled. Nor is he yet forgotten by them. Now and then a white-bearded old sepoy may still be found, who loves to talk of Porto Novo and Pollilore. It is but a short time since one of those aged men came to present a memorial to an English officer, who holds one of the highest employments in India. A print of Coote hung in the room. The veteran recognized at once that face and figure which he had not seen for more than half a century, and, forgetting his salam to the living, halted, drew himself up, lifted his hand, and with solemn reverence paid his military obeisance to the dead.

Coote, though he did not, like Barwell, vote constantly with the Governor-General, was by no means inclined to join in systematic opposition, and on most questions concurred with Hastings, who did his best, by assiduous courtship, and by readily granting the most exorbitant allowances, to gratify the strongest passions of the old soldier.

It seemed likely at this time that a general reconciliation would put an end to the quarrels which had, during some years, weakened and disgraced the government of Bengal. The dangers of the empire might well induce men of patriotic feeling,—and of patriotic feeling neither Hastings nor Francis was destitute,—to forget private enmities, and to co-operate heartily for the general good. Coote had never been concerned in faction. Wheler was thoroughly tired of it. Barwell had made an ample fortune, and, though he had promised that he would not leave Calcutta while his help was needed in Council, was most desirous to return to England, and exerted himself to promote an arrangement which would set him at liberty.

A compact was made, by which Francis agreed to desist from opposition, and Hastings engaged that the friends of Francis should be admitted to a fair share of the honors and emoluments of the service. During a few months after this treaty there was apparent harmony at the council-board.

Harmony, indeed, was never more necessary; for at this moment internal calamities, more formidable than war itself, menaced Bengal. The authors of the Regulating Act of 1773 had established two independent powers, the one judicial, the other political; and, with a carelessness scandalously common in English legislation, had omitted to define the limits of either. The judges took advantage of the indistinctness, and attempted to draw to themselves supreme authority, not only within Calcutta, but through the whole of the great territory subject to the Presidency of Fort William. There are few Englishmen who will not admit that the English law, in spite of modern improvements, is neither so cheap nor so speedy [1] as might be wished. Still, it is a system which has grown up among us. In some points, it has been fashioned to suit our feelings; in others, it has gradually fashioned our feelings to suit itself. Even to its worst evils we are accustomed; and therefore, though we may complain of them, they do not strike us with the horror and dismay which would be produced by a new grievance of smaller severity. In India the case is widely different. English law, transplanted to that country, has all the vices from which we suffer here; it has them all in a far higher degree; and it has other vices, compared with which the worst vices from which we suffer are trifles. Dilatory here, it is far more dilatory in a land where the help of an interpreter is needed by every judge and by every advocate. Costly here, it is far more costly in a land into which the legal practitioners must be imported from an immense distance. All English labor in India, from the labor of the Governor-General and the Commander-in-Chief, down to that of a groom or a watchmaker, must be paid for at a higher rate than at home. No man will be banished, and banished to the torrid zone, for nothing. The rule holds good with respect to the legal profession. No English barrister will work, fifteen thousand miles from all his friends, with the thermometer at ninety-six in the shade, for the emoluments which will content him in chambers that overlook the Thames. Accordingly, the fees at Calcutta are about three times as great as the fees of Westminster Hall; and this, though the people of India are, beyond all comparison, poorer than the people of England. Yet the delay and the expense, grievous as they are, form the smallest part of the evil which English law, imported without modifications into India, could not fail to produce. The strongest feelings of our nature, honor, religion, female modesty, rose up against the innovation. Arrest on mesne process was the first step in most civil proceedings; and to a native of rank arrest was not merely a restraint, but a foul personal indignity. Oaths were required in every stage of every suit; and the feeling of a Quaker about an oath is hardly stronger than that of a respectable native. That the apartments of a woman of quality should be entered by strange men, or that her face should be seen by them, are, in the East, intolerable outrages, outrages which are more dreaded than death, and which can be expiated only by the shedding of blood. To these outrages the most distinguished families of Bengal, Bahar, and Orissa, were now exposed. Imagine what the state of our own country would be, if a jurisprudence were on a sudden introduced among us, which should be to us what our jurisprudence was to our Asiatic subjects. Imagine what the state of our country would be, if it were enacted that any man, by merely swearing that a debt was due to him, should acquire a right to insult the persons of men of the most honorable and sacred callings and of women of the most shrinking delicacy, to horsewhip a general officer, to put a bishop in the stocks, to treat ladies in the way which called forth the blow of Wat Tyler. Something like this was the effect of the attempt which the Supreme Court made to extend its jurisdiction over the whole of the Company's territory.

A reign of terror began, of terror heightened by mystery; for even that which was endured was less horrible than that which was anticipated. No man knew what was next to be expected from this strange tribunal. It came from beyond the black water, as the people of India, with mysterious horror, call the sea. It consisted of judges not one of whom was familiar with the usages of the millions over whom they claimed boundless authority. Its records were kept in unknown characters; its sentences were pronounced in unknown sounds. It had already collected round itself an army of the worst part of the native population, informers, and false witnesses, and common barrators, and agents of chicane, and above all, a banditti of bailiffs' followers, compared with whom the retainers of the worst English spunging-houses, in the worst times, might be considered as upright and tender-hearted. Many natives, highly considered among their countrymen, were seized, hurried up to Calcutta, flung into the common gaol, not for any crime even imputed, not for any debt that had been proved, but merely as a precaution till their cause should come to trial. There were instances in which men of the most venerable dignity, persecuted without a cause by extortioners, died of rage and shame in the grip of the vile alguazils [1] of Impey. The harems of noble Mahommedans, sanctuaries respected in the East by governments which respected nothing else, were burst open by gangs of bailiffs. The Mussulmans, braver and less accustomed to submission than the Hindoos, sometimes stood on their defence; and there were instances in which they shed their blood in the doorway, while defending, sword in hand, the sacred apartments of their women. Nay, it seemed as if even the faint-hearted Bengalee, who had crouched at the feet of Surajah Dowlah, who had been mute during the administration of Vansittart, would at length find courage in despair. No Mahratta invasion had ever spread through the province such dismay as this inroad of English lawyers. All the injustice of former oppressors, Asiatic and European, appeared as a blessing when compared with the justice of the Supreme Court.

Every class of the population, English and native, with the exception of the ravenous pettifoggers who fattened on the misery and terror of an immense community, cried out loudly against this fearful oppression. But the judges were immovable. If a bailiff was resisted, they ordered the soldiers to be called out. If a servant of the Company, in conformity with the orders of the government, withstood the miserable catchpoles who, with Impey's writs in their hands, exceeded the insolence and rapacity of gang-robbers, he was flung into prison for a contempt. The lapse of sixty years, the virtue and wisdom of many eminent magistrates who have during that time administered justice in the Supreme Court, have not effaced from the minds of the people of Bengal the recollection of those evil days.

The members of the government were, on this subject, united as one man. Hastings had courted the judges, he had found them useful instruments; but he was not disposed to make them his own masters, or the masters of India. His mind was large; his knowledge of the native character most accurate. He saw that the system pursued by the Supreme Court was degrading to the government and ruinous to the people; and he resolved to oppose it manfully. The consequence was, that the friendship, if that be the proper word for such a connection, which had existed between him and Impey, was for a time completely dissolved. The government placed itself firmly between the tyrannical tribunal and the people. The Chief Justice proceeded to the wildest excesses. The Governor-General and all the members of Council were served with writs, calling on them to appear before the King's justices, and to answer for their public acts. This was too much. Hastings, with just scorn, refused to obey the call, set at liberty the persons wrongfully detained by the Court, and took measures for resisting the outrageous proceedings of the sheriffs' officers, if necessary, by the sword. But he had in view another device which might prevent the necessity of an appeal to arms. He was seldom at a loss for an expedient; and he knew Impey well. The expedient, in this case, was a very simple one, neither more nor less than a bribe. Impey was, by act of Parliament, a judge, independent of the government of Bengal, and entitled to a salary of eight thousand a year. Hastings proposed to make him also a judge in the Company's service, removable at the pleasure of the government of Bengal; and to give him, in that capacity, about eight thousand a year more. It was understood that, in consideration of this new salary, Impey would desist from urging the high pretensions of his Court. If he did urge these pretensions, the government could, at a moment's notice, eject him from the new place which had been created for him. The bargain was struck; Bengal was saved; an appeal to force was averted; and the Chief Justice was rich, quiet, and infamous.[1]

Of Impey's conduct it is unnecessary to speak. It was of a piece with almost every part of his conduct that comes under the notice of history. No other such judge has dishonored the English ermine, since Jeffreys[2] drank himself to death in the Tower. But we cannot agree with those who have blamed Hastings for this transaction. The case stood thus. The negligent manner in which the Regulating Act[3] had been framed put it in the power of the Chief Justice to throw a great country into the most dreadful confusion. He was determined to use his power to the utmost, unless he was paid to be still; and Hastings consented to pay him. The necessity was to be deplored. It is also to be deplored that pirates should be able to exact ransom, by threatening to make their captives walk the plank. But to ransom a captive from pirates has always been held a humane and Christian act; and it would be absurd to charge the payer of the ransom with corrupting the virtue of the corsair. This, we seriously think, is a not unfair illustration of the relative position of Impey, Hastings, and the people of India. Whether it was right in Impey to demand or to accept a price for powers which, if they really belonged to him, he could not abdicate, which, if they did not belong to him, he ought never to have usurped, and which in neither case he could honestly sell, is one question. It is quite another question, whether Hastings was not right to give any sum, however large, to any man, however worthless, rather than either surrender millions of human beings to pillage, or rescue them by civil war.

Francis strongly opposed this arrangement. It may, indeed, be suspected that personal aversion to Impey was as strong a motive with Francis as regard for the welfare of the province. To a mind burning with resentment, it might seem better to leave Bengal to the oppressors than to redeem it by enriching them. It is not improbable, on the other hand, that Hastings may have been the more willing to resort to an expedient agreeable to the Chief Justice, because that high functionary had already been so serviceable, and might, when existing dissensions were composed, be serviceable again.

But it was not on this point alone that Francis was now opposed to Hastings. The peace between them proved to be only a short and hollow truce, during which their mutual aversion was constantly becoming stronger. At length an explosion took place. Hastings publicly charged Francis with having deceived him, and with having induced Barwell to quit the service by insincere promises. Then came a dispute, such as frequently arises even between honorable men when they may make important agreements by mere verbal communication. An impartial historian will probably be of the opinion that they had misunderstood each other; but their minds were so much embittered that they imputed to each other nothing less than deliberate villainy. "I do not," said Hastings, in a minute recorded on the Consultations of the Government, "I do not trust to Mr. Francis's promises of candor, convinced that he is incapable of it. I judge of his public conduct by his private, which I have found to be void of truth and honor." After the Council had risen, Francis put a challenge into the Governor-General's hand. It was instantly accepted. They met, and fired. Francis was shot through the body. He was carried to a neighboring house, where it appeared that the wound, though severe, was not mortal. Hastings inquired repeatedly after his enemy's health, and proposed to call on him; but Francis coldly declined the visit. He had a proper sense, he said, of the Governor-General's politeness, but could not consent to any private interview. They could meet only at the council-board.

In a very short time it was made signally manifest to how great a danger the Governor-General had, on this occasion, exposed his country. A crisis arrived with which he, and he alone, was competent to deal. It is not too much to say that, if he had been taken from the head of affairs, the years 1780 and 1781 would have been as fatal to our power in Asia as to our power in America.

The Mahrattas had been the chief objects of apprehension to Hastings. The measures which he had adopted for the purpose of breaking their power, had at first been frustrated by the errors of those whom he was compelled to employ; but his perseverance and ability seemed likely to be crowned with success, when a far more formidable danger [1] showed itself in a distant quarter.

About thirty years before this time, a Mahommedan soldier had begun to distinguish himself in the wars of Southern India. His education had been neglected; his extraction was humble. His father had been a petty officer of revenue; his grandfather a wandering dervise. But though thus meanly descended, though ignorant even of the alphabet, the adventurer had no sooner been placed at the head of a body of troops than he approved himself a man born for conquest and command. Among the crowd of chiefs who were struggling for a share of India, none could compare with him in the qualities of the captain and the statesman. He became a general; he became a sovereign. Out of the fragments of old principalities, which had gone to pieces in the general wreck, he formed for himself a great, compact, and vigorous empire. That empire he ruled with the ability, severity, and vigilance of Lewis the Eleventh.[1] Licentious in his pleasures, implacable in his revenge, he had yet enlargement of mind enough to perceive how much the prosperity of subjects adds to the strength of governments. He was an oppressor; but he had at least the merit of protecting his people against all oppression except his own. He was now in extreme old age; but his intellect was as clear, and his spirit as high, as in the prime of manhood. Such was the great Hyder Ali, the founder of the Mahommedan kingdom of Mysore, and the most formidable enemy[2] with whom the English conquerors of India have ever had to contend.

Had Hastings been governor of Madras, Hyder would have been either made a friend, or vigorously encountered as an enemy. Unhappily the English authorities in the south provoked their powerful neighbor's hostility, without being prepared to repel it. On a sudden, an army of ninety thousand men, far superior in discipline and efficiency to any other native force that could be found in India, came pouring through those wild passes which, worn by mountain torrents, and dark with jungle, lead down from the table-land of Mysore to the plains of the Carnatic. This great army was accompanied by a hundred pieces of cannon; and its movements were guided by many French officers, trained in the best military schools of Europe.

Hyder was everywhere triumphant. The sepoys in many British garrisons flung down their arms. Some forts were surrendered by treachery and some by despair. In a few days the whole open country north of the Coleroon had submitted. The English inhabitants of Madras could already see by night, from the top of Mount St. Thomas, the western sky reddened by a vast semicircle of blazing villages. The white villas, to which our countrymen retire after the daily labors of government and of trade, when the cool evening breeze springs up from the bay, were now left without inhabitants; for bands of the fierce horsemen of Mysore had already been seen prowling among the tulip-trees and near the gay verandas. Even the town was not thought secure, and the British merchants and public functionaries made haste to crowd themselves behind the cannon of Fort St. George.

There were the means, indeed, of assembling an army which might have defended the presidency, and even driven the invader back to his mountains. Sir Hector Munro was at the head of one considerable force; Baillie was advancing with another. United, they might have presented a formidable front even to such an enemy as Hyder. But the English commanders, neglecting those fundamental rules of the military art of which the propriety is obvious even to men who have never received a military education, deferred their junction, and were separately attacked. Baillie's detachment was destroyed. Munro was forced to abandon his baggage, to fling his guns into the tanks, and to save himself by a retreat which might be called a flight. In three weeks from the commencement of the war, the British empire in Southern India had been brought to the verge of ruin. Only a few fortified places remained to us. The glory of our arms had departed. It was known that a great French expedition might soon be expected on the coast of Coromandel. England, beset by enemies on every side, was in no condition to protect such remote dependencies.

Then it was that the fertile genius and serene courage of Hastings achieved their most signal triumph. A swift ship, flying before the south-west monsoon, brought the evil tidings in few days to Calcutta. In twenty-four hours the Governor-General had framed a complete plan of policy adapted to the altered state of affairs. The struggle with Hyder was a struggle for life and death. All minor objects must be sacrificed to the preservation of the Carnatic. The disputes with the Mahrattas must be accommodated. A large military force and a supply of money must be instantly sent to Madras. But even these measures would be insufficient, unless the war, hitherto so grossly mismanaged, were placed under the direction of a vigorous mind. It was no time for trifling. Hastings determined to resort to an extreme exercise of power, to suspend the incapable governor of Fort St. George, to send Sir Eyre Coote to oppose Hyder, and to intrust that distinguished general with the whole administration of the war.

In spite of the sullen opposition of Francis, who had now recovered from his wound, and had returned to the Council, the Governor-General's wise and firm policy was approved by the majority of the board. The reinforcements were sent off with great expedition, and reached Madras before the French armament arrived in the Indian seas. Coote, broken by age and disease, was no longer the Coote of Wandewash; but he was still a resolute and skilful commander. The progress of Hyder was arrested; and in a few months the great victory of Porto Novo retrieved the honor of the English arms.

In the meantime Francis had returned to England, and Hastings was now left perfectly unfettered. Wheler had gradually been relaxing in his opposition, and, after the departure of his vehement and implacable colleague, co-operated heartily with the Governor-General, whose influence over the British in India, always great, had, by the vigor and success of his recent measures, been considerably increased.

But, though the difficulties arising from factions within the Council were at an end, another class of difficulties had become more pressing than ever. The financial embarrassment was extreme. Hastings had to find the means, not only of carrying on the government of Bengal, but of maintaining a most costly war against both Indian and European enemies in the Carnatic, and of making remittances to England. A few years before this time he had obtained relief by plundering the Mogul and enslaving the Rohillas; nor were the resources of his fruitful mind by any means exhausted.

His first design was on Benares, a city which in wealth, population, dignity, and sanctity, was among the foremost of Asia. It was commonly believed that half a million of human beings was crowded into that labyrinth of lofty alleys, rich with shrines, and minarets, and balconies, and carved oriels, to which the sacred apes clung by hundreds. The traveller could scarcely make his way through the press of holy mendicants and not less holy bulls. The broad and stately flights of steps which descended from these swarming haunts to the bathing-places along the Ganges were worn every day by the footsteps of an innumerable multitude of worshippers. The schools and temples drew crowds of pious Hindoos from every province where the Brahminical faith was known. Hundreds of devotees came thither every month to die: for it was believed that a peculiarly happy fate awaited the man who should pass from the sacred city into the sacred river. Nor was superstition the only motive which allured strangers to that great metropolis. Commerce had as many pilgrims as religion. All along the shores of the venerable stream lay great fleets of vessels laden with rich merchandise. From the looms of Benares went forth the most delicate silks that adorned the balls of St. James's and of Versailles; and in the bazaars the muslins of Bengal and the sabres of Oude were mingled with the jewels of Golconda and the shawls of Cashmere. This rich capital, and the surrounding tract, had long been under the immediate rule of a Hindoo prince, who rendered homage to the Mogul emperors. During the great anarchy of India, the lords of Benares became independent of the court of Delhi, but were compelled to submit to the authority of the Nabob of Oude. Oppressed by this formidable neighbor, they invoked the protection of the English. The English protection was given; and at length the Nabob Vizier, by a solemn treaty, ceded all his rights over Benares to the Company. From that time the Rajah was the vassal of the government of Bengal, acknowledged its supremacy, and engaged to send an annual tribute to Fort William. This tribute Cheyte Sing, the reigning prince, had paid with strict punctuality.

About the precise nature of the legal relation between the Company and the Rajah of Benares, there has been much warm and acute controversy. On the one side, it has been maintained that Cheyte Sing was merely a great subject on whom the superior power had a right to call for aid in the necessities of the empire. On the other side, it has been contended that he was an independent prince, that the only claim which the Company had upon him was for a fixed tribute, and that, while the fixed tribute was regularly paid, as it assuredly was, the English had no more right to exact any further contribution from him than to demand subsidies from Holland or Denmark. Nothing is easier than to find precedents and analogies in favor of either view.

Our own impression is that neither view is correct. It was too much the habit of English politicians to take it for granted that there was in India a known and definite constitution by which questions of this kind were to be decided. The truth is that, during the interval which elapsed between the fall of the house of Tamerlane[1] and the establishment of the British ascendency, there was no such constitution.[2] The old order of things had passed away; the new order of things was not yet formed. All was transition, confusion, obscurity. Everybody kept his head as he best might, and scrambled for whatever he could get. There have been similar seasons in Europe. The time of the dissolution of the Carlovingian empire is an instance. Who would think of seriously discussing the question, what extent of pecuniary aid and of obedience Hugh Capet[3] had a constitutional right to demand from the Duke of Britanny or the Duke of Normandy? The words "constitutional right" had, in that state of society, no meaning. If Hugh Capet laid hands on all the possessions of the Duke of Normandy, this might be unjust and immoral; but it would not be illegal, in the sense in which the ordinances of Charles the Tenth[4] were illegal. If, on the other hand, the Duke of Normandy made war on Hugh Capet, this might be unjust and immoral; but it would not be illegal, in the sense in which the expedition of Prince Louis Bonaparte was illegal.

Very similar to this the state of India sixty years ago. Of the existing governments not a single one could lay claim to legitimacy, or could plead any other title than recent occupation. There was scarcely a province in which the real sovereignty and the nominal sovereignty were not disjoined. Titles and forms were still retained which implied that the heir of Tamerlane was an absolute ruler, and that the Nabobs of the provinces were his lieutenants. In reality, he was a captive. The Nabobs were in some places independent princes. In other places, as in Bengal and the Carnatic, they had, like their master, become mere phantoms, and the Company was supreme. Among the Mahrattas, again, the heir of Sevajee still kept the title of Rajah; but he was a prisoner, and his prime minister, the Peshwa, had become the hereditary chief of the state. The Peshwa, in his turn, was fast sinking into the same degraded situation to which he had reduced the Rajah. It was, we believe, impossible to find, from the Himalayas to Mysore, a single government which was at once a government *de facto* and a government *de jure,* which possessed the physical means of making itself feared by its neighbors and subjects, and which had at the same time the authority derived from law and long prescription.

Hastings clearly discerned, what was hidden from most of his contemporaries, that such a state of things gave immense advantages to a ruler of great talents and few scruples. In every international question that could arise, he had his option between the *de facto* ground and the *de jure* ground; and the probability was that one of those grounds would sustain any claim that it might be convenient for him to make, and enable him to resist any claim made by others. In every controversy, accordingly, he resorted to the plea which suited his immediate purpose, without troubling himself in the least about consistency; and thus he scarcely ever failed to find what, to persons of short memories and scanty information, seemed to be a justification for what he wanted to do. Sometimes the Nabob of Bengal is a shadow, sometimes a monarch. Sometimes the Vizier is a mere deputy, sometimes an independent potentate. If it is expedient for the Company to show some legal title to the revenues of Bengal, the grant under the seal of the Mogul is brought forward as an instrument of the highest authority. When the Mogul asks for the rents which were reserved to him by that very grant, he is told that he is a mere pageant, that the English power rests on a very different foundation from a charter given by him, that he is welcome to play at royalty as long as he likes, but that he must expect no tribute from the real masters of India.

It is true that it was in the power of others, as well as of Hastings, to practise this legerdemain;[1] but in the controversies of governments, sophistry is of little use unless it be backed by power. There is a principle which Hastings was fond of asserting in the strongest terms, and on which he acted with undeviating steadiness. It is a principle which, we must own, though it may be grossly abused, can hardly be disputed in the present state of public law. It is this, that where an ambiguous question arises between two governments, there is, if they cannot agree, no appeal except to force, and that the opinion of the stronger must prevail. Almost every question was ambiguous in India. The English government was the strongest in India. The consequences are obvious. The English government might do exactly what it chose.

The English government now chose to wring money out of Cheyte Sing. It had formerly been convenient to treat him as a sovereign prince; it was now convenient to treat him as a subject. Dexterity inferior to that of Hastings could easily find, in the general chaos of laws and customs, arguments for either course. Hastings wanted a great supply. It was known that Cheyte Sing had a large revenue, and it was suspected that he had accumulated a treasure. Nor was he a favorite at Calcutta. He had, when the Governor-General was in great difficulties, courted the favor of Francis and Clavering. Hastings who, less perhaps from evil passions than from policy, seldom left an injury unpunished, was not sorry that the fate of Cheyte Sing should teach neighboring princes the same lesson which the fate of Nuncomar had already impressed on the inhabitants of Bengal.

In 1778, on the first breaking out of the war with France, Cheyte Sing was called upon to pay, in addition to his fixed tribute, an extraordinary contribution of fifty thousand pounds. In 1779, an equal sum was exacted. In 1780, the demand was renewed. Cheyte Sing, in the hope of obtaining some indulgence, secretly offered the Governor-General a bribe of twenty thousand pounds. Hastings took the money, and his enemies have maintained that he took it intending to keep it. He certainly concealed the transaction, for a time, both from the Council in Bengal and from the Directors at home; nor did he ever give any satisfactory reason for the concealment. Public spirit, or the fear of detection, at last determined him to withstand the temptation. He paid over the bribe to the Company's treasury, and insisted that the Rajah should instantly comply with the demands of the English government. The Rajah, after the fashion of his countrymen, shuffled, solicited, and pleaded poverty. The grasp of Hastings was not to be so eluded. He added to the requisition another ten thousand pounds as a fine for delay, and sent troops to exact the money.

The money was paid. But this was not enough. The late events in the south of India had increased the financial embarrassments of the Company. Hastings was determined to plunder Cheyte Sing, and, for that end, to fasten a quarrel on him. Accordingly, the Rajah was now required to keep a body of cavalry for the service of the British government. He objected and evaded. This was exactly what the Governor-General wanted. He had now a pretext for treating the wealthiest of his vassals as a criminal. "I resolved,"—these are the words of Hastings himself, —"to draw from his guilt the means of relief of the Company's distresses, to make him pay largely for his pardon, or to exact a severe vengeance for past delinquency." The plan was simply this, to demand larger and larger contributions till the Rajah should be driven to remonstrate, then to call his remonstrance a crime, and to punish him by confiscating all his possessions.

Cheyte Sing was in the greatest dismay. He offered two hundred thousand pounds to propitiate the British government. But Hastings replied that nothing less than half a million would be accepted. Nay, he began to think of selling Benares to Oude, as he had formerly sold Allahabad and Rohilcund. The matter was one which could not be well managed at a distance; and Hastings resolved to visit Benares.

Cheyte Sing received his liege lord with every mark of reverence, came near sixty miles, with his guards, to meet and escort the illustrious visitor, and expressed his deep concern at the displeasure of the English. He even took off his turban, and laid it in the lap of Hastings, a gesture which in India marks the most profound submission and devotion. Hastings behaved with cold and repulsive severity. Having arrived at Benares,[1] he sent to the Rajah a paper containing the demands of the government of Bengal. The Rajah, in reply, attempted to clear himself from the accusations brought against him. Hastings, who wanted money and not excuses, was not to be put off by the ordinary artifices of Eastern negotiation. He instantly ordered the Rajah to be arrested and placed under the custody of two companies of sepoys.

In taking these strong measures, Hastings scarcely showed his usual judgment. It is possible that, having had little opportunity of personally observing any part of the population of India, except the Bengalees, he was not fully aware of the difference between their character and that of the tribes which inhabit the upper provinces. He was now in a land far more favorable to the vigor of the human frame than the Delta of the Ganges; in a land fruitful of soldiers, who have been found worthy to follow English battalions to the charge and into the breach. The Rajah was popular among his subjects. His administration had been mild; and the prosperity of the district which he governed presented a striking contrast to the depressed state of Bahar under our rule, and a still more striking contrast to the misery of the provinces which were cursed by the tyranny of the Nabob Vizier. The national and religious prejudices with which the English were regarded throughout India were peculiarly intense in the metropolis of the Brahminical superstition. It can therefore scarcely be doubted that the Governor-General, before he outraged the dignity of Cheyte Sing by an arrest, ought to have assembled a force capable of bearing down all opposition. This had not been done. The handful of sepoys who attended Hastings would probably have been sufficient to overawe Moorshedabad, or the Black Town of Calcutta. But they were unequal to a conflict with the hardy rabble of Benares. The streets surrounding the palace were filled with an immense multitude, of whom a large proportion, as is usual in Upper India, wore arms. The tumult became a fight, and the fight a massacre. The English officers defended themselves with desperate courage against overwhelming numbers, and fell, as became them, sword in hand. The sepoys were butchered. The gates were forced. The captive prince, neglected by his jailers during the confusion, discovered an outlet which opened on the precipitous bank of the Ganges, let himself down to the water by a string made of the turbans of his attendants, found a boat, and escaped to the opposite shore.

If Hastings had, by indiscreet violence, brought himself into a difficult and perilous situation, it is only just to acknowledge that he extricated himself with even more than his usual ability and presence of mind. He had only fifty men with him. The building in which he had taken up his residence was on every side blockaded by the insurgents. But his fortitude remained unshaken. The Rajah from the other side of the river sent apologies and liberal offers. They were not even answered. Some subtle and enterprising men were found who undertook to pass through the throng of enemies, and to convey the intelligence of the late events to the English cantonments. It is the fashion of the natives of India to wear large earrings of gold. When they travel, the rings are laid aside, lest the precious metal should tempt some gang of robbers; and, in place of the ring, a quill or a roll of paper is inserted in the orifice to prevent it from closing. Hastings placed in the ears of his messengers letters rolled up in the smallest compass. Some of these letters were addressed to the commanders of the English troops. One was written to assure his wife of his safety. One was to the envoy whom he had sent to negotiate with the Mahrattas. Instructions for the negotiation were needed; and the Governor-General framed them in that situation of extreme danger, with as much composure as if he had been writing in his palace at Calcutta.

Things, however, were not yet at the worst. An English officer of more spirit than judgment, eager to distinguish himself, made a premature attack on the insurgents beyond the river. His troops were entangled in narrow streets, and assailed by a furious population. He fell, with many of his men; and the survivors were forced to retire.

This event produced the effect which has never failed to follow every check, however slight, sustained in India by the English arms. For hundreds of miles around, the whole country was in commotion. The entire population of the district of Benares took arms. The fields were abandoned by the husbandmen, who thronged to defend their prince. The infection spread to Oude. The oppressed people of that province rose up against the Nabob Vizier, refused to pay their imposts, and put the revenue officers to flight. Even Bahar was ripe for revolt. The hopes of Cheyte Sing began to rise. Instead of imploring mercy in the humble style of a vassal, he began to talk the language of a conqueror, and threatened, it was said, to sweep the white usurpers out of the land. But the English troops were now assembling fast. The officers, and even the private men, regarded the Governor-General with enthusiastic attachment, and flew to his aid with an alacrity which, as he boasted, had never been shown on any other occasion. Major Popham, a brave and skilful soldier, who had highly distinguished himself in the Mahratta war, and in whom the Governor-General reposed the greatest confidence, took the command. The tumultuary army of the Rajah was put to rout. His fastnesses were stormed. In a few hours, above thirty thousand men left his standard, and returned to their ordinary avocations. The unhappy prince fled from his country for ever. His fair domain was added to the British dominions. One of his relations indeed was appointed rajah; but the Rajah of Benares was henceforth to be, like the Nabob of Bengal, a mere pensioner.

By this revolution, an addition of two hundred thousand pounds a year was made to the revenues of the Company. But the immediate relief was not as great as had been expected. The treasure laid up by Cheyte Sing had been popularly estimated at a million sterling. It turned out to be about a fourth part of that sum; and, such as it was, it was seized by the army, and divided as prize-money.

Disappointed in his expectations from Benares, Hastings was more violent than he would otherwise have been, in his dealings with Oude. Sujah Dowlah had long been dead. His son and successor, Asaph-ul-Dowlah, was one of the weakest and most vicious even of Eastern princes. His life was divided between torpid repose and the most odious forms of sensuality. In his court there was boundless waste, throughout his dominions wretchedness and disorder. He had been, under the skilful management of the English government, gradually sinking from the rank of an independent prince to that of a vassal of the Company. It was only by the help of a British brigade that he could be secure from the aggressions of neighbors who despised his weakness, and from the vengeance of subjects who detested his tyranny. A brigade was furnished; and he engaged to defray the charge of paying and maintaining it. From that time his independence was at an end. Hastings was not a man to lose the advantage which he had thus gained. The Nabob soon began to complain of the burden which he had undertaken to bear. His revenues, he said, were falling off; his servants were unpaid; he could no longer support the expense of the arrangement which he had sanctioned. Hastings would not listen to these representations. The Vizier, he said, had invited the government of Bengal to send him troops and had promised to pay for them. The troops had been sent. How long the troops were to remain in Oude was a matter not settled by the treaty. It remained, therefore, to be settled between the contracting parties. But the contracting parties differed. Who then must decide? The stronger.

Hastings also argued that, if the English force was withdrawn, Oude would certainly become a prey to anarchy, and would probably be overrun by a Mahratta army. That the finances of Oude were embarrassed he admitted. But he contended, not without reason, that the embarrassment was to be attributed to the incapacity and vices of Asaph-ul-Dowlah himself, and that, if less were spent on the troops, the only effect would be that more would be squandered on worthless favorites.

Hastings had intended, after settling the affairs of Benares, to visit Lucknow, and there to confer with Asaph-ul-Dowlah. But the obsequious courtesy of the Nabob Vizier prevented this visit. With a small train he hastened to meet the Governor-General. An interview took place in the fortress which, from the crest of the precipitous rock of Chunar, looks down on the waters of the Ganges.

At first sight it might appear impossible that the negotiations should come to an amicable close. Hastings wanted an extraordinary supply of money. Asaph-ul-Dowlah wanted to obtain a remission of what he already owed. Such a difference seemed to admit of no compromise. There was, however, one course satisfactory to both sides, one course by which it was possible to relieve the finances both of Oude and of Bengal; and that course was adopted. It was simply this, that the Governor General and the Nabob Vizier should join to rob a third party; and the third party whom they determined to rob was the parent of one of the robbers.

The mother of the late Nabob, and his wife, who was the mother of the present Nabob, were known as the Begums or Princesses of Oude. They had possessed great influence over Sujah Dowlah, and had, at his death, been left in possession of a splendid dotation. The domains of which they received the rents and administered the government were of wide extent. The treasure hoarded by the late Nabob, a treasure which was popularly estimated at near three millions sterling, was in their hands. They continued to occupy his favorite palace at Fyzabad, the Beautiful Dwelling; while Asaph-ul-Dowlah held his court in the stately Lucknow, which he had built for himself on the shores of the Goomti, and had adorned with noble mosques and colleges.

Asaph-ul-Dowlah had already extorted considerable sums from his mother. She had at length appealed to the English; and the English had interfered. A solemn compact had been made, by which she consented to give her son some pecuniary assistance, and he in his turn promised never to commit any further invasion of her rights. This compact was formally guaranteed by the government of Bengal. But times had changed; money was wanted; and the power which had given the guarantee was not ashamed to instigate the spoiler to excesses such that even he shrank from them.

It was necessary to find some pretext for a confiscation inconsistent, not merely with plighted faith, not merely with the ordinary rules of humanity and justice, but also with that great law of filial piety which, even in the wildest tribes of savages, even in those more degraded communities which wither under the influence of a corrupt half-civilization, retains a certain authority over the human mind. A pretext was the last thing that Hastings was likely to want. The insurrection at Benares had produced disturbances in Oude. These disturbances it was convenient to impute to the

Princesses. Evidence for the imputation there was scarcely any; unless reports wandering from one mouth to another, and gaining something by every transmission, may be called evidence. The accused were furnished with no charge; they were permitted to make no defence; for the Governor-General wisely considered that, if he tried them, he might not be able to find a ground for plundering them. It was agreed between him and the Nabob Vizier that the noble ladies should, by a sweeping act of confiscation, be stripped of their domains and treasures for the benefit of the Company, and that the sums thus obtained should be accepted by the government of Bengal in satisfaction of its claims on the government of Oude.

While Asaph-ul-Dowlah was at Chunar, he was completely subjugated by the clear and commanding intellect of the English statesman. But, when they had separated, the Vizier began to reflect with uneasiness on the engagements into which he had entered. His mother and grandmother protested and implored. His heart, deeply corrupted by absolute power and licentious pleasures, yet not naturally unfeeling, failed him in this crisis. Even the English resident at Lucknow, though hitherto devoted to Hastings, shrank from extreme measures. But the Governor-General was inexorable. He wrote to the resident in terms of the greatest severity, and declared that, if the spoliation which had been agreed upon were not instantly carried into effect, he would himself go to Lucknow, and do that from which feebler minds recoil with dismay.

The resident, thus menaced, waited on his Highness, and insisted that the treaty of Chunar should be carried into full and immediate effect. Asaph-ul-Dowlah yielded, making at the same time a solemn protestation that he yielded to compulsion. The lands were resumed; but the treasure was not so easily obtained. It was necessary to use violence. A body of the Company's troops marched to Fyzabad, and forced the gates of the palace. The Princesses were confined to their own apartments. But still they refused to submit. Some more stringent mode of coercion was to be found. A mode was found of which, even at this distance of time, we cannot speak without shame and sorrow.

There were at Fyzabad two ancient men, belonging to that unhappy class which a practice, of immemorial antiquity in the East, has excluded from the pleasures of love and from the hope of posterity. It has always been held in Asiatic courts that beings thus estranged from sympathy with their kind are those whom princes may most safely trust. Sujah Dowlah had been of this opinion. He had given his entire confidence to the two eunuchs; and after his death they remained at the head of the household of his widow.

These men were, by the orders of the British government, seized, imprisoned, ironed, starved almost to death, in order to extort money from the Princesses. After they had been two months in confinement, their health gave way. They implored permission to take a little exercise in the garden of their prison. The officer who was in charge of them stated that, if they were allowed this indulgence, there was not the smallest chance of their escaping, and that their irons really added nothing to the security of the custody in which they were kept. He did not understand the plan of his superiors. Their object in these inflictions was not security, but torture; and all mitigation was refused. Yet this was not the worst. It was resolved by an English government that these two infirm old men should be delivered to the tormentors. For that purpose they were removed to Lucknow. What horrors their dungeons there witnessed can only be guessed. But there remains on the records of Parliament, this letter, written by a British resident to a British soldier.

"Sir, The Nabob having determined to inflict corporal punishment upon the prisoners under your guard, this is to desire that his officers, when they shall come, may have free access to the prisoners, and be permitted to do with them as they shall see proper."

While these barbarities were perpetrated at Lucknow, the Princesses were still under duress at Fyzabad. Food was allowed to enter their apartments only in such scanty quantities that their female attendants were in danger of perishing with hunger. Month after month this cruelty continued, till at length, after twelve hundred thousand pounds had been wrung out of the Princesses, Hastings began to think that he had really got to the bottom of their coffers, and that no rigor could extort more. Then at length the wretched men who were detained at Lucknow regained their liberty. When their irons were knocked off, and the doors of their prisons opened, their quivering lips, the tears which ran down their cheeks, and the thanksgivings which they poured forth to the common Father of Mussulmans and Christians, melted even the stout hearts of the English warriors who stood by.

But we must not forget to do justice to Sir Elijah Impey's conduct on this occasion. It was not indeed easy for him to intrude himself into a business so entirely alien from all his official duties. But there was something inexpressibly alluring, we must suppose, in the peculiar rankness of the infamy which was then to be got at Lucknow. He hurried thither as fast as relays of palanquin-bearers could carry him. A crowd of people came before him with affidavits against the Begums, ready drawn in their hands. Those affidavits he did not read. Some of them, indeed, he could not read; for they were in the dialects of Northern India, and no interpreter was employed. He administered the oath to the deponents with all possible expedition, and asked not a single question, not even whether they had perused the statements to which they swore. This work performed, he got again into his palanquin, and posted back to Calcutta, to be in time for the opening of term. The cause was one which, by his own confession, lay altogether out of his jurisdiction. Under the charter of justice, he had no more right to inquire into crimes committed by Asiatics in Oude than the Lord President of the Court of Session of Scotland to hold an assize at Exeter. He had no right to try the Begums, nor did he pretend to try them. With what object, then, did he undertake so long a journey? Evidently in order that he might give, in an irregular manner, the sanction which in a regular manner he could not give, to the crimes of those who had recently hired him; and in order that a confused mass of testimony which he did not sift, which he did not even read, might acquire an authority not properly belonging to it, from the signature of the highest judicial functionary in India.

The time was approaching,[1] however, when he was to be stripped of that robe which has never, since the Revolution, been disgraced so foully as by him. The state of India had for some time occupied much of the attention of the British Parliament. Towards the close of the American war, two committees of the Commons sat on Eastern affairs. In one Edmund Burke took the lead. The other was under the presidency of the able and versatile Henry Dundas, then Lord Advocate of Scotland. Great as are the changes which, during the last sixty years, have taken place in our Asiatic dominions, the reports which those committees laid on the table of the House will still be found most interesting and instructive.

There was as yet no connection between the Company and either of the great parties in the state. The ministers had no motive to defend Indian abuses. On the contrary, it was for their interest to show, if possible, that the government and patronage of our Oriental empire might, with advantage, be transferred to themselves. The votes, therefore, which, in consequence of the reports made by the two committees, were passed by the Commons, breathed the spirit of stern and indignant justice. The severest epithets were applied to several of the measures of Hastings, especially to the Rohilla war; and it was resolved, on the motion of Mr. Dundas, that the Company ought to recall a Governor-General who had brought such calamities on the Indian people, and such dishonor on the British name. An act was passed for limiting the jurisdiction of the Supreme Court. The bargain which Hastings had made with the Chief Justice was condemned in the strongest terms; and an address was presented to the king, praying that Impey might be summoned home to answer for his misdeeds.

Impey was recalled by a letter from the Secretary of State. But the proprietors of India Stock resolutely refused to dismiss Hastings from their service, and passed a resolution affirming, what was undeniably true, that they were intrusted by law with the right of naming and removing their Governor-General, and that they were not bound to obey the directions of a single branch of the legislature with respect to such nomination or removal.

Thus supported by his employers, Hastings remained at the head of the government of Bengal till the spring of 1785. His administration, so eventful and stormy, closed in almost perfect quiet. In the Council there was no regular opposition to his measures. Peace was restored to India. The Mahratta war had ceased. Hyder was no more. A treaty had been concluded with his son, Tippoo; and the Carnatic had been evacuated by the armies of Mysore. Since the termination of the American war, England had no European enemy or rival in the Eastern seas.

On a general review of the long administration of Hastings, it is impossible to deny that, against the great crimes by which it is blemished, we have to set off great public services. England had passed through a perilous crisis. She still, indeed, maintained her place in the foremost rank of European powers; and the manner in which she had defended herself against fearful odds had inspired surrounding nations with a high opinion both of her spirit and of her strength. Nevertheless, in every part of the world, except one, she had been a loser. Not only had she been compelled to acknowledge the independence of thirteen colonies peopled by her children, and to conciliate the Irish by giving up the right of legislating for them; but, in the Mediterranean, in the Gulf of Mexico, on the coast of Africa, on the continent of America, she had been compelled to cede the fruits of her victories in former wars. Spain regained Minorca and Florida; France regained Senegal, Goree, and several West Indian Islands. The only quarter of the world in which Britain had lost nothing was the quarter in which her interests had been committed to the care of Hastings. In spite of the utmost exertions both of European and Asiatic enemies, the power of our country in the East had been greatly augmented. Benares was subjected; the Nabob Vizier reduced to vassalage. That our influence had been thus extended, nay, that Fort William and Fort St.

George had not been occupied by hostile armies, was owing, if we may trust the general voice of the English in India, to the skill and resolution of Hastings.

His internal administration, with all its blemishes, gives him a title to be considered as one of the most remarkable men in our history. He dissolved the double government. He transferred the direction of affairs to English hands. Out of a frightful anarchy, he educed at least a rude and imperfect order. The whole organization by which justice was dispensed, revenue collected, peace maintained throughout a territory not inferior in population to the dominions of Lewis the Sixteenth or of the Emperor Joseph, was formed and superintended by him. He boasted that every public office, without exception, which existed when he left Bengal, was his creation. It is quite true that this system, after all the improvements suggested by the experience of sixty years, still needs improvement, and that it was at first far more defective than it now is. But whoever seriously considers what it is to construct from the beginning the whole of a machine so vast and complex as a government, will allow that what Hastings effected deserves high admiration. To compare the most celebrated European ministers to him seems to us as unjust as it would be to compare the best baker in London with Robinson Crusoe, who, before he could bake a single loaf, had to make his plough and his harrow, his fences and his scarecrows, his sickle and his flail, his mill and his oven.

The just fame of Hastings rises still higher, when

we reflect that he was not bred a statesman; that he was sent from school to a counting-house; and that he was employed during the prime of his manhood as a commercial agent, far from all intellectual society.

Nor must we forget that all, or almost all, to whom, when placed at the head of affairs, he could apply for assistance, were persons who owed as little as himself, or less than himself, to education. A minister in Europe finds himself, on the first day on which he commences his functions, surrounded by experienced public servants, the depositaries of official traditions. Hastings had no such help. His own reflection, his own energy, were to supply the place of all Downing Street [1] and Somerset House.[2] Having had no facilities for learning, he was forced to teach. He had first to form himself, and then to form his instruments; and this not in a single department, but in all the departments of the administration.

It must be added that, while engaged in this most arduous task, he was constantly trammelled by orders from home, and frequently borne down by a majority in council. The preservation of an Empire from a formidable combination of foreign enemies, the construction of a government in all its parts, were accomplished by him, while every ship brought out bales of censure from his employers, and while the records of every consultation were filled with acrimonious minutes by his colleagues. We believe that there never was a public man whose temper was so severely tried; not Marlborough, when thwarted by the Dutch Deputies; not Wellington, when he had to deal at once with the Portuguese Regency, the Spanish Juntas, and Mr. Percival. But the temper of Hastings was equal to almost any trial. It was not sweet; but it was calm. Quick and vigorous as his intellect was, the patience with which he endured the most cruel vexations, till a remedy could be found, resembled the patience of stupidity. He seems to have been capable of resentment, bitter and long-enduring; yet his resentment so seldom hurried him into any blunder, that it may be doubted whether what appeared to be revenge was anything but policy.

The effect of this singular equanimity was that he always had the full command of all the resources of one of the most fertile minds that ever existed. Accordingly no complication of perils and embarrassments could perplex him. For every difficulty he had a contrivance ready; and, whatever may be thought of the justice and humanity of some of his contrivances, it is certain that they seldom failed to serve the purpose for which they were designed.

Together with this extraordinary talent for devising expedients, Hastings possessed, in a very high degree, another talent scarcely less necessary to a man in his situation; we mean the talent for conducting political controversy. It is as necessary to an English statesman in the East that he should be able to write, as it is to a minister in this country that he should be able to speak. It is chiefly by the oratory of a public man here that the nation judges of his powers. It is from the letters and reports of a public man in India that the dispensers of patronage form their estimate of him. In each case, the talent which receives peculiar encouragement is developed, perhaps at the expense of the other powers. In this country, we sometimes hear men speak above their abilities. It is not very unusual to find gentlemen in the Indian service who write above their abilities. The English politician is a little too much of a debater; the Indian politician a little too much of an essayist.

Of the numerous servants of the Company who have distinguished themselves as framers of minutes and despatches, Hastings stands at the head. He was indeed the person who gave to the official writing of the Indian governments the character which it still retains. He was matched against no common antagonist. But even Francis was forced to acknowledge, with sullen and resentful candor, that there was no contending against the pen of Hastings. And, in truth, the Governor-General's power of making out a case, of perplexing what it was inconvenient that people should understand, and of setting in the clearest point of view whatever would bear the light, was incomparable. His style must be praised with some reservation. It was in general forcible, pure, and polished; but it was sometimes, though not often, turgid, and, on one or two occasions, even bombastic. Perhaps the fondness of Hastings for Persian literature may have tended to corrupt his taste.

And, since we have referred to his literary tastes,

it would be most unjust not to praise the judicious encouragement which, as a ruler, he gave to liberal studies and curious researches. His patronage was extended, with prudent generosity, to voyages, travels, experiments, publications. He did little, it is true, towards introducing into India the learning of the West. To make the young natives of Bengal familiar with Milton and Adam Smith, to substitute the geography, astronomy, and surgery of Europe for the dotages of the Brahminical superstition, or for the imperfect science of ancient Greece transfused through Arabian expositions, this was a scheme reserved to crown the beneficent administration of a far more virtuous ruler.[1] Still it is impossible to refuse high commendation to a man who, taken from a ledger to govern an empire, overwhelmed by public business, surrounded by people as busy as himself, and separated by thousands of leagues from almost all literary society, gave, both by his example and by his munificence, a great impulse to learning. In Persian and Arabic literature he was deeply skilled. With the Sanscrit he was not himself acquainted; but those who first brought that language to the knowledge of European students owed much to his encouragement. It was under his protection that the Asiatic Society commenced its honorable career. That distinguished body selected him to be its first president; but, with excellent taste and feeling, he declined the honor in favor of Sir William Jones. But the chief advantage which the students of Oriental letters derived from his patronage remains to be mentioned. The Pundits [1] of Bengal had always looked with great jealousy on the attempts of foreigners to pry into those mysteries which were locked up in the sacred dialect. The Brahminical religion had been persecuted by the Mahommedans. What the Hindoos knew of the spirit of the Portuguese government might warrant them in apprehending persecution from Christians. That apprehension the wisdom and moderation of Hastings removed. He was the first foreign ruler who succeeded in gaining the confidence of the hereditary priests of India, and who induced them to lay open to English scholars the secrets of the old Brahminical theology and jurisprudence.

It is indeed impossible to deny that, in the great art of inspiring large masses of human beings with confidence and attachment, no ruler ever surpassed Hastings. If he had made himself popular with the English by giving up the Bengalees to extortion and oppression, or if, on the other hand, he had conciliated the Bengalees and alienated the English, there would have been no cause for wonder. What is peculiar to him is that, being the chief of a small band of strangers who exercised boundless power over a great indigenous population, he made himself beloved both by the subject many and by the dominant few. The affection felt for him by the civil service was singularly ardent and constant. Through all his disasters and perils, his brethren stood by him with steadfast loyalty. The army, at the same time, loved him as armies have seldom loved any but the greatest chiefs who have led them to victory. Even in his disputes with distinguished military men, he could always count on the support of the military profession. While such was his empire over the hearts of his countrymen, he enjoyed among the natives a popularity, such as other governors have perhaps better merited, but such as no other governor has been able to attain. He spoke their vernacular dialects with facility and precision. He was intimately acquainted with their feelings and usages. On one or two occasions, for great ends, he deliberately acted in defiance of their opinion; but on such occasions he gained more in their respect than he lost in their love. In general, he carefully avoided all that could shock their national or religious prejudices. His administration was indeed in many respects faulty; but the Bengalee standard of good government was not high. Under the Nabobs, the hurricane of Mahratta cavalry had passed annually over the rich alluvial plain. But even the Mahratta shrank from a conflict with the mighty children of the sea; and the immense rice harvests of the Lower Ganges were safely gathered in, under the protection of the English sword. The first English conquerors had been more rapacious and merciless even than the Mahrattas; but that generation had passed away. Defective as was the police, heavy as were the public burdens, it is probable that the oldest man in Bengal could not recollect a season of equal security and prosperity. For the first time within living memory, the province was placed under a government strong enough to prevent others from robbing, and not inclined to play the robber itself. These things inspired good-will. At the same time, the constant success of Hastings and the manner in which he extricated himself from every difficulty made him an object of superstitious admiration; and the more than regal splendor which he sometimes displayed dazzled a people who have much in common with children. Even now, after the lapse of more than fifty years, the natives of India still talk of him as the greatest of the English; and nurses sing children to sleep with a jingling ballad about the fleet horses and richly caparisoned elephants of Sahib Warren Hostein.

The gravest offences of which Hastings was guilty did not affect his popularity with the people of Bengal; for those offences were committed against neighboring states. Those offences, as our readers must have perceived, we are not disposed to vindicate; yet, in order that the censure may be justly apportioned to the transgression, it is fit that the motive of the criminal should be taken into consideration. The motive which prompted the worst acts of Hastings was misdirected and ill-regulated public spirit. The rules of justice, the sentiments of humanity, the plighted faith of treaties, were in his view as nothing, when opposed to the immediate interest of the state. This is no justification, according to the principles either of morality, or of what we believe to be identical with morality, namely, far-sighted policy. Nevertheless the common-sense of mankind, which in questions of this kind seldom goes far wrong, will always recognize a distinction between crimes which originate in an inordinate zeal for the commonwealth, and crimes which originate in selfish cupidity. To the benefit of this distinction Hastings is fairly entitled. There is, we conceive, no reason to suspect that the Rohilla war, the revolution of Benares, or the spoliation of the Princesses of Oude, added a rupee to his fortune. We will not affirm that, in all pecuniary dealings, he showed that punctilious integrity, that dread of the faintest appearance of evil, which is now the glory of the Indian civil service. But when the school in which he had been trained and the temptations to which he was exposed are considered, we are more inclined to praise him for his general uprightness with respect to money, than rigidly to blame him for a few transactions which would now be called indelicate and irregular, but which even now would hardly be designated as corrupt. A rapacious man he certainly was not. Had he been so, he would infallibly have returned to his country the richest subject in Europe. We speak within compass, when we say that, without applying any extraordinary pressure he might easily have obtained from the zemindars [1] of the Company's provinces and from neighboring princes, in the course of thirteen years, more than three millions sterling, and might have outshone the splendor of Carlton House [2] and of the *Palais Royal*. He brought home a fortune such as a Governor-General, fond of state, and careless of thrift, might easily, during so long a tenure of office, save out of his legal salary. Mrs. Hastings, we are afraid, was less scrupulous. It was generally believed that she accepted presents with great alacrity, and that she thus formed, without the connivance of her husband, a private hoard amounting to several lacs [1] of rupees. We are the more inclined to give credit to this story, because Mr. Gleig, who cannot but have heard it, does not, as far as we have observed, notice or contradict it.

The influence of Mrs. Hastings over her husband was indeed such that she might easily have obtained much larger sums than she was ever accused of receiving. At length her health began to give way; and the Governor-General, much against his will, was compelled to send her to England. He seems to have loved her with that love which is peculiar to men of strong minds, to men whose affection is not easily won or widely diffused. The talk of Calcutta ran for some time on the luxurious manner in which he fitted up the round-house of an Indiaman for her accommodation, on the profusion of sandal-wood and carved ivory which adorned her cabin, and on the thousands of rupees which had been expended in order to procure for her the society of an agreeable female companion during the voyage. We may remark here that the letters of Hastings to his wife are exceedingly characteristic. They are tender, and full of indications of esteem and confidence; but, at the same time, a little more ceremonious than is usual in so intimate a relation. The solemn courtesy with which he compliments "his elegant Marian" reminds us now and then of the dignified air with which

Sir Charles Grandison [1] bowed over Miss Byron's hand in the cedar parlor.

After some months, Hastings prepared to follow his wife to England. When it was announced that he was about to quit his office, the feeling of the society which he had so long governed manifested itself by many signs. Addresses poured in from Europeans and Asiatics, from civil functionaries, soldiers, and traders. On the day on which he delivered up the keys of office, a crowd of friends and admirers formed a lane to the quay where he embarked. Several barges escorted him far down the river; and some attached friends refused to quit him till the low coast of Bengal was fading from the view, and till the pilot was leaving the ship.

Of his voyage little is known, except that he amused himself with his books and with his pen; and that among the compositions by which he beguiled the tediousness of that long leisure, was a pleasing imitation of Horace's *Otium Divos rogat*. This little poem was inscribed to Mr. Shore, afterwards Lord Teignmouth, a man of whose integrity, humanity, and honor it is impossible to speak too highly, but who, like some other excellent members of the civil service, extended to the conduct of his friend Hastings an indulgence of which his own conduct never stood in need.

The voyage was, for those times, very speedy. Hastings was little more than four months on the sea. In June, 1785, he landed at Plymouth, posted to London, appeared at Court, paid his respects in Leadenhall Street, and then retired with his wife to Cheltenham.

He was greatly pleased with his reception. The King treated him with marked distinction. The Queen, who had already incurred much censure on account of the favor which, in spite of the ordinary severity of her virtue, she had shown to the "elegant Marian," was not less gracious to Hastings. The Directors received him in a solemn sitting; and their chairman read to him a vote of thanks which they had passed without one dissentient voice. "I find myself," said Hastings, in a letter written about a quarter of a year after his arrival in England, "I find myself everywhere, and universally, treated with evidences, apparent even to my own observation, that I possess the good opinion of my country."

The confident and exulting tone of his correspondence about this time is the more remarkable, because he had already received ample notice of the attack which was in preparation. Within a week after he landed at Plymouth, Burke gave notice [1] in the House of Commons of a motion seriously affecting a gentleman lately returned from India. The session, however, was then so far advanced, that it was impossible to enter on so extensive and important a subject.

Hastings, it is clear, was not sensible of the danger of his position. Indeed that sagacity, that judgment, that readiness in devising expedients, which had distinguished him in the East, seemed now to have forsaken him; not that his abilities were at all impaired; not that he was not still the same man who had triumphed over Francis and Nuncomar, who had made the Chief Justice and the Nabob Vizier his tools, who had deposed Cheyte Sing, and repelled Hyder Ali. But an oak, as Mr. Grattan finely said, should not be transplanted at fifty. A man who, having left England when a boy, returns to it after thirty or forty years passed in India, will find, be his talents what they may, that he has much both to learn and to unlearn before he can take a place among English statesmen. The working of a representative system, the war of parties, the arts of debate, the influence of the press, are startling novelties to him. Surrounded on every side by new machines and new tactics, he is as much bewildered as Hannibal would have been at Waterloo, or Themistocles at Trafalgar. His very acuteness deludes him. His very vigor causes him to stumble. The more correct his maxims, when applied to the state of society to which he is accustomed, the more certain they are to lead him astray. This was strikingly the case with Hastings. In India he had a bad hand;[1] but he was master of the game, and he won every stake. In England he held excellent cards, if he had known how to play them; and it was chiefly by his own errors that he was brought to the verge of ruin.

Of all his errors the most serious was perhaps the choice of a champion. Clive, in similar circumstances, had made a singularly happy selection. He put himself into the hands of Wedderburn, afterwards Lord Loughborough, one of the few great advocates who have also been great in the House of Commons. To the defence of Clive, therefore, nothing was wanting, neither learning nor knowledge of the world, neither forensic acuteness nor that eloquence which charms political assemblies. Hastings intrusted his interests to a very different person, a major in the Bengal army, named Scott. This gentleman had been sent over from India some time before as an agent of the Governor-General. It was rumored that his services were rewarded with Oriental munificence; and we believe that he received much more than Hastings could conveniently spare. The Major obtained a seat in Parliament, and was there regarded as the organ of his employer. It was evidently impossible that a gentleman so situated could speak with the authority which belongs to an independent position. Nor had the agent of Hastings the talents necessary for obtaining the ear of an assembly which, accustomed to listen to great orators, had naturally become fastidious. He was always on his legs; he was very tedious; and he had only one topic, the merits and wrongs of Hastings. Everybody who knows the House of Commons will easily guess what followed. The Major was soon considered as the greatest bore of his time. His exertions were not confined to Parliament. There was hardly a day on which the newspapers did not contain some puff upon Hastings, signed *Asiaticus* or *Bengalensis*, but known to be written by the indefatigable Scott; and hardly a month in which some bulky pamphlet on the same subject, and from the same pen, did not pass to the trunk-makers and the pastry-cooks. As to this gentleman's capacity for conducting a delicate question through

Parliament, our readers will want no evidence beyond that which they will find in letters preserved in these volumes. We will give a single specimen of his temper and judgment. He designated the greatest man then living as "that reptile Mr. Burke."

In spite, however, of this unfortunate choice, the general aspect of affairs was favorable to Hastings. The King was on his side. The Company and its servants were zealous in his cause. Among public men he had many ardent friends. Such were Lord Mansfield, who had outlived the vigor of his body, but not that of his mind; and Lord Lansdowne, who, though unconnected with any party, retained the importance which belongs to great talents and knowledge. The ministers were generally believed to be favorable to the late Governor-General. They owed their power to the clamor which had been raised against Mr. Fox's East India Bill. The authors of that bill, when accused of invading vested rights, and of setting up powers unknown to the constitution, had defended themselves by pointing to the crimes of Hastings, and by arguing that abuses so extraordinary justified extraordinary measures. Those who, by opposing that bill, had raised themselves to the head of affairs, would naturally be inclined to extenuate the evils which had been made the plea for administering so violent a remedy; and such, in fact, was their general disposition. The Lord Chancellor Thurlow, in particular, whose great place and force of intellect gave him a weight in the government inferior only to that of Mr. Pitt, espoused the cause of

Hastings with indecorous violence. Mr. Pitt, though he had censured many parts of the Indian system, had studiously abstained from saying a word against the late chief of the Indian government. To Major Scott, indeed, the young minister had in private extolled Hastings as a great, a wonderful man, who had the highest claims on the government. There was only one objection to granting all that so eminent a servant of the public could ask. The resolution of censure still remained on the journals of the House of Commons. That resolution was, indeed, unjust; but, till it was rescinded, could the minister advise the King to bestow any mark of approbation on the person censured? If Major Scott is to be trusted, Mr. Pitt declared that this was the only reason which prevented the advisers of the Crown from conferring a peerage on the late Governor-General. Mr. Dundas was the only important member of the administration who was deeply committed to a different view of the subject. He had moved the resolution which created the difficulty; but even from him little was to be apprehended. Since he had presided over the committee on Eastern affairs, the great changes had taken place. He was surrounded by new allies; he had fixed his hopes on new objects; and whatever may have been his good qualities,—and he had many,—flattery itself never reckoned rigid consistency in the number.

From the ministry, therefore, Hastings had every reason to expect support; and the ministry was very powerful. The opposition was loud and vehement against him. But the opposition,[1] though formidable from the wealth and influence of some of its members, and from the admirable talents and eloquence of others, was outnumbered in Parliament, and odious throughout the country. Nor, as far as we can judge, was the opposition generally desirous to engage in so serious an undertaking as the impeachment of an Indian Governor. Such an impeachment must last for years. It must impose on the chiefs of the party an immense load of labor. Yet it could scarcely, in any manner, affect the event of the great political game. The followers of the coalition were therefore more inclined to revile Hastings than to prosecute him. They lost no opportunity of coupling his name with the names of the most hateful tyrants of whom history makes mention. The wits of Brooks's [2] aimed their keenest sarcasms both at his public and at his domestic life. Some fine diamonds which he had presented, as it was rumored, to the royal family, and a certain richly carved ivory bed which the Queen had done him the honor to accept from him, were favorite subjects of ridicule. One lively poet proposed that the great acts of the fair Marian's present husband should be immortalized by the pencil of his predecessor; and that Imhoff should be employed to embellish the House of Commons with paintings of the bleeding Rohillas, of Nuncomar swinging, of Cheyte Sing letting himself down to the Ganges. Another, in an exquisitely humorous parody of Virgil's third eclogue, propounded the question, what that mineral could be of which the rays had power to make the most austere of princesses the friend of a wanton. A third described, with gay malevolence, the gorgeous appearance of Mrs. Hastings at St. James's, the galaxy of jewels, torn from Indian Begums, which adorned her head dress, her necklace gleaming with future votes, and the depending questions that shone upon her ears. Satirical attacks of this description, and perhaps a motion for a vote of censure, would have satisfied the great body of the opposition. But there were two men whose indignation was not to be so appeased, Philip Francis and Edmund Burke.

Francis had recently entered the House of Commons, and had already established a character there for industry and ability. He labored indeed under one most unfortunate defect, want of fluency. But he occasionally expressed himself with a dignity and energy worthy of the greatest orators. Before he had been many days in Parliament, he incurred the bitter dislike of Pitt, who constantly treated him with as much asperity as the laws of debate would allow. Neither lapse of years nor change of scene had mitigated the enmities which Francis had brought back from the East. After his usual fashion, he mistook his malevolence for virtue, nursed it, as preachers tell us that we ought to nurse our good dispositions, and paraded it on all occasions with Pharisaical ostentation.[1]

The zeal of Burke was still fiercer; but it was far purer. Men unable to understand the elevation of his mind have tried to find out some discreditable motive for the vehemence and pertinacity which he showed on this occasion. But they have altogether failed. The idle story that he had some private slight to revenge has long been given up, even by the advocates of Hastings. Mr. Gleig supposes that Burke was actuated by party spirit, that he retained a bitter remembrance of the fall of the coalition,[1] that he attributed that fall to the exertions of the East India interest, and that he considered Hastings as the head and the representative of that interest. This explanation seems to be sufficiently refuted by a reference to dates. The hostility of Burke to Hastings commenced long before the coalition; and lasted long after Burke had become a strenuous supporter of those by whom the coalition had been defeated. It began when Burke and Fox, closely allied together, were attacking the influence of the crown, and calling for peace with the American republic. It continued till Burke, alienated from Fox, and loaded with the favors of the crown, died, preaching a crusade against the French republic. We surely cannot attribute to the events of 1784 an enmity which began in 1781, and which retained undiminished force long after persons far more deeply implicated than Hastings in the events of 1784 had been cordially forgiven. And why should we look for any other explanation of Burke's conduct than that which we find on the surface? The plain truth is that Hastings had committed some great crimes, and that the thought of those crimes made the blood of Burke boil in his veins. For Burke was a man in whom compassion for suffering, and hatred of injustice and tyranny, were as strong as in Las Casas or Clarkson. And although in him, as in Las Casas and in Clarkson, these noble feelings were alloyed with the infirmity which belongs to human nature, he is, like them, entitled to this great praise, that he devoted years of intense labor to the service of a people with whom he had neither blood nor language, neither religion nor manners in common, and from whom no requital, no thanks, no applause could be expected.

His knowledge of India [1] was such as few, even of those Europeans who have passed many years in that country, have attained, and such as certainly was never attained by any public man who had not quitted Europe. He had studied the history, the laws, and the usages of the East with an industry, such as is seldom found united to so much genius and so much sensibility. Others have perhaps been equally laborious, and have collected an equal mass of materials. But the manner in which Burke brought his higher powers of intellect to work on statements of facts, and on tables of figures, was peculiar to himself. In every part of those huge bales of Indian information which repelled almost all other readers, his mind, at once philosophical and poetical, found something to instruct or to delight. His reason analyzed and digested those vast and shapeless masses; his imagination animated and colored them. Out of darkness, and dulness, and confusion, he formed a multitude of ingenious theories and vivid pictures. He had, in the highest degree, that noble faculty whereby man is able to live in the past and in the future, in the distant and in the unreal. India and its inhabitants were not to him, as to most Englishmen, mere names and abstractions, but a real country and a real people. The burning sun, the strange vegetation of the palm and the cocoa tree, the rice-field, the tank, the huge trees, older than the Mogul empire, under which the village crowds assemble, the thatched roof of the peasant's hut, the rich tracery of the mosque where the imaum prays with his face to Mecca,[1] the drums, and banners and gaudy idols, the devotee swinging in the air, the graceful maiden, with the pitcher on her head, descending the steps to the river-side, the black faces, the long beards, the yellow streaks of sect, the turbans and the flowing robes, the spears and the silver maces, the elephants with their canopies of state, the gorgeous palanquin of the prince, and the close litter of the noble lady, all these things were to him as the objects amidst which his own life had been passed, as the objects which lay on the road between Beaconsfield and St. James's Street.[2] All India was present to the eye of his mind, from the halls where suitors laid gold and perfumes at the feet of sovereigns to the wild moor where the gypsy camp was pitched, from the bazar, humming like a bee-hive with the crowd of buyers and sellers, to the jungle where the lonely courier shakes his bunch of iron rings to scare away the hyænas. He had just as lively an idea of the insurrection at Benares as of Lord George Gordon's[3] riots, and of the execution of

Nuncomar as of the execution of Dr. Dodd. Oppression in Bengal was to him the same thing as oppression in the streets of London.

He saw that Hastings had been guilty of some most unjustifiable acts. All that followed was natural and necessary in a mind like Burke's. His imagination and his passions, once excited, hurried him beyond the bounds of justice and good sense. His reason, powerful as it was, became the slave of feelings which it should have controlled. His indignation, virtuous in its origin, acquired too much of the character of personal aversion. He could see no mitigating circumstance, no redeeming merit. His temper, which, though generous and affectionate, had always been irritable, had now been made almost savage by bodily infirmities and mental vexations. Conscious of great powers and great virtues, he found himself, in age and poverty, a mark for the hatred of a perfidious court and a deluded people. In Parliament his eloquence was out of date. A young generation, which knew him not, had filled the House. Whenever he rose to speak, his voice was drowned by the unseemly interruption of lads who were in their cradles when his orations on the Stamp Act called forth the applause of the great Earl of Chatham. These things had produced on his proud and sensitive spirit an effect at which we cannot wonder. He could no longer discuss any question with calmness, or make allowance for honest differences of opinion. Those who think that he was more violent and acrimonious in debates about India than on other occasions are ill informed respecting the last years of his life. In the discussions on the Commercial Treaty with the Court of Versailles, on the Regency, on the French Revolution, he showed even more virulence than in conducting the impeachment. Indeed it may be remarked that the very persons who call him a mischievous maniac, for condemning in burning words the Rohilla war and the spoliation of the Begums, exalted him into a prophet as soon as he began to declaim, with greater vehemence, and not with greater reason, against the taking of the Bastile and the insults offered to Marie Antoinette. To us he appears to have been neither a maniac in the former case, nor a prophet in the latter, but in both cases a great and good man, led into extravagance by a sensibility [1] which domineered over all his faculties.

It may be doubted whether the personal antipathy of Francis or the nobler indignation of Burke, would have led their party to adopt extreme measures against Hastings, if his own conduct had been judicious. He should have felt that, great as his public services had been, he was not faultless, and should have been content to make his escape, without aspiring to the honors of a triumph. He and his agent took a different view. They were impatient for the rewards which, as they conceived, were deferred only till Burke's attack should be over. They accordingly resolved to force on a decisive action with an enemy for whom, if they had been wise, they would have made a bridge of gold.[2] On the first day of the session in 1786, Major Scott reminded Burke of the notice given in the preceding year, and asked whether it was seriously intended to bring any charge against the late Governor-General. This challenge left no course open to Opposition, except to come forward as accusers, or to acknowledge themselves calumniators. The administration of Hastings had not been so blameless, nor was the great party of Fox and North so feeble, that it could be prudent to venture on so bold a defiance. The leaders of the Opposition instantly returned the only answer which they could with honor return; and the whole party was irrevocably pledged to a prosecution.

Burke began his operations by applying for Papers. Some of the documents for which he asked were refused by the ministers, who, in the debate, held language such as strongly confirmed the prevailing opinion, that they intended to support Hastings. In April, the charges were laid on the table. They had been drawn by Burke with great ability, though in a form too much resembling that of a pamphlet. Hastings was furnished with a copy of the accusations; and it was intimated to him that he might, if he thought fit, be heard in his own defence at the bar of the Commons.

Here again Hastings was pursued by the same fatality which had attended him ever since the day when he set foot on English ground. It seemed to be decreed that this man, so politic and so successful in the East, should commit nothing but blunders in Europe. Any judicious adviser would have told him that the best thing which he could do would be to make an eloquent, forcible, and affecting oration at the bar of the House; but that, if he could not trust himself to speak, and found it necessary to read, he ought to be as concise as possible. Audiences accustomed to extemporaneous debating of the highest excellence are always impatient of long written compositions. Hastings, however, sat down as he would have done at the Government-house in Bengal, and prepared a paper of immense length. That paper, if recorded on the consultations of an Indian administration, would have been justly praised as a very able minute. But it was now out of place. It fell flat, as the best written defence must have fallen flat, on an assembly accustomed to the animated and strenuous conflicts of Pitt and Fox. The members, as soon as their curiosity about the face and demeanor of so eminent a stranger was satisfied, walked away to dinner, and left Hastings to tell his story till midnight to the clerks and the Serjeant-at-arms.

All preliminary steps having been duly taken, Burke, in the beginning of June, brought forward the charge relating to the Rohilla war. He acted discreetly in placing this accusation in the van; for Dundas had formerly moved, and the House had adopted, a resolution condemning, in the most severe terms, the policy followed by Hastings with regard to Rohilcund. Dundas had little, or rather nothing, to say in defence of his own consistency; but he put a bold face on the matter, and opposed the motion. Among other things, he declared that, though he still thought the Rohilla war was unjustifiable, he considered the services which Hastings had subsequently rendered to the state as sufficient to atone even for so great an offence. Pitt did not speak, but voted with Dundas; and Hastings was absolved by a hundred and nineteen votes against sixty-seven.

Hastings was now confident of victory. It seemed, indeed, that he had reason to be so. The Rohilla war was, of all his measures, that which his accusers might with greatest advantage assail. It had been condemned by the Court of Directors. It had been condemned by the House of Commons. It had been condemned by Mr. Dundas, who had since become the chief minister of the Crown for Indian affairs. Yet Burke, having chosen this strong ground, had been completely defeated on it. That, having failed here, he should succeed on any point, was generally thought impossible. It was rumored at the clubs and coffee-houses that one or perhaps two more charges would be brought forward; that if, on those charges, the sense of the House of Commons should be against impeachment, the Opposition would let the matter drop, that Hastings would be immediately raised to the peerage, decorated with the star of the Bath,[1] sworn of the privy council,[2] and invited to lend the assistance of his talents and experience to the India board. Lord Thurlow, indeed, some months before, had spoken with contempt of the scruples which prevented Pitt from calling Hastings to the House of

Lords; and had even said that, if the Chancellor of the Exchequer was afraid of the Commons, there was nothing to prevent the Keeper of the Great Seal from taking the royal pleasure about a patent of peerage. The very title was chosen. Hastings was to be Lord Daylesford. For, through all changes of scene and changes of fortune, remained unchanged his attachment to the spot which had witnessed the greatness and the fall of his family, and which had borne so great a part in the first dreams of his young ambition.

But in a very few days these fair prospects were overcast. On the thirteenth of June, Mr. Fox brought forward, with great ability and eloquence, the charge respecting the treatment of Cheyte Sing. Francis followed on the same side. The friends of Hastings were in high spirits when Pitt rose. With his usual abundance and felicity of language, the minister gave his opinion on the case. He maintained that the Governor-General was justified in calling on the Rajah of Benares for pecuniary assistance, and in imposing a fine when that assistance was contumaciously withheld. He also thought that the conduct of the Governor-General during the insurrection had been distinguished by ability and presence of mind. He censured, with great bitterness, the conduct of Francis, both in India and in Parliament, as most dishonest and malignant. The necessary inference from Pitt's arguments seemed to be that Hastings ought to be honorably acquitted; and both the friends and the opponents of the Minister expected from him a declaration to that effect. To the astonishment of all parties, he concluded by saying that, though he thought it right in Hastings to fine Cheyte Sing for contumacy, yet the amount of the fine was too great for the occasion. On this ground, and on this ground alone, did Mr. Pitt, applauding every other part of the conduct of Hastings with regard to Benares, declare that he should vote in favor of Mr. Fox's motion.

The House was thunderstruck; and it well might be so. For the wrong done to Cheyte Sing, even had it been as flagitious as Fox and Francis contended, was a trifle when compared with the horrors which had been inflicted on Rohilcund. But if Mr. Pitt's view of the case of Cheyte Sing were correct, there was no ground for an impeachment, or even for a vote of censure. If the offence of Hastings was really no more than this, that, having a right to impose a mulct, the amount of which mulct was not defined, but was left to be settled by his discretion, he had, not for his own advantage, but for that of the state, demanded too much, was this an offence which required a criminal proceeding of the highest solemnity, a criminal proceeding, to which, during sixty years, no public functionary had been subjected? We can see, we think, in what way a man of sense and integrity might have been induced to take any course respecting Hastings, except the course which Mr. Pitt took. Such a man might have thought a great example necessary, for the preventing of injustice, and for the vindicating of the national honor, and might, on that ground, have voted for impeachment both on the Rohilla charge, and on the Benares charge. Such a man might have thought that the offences of Hastings had been atoned for by great services, and might, on that ground, have voted against the impeachment, on both charges. With great diffidence, we give it as our opinion that the most correct course would, on the whole, have been to impeach on the Rohilla charge, and to acquit on the Benares charge. Had the Benares charge appeared to us in the same light in which it appeared to Mr. Pitt, we should without hesitation have voted for acquittal on that charge. The one course which it is inconceivable that any man of a tenth part of Mr. Pitt's abilities can have honestly taken was the course which he took. He acquitted Hastings on the Rohilla charge. He softened down the Benares charge till it became no charge at all; and then he pronounced that it contained matter for impeachment.

Nor must it be forgotten that the principal reason assigned by the ministry for not impeaching Hastings on account of the Rohilla war was this, that the delinquencies of the early part of his administration had been atoned for by the excellence of the later part. Was it not most extraordinary that men who had held this language could afterwards vote that the later part of his administration furnished matter for no less than twenty articles of impeachment? They first represented the conduct of Hastings in 1780 and 1781 as so highly meritorious that, like works of supererogation[1] in the Catholic theology, it ought to be efficacious for the cancelling of former offences; and they then prosecuted him for his conduct in 1780 and 1781.

The general astonishment was the greater, because, only twenty-four hours before, the members on whom the minister could depend had received the usual notes from the Treasury, begging them to be in their places and to vote against Mr. Fox's motion. It was asserted by Mr. Hastings, that, early on the morning of the very day on which the debate took place, Dundas called on Pitt, woke him, and was closeted with him many hours. The result of this conference was a determination to give up the late Governor-General to the vengeance of the Opposition. It was impossible even for the most powerful minister to carry all his followers with him in so strange a course. Several persons high in office, the Attorney-General, Mr. Grenville, and Lord Mulgrave, divided against Mr. Pitt. But the devoted adherents who stood by the head of the government without asking questions, were sufficiently numerous to turn the scale. A hundred and nineteen members voted for Mr. Fox's motion; seventy-nine against it. Dundas silently followed Pitt.

That good and great man, the late William Wilberforce,[1] often related the events of this remarkable night. He described the amazement of the House, and the bitter reflections which were muttered against the Prime Minister by some of the habitual supporters of government. Pitt himself appeared to feel that his conduct required some explanation. He left the treasury bench, sat for some time next to Mr. Wilberforce, and very earnestly declared that he had found it impossible, as a man of conscience, to stand any longer by Hastings. The business, he said, was too bad. Mr. Wilberforce, we are bound to add, fully believed that his friend was sincere, and that the suspicions to which this mysterious affair gave rise were altogether unfounded.

Those suspicions, indeed, were such as it is painful to mention. The friends of Hastings, most of whom, it is to be observed, generally supported the administration, affirmed that the motive of Pitt and Dundas was jealousy. Hastings was personally a favorite with the King. He was the idol of the East India Company and of its servants. If he were absolved by the Commons, seated among the Lords, admitted to the Board of Control, closely allied with the strong-minded and imperious Thurlow, was it not almost certain that he would soon draw to himself the entire management of Eastern affairs? Was it not possible that he might become a formidable rival in the cabinet? It had probably got abroad that very singular communications had taken place between Thurlow and Major Scott, and that, if the First Lord of the Treasury was afraid to recommend Hastings for a peerage, the Chancellor was ready to take the responsibility of that step on himself. Of all ministers, Pitt was the least likely to submit with patience to such an encroachment on his functions. If the Commons impeached Hastings, all danger was at an end. The proceeding, however it might terminate, would probably last some years. In the meantime, the accused person would be excluded from honors and public employments, and could scarcely venture even to pay his duty at court. Such were the motives attributed by a great part of the public to the young minister, whose ruling passion was generally believed to be avarice of power.

The prorogation [1] soon interrupted the discussions respecting Hastings. In the following year, those discussions were resumed. The charge touching the spoliation of the Begums [2] was brought forward by Sheridan,[3] in a speech which was so imperfectly reported that it may be said to be wholly lost, but which was, without doubt, the most elaborately brilliant of all the productions of his ingenious mind. The impression which it produced was such as has never been equalled. He sat down, not merely amidst cheering, but amidst the loud clapping of hands, in which the Lords below the bar and the strangers in the gallery joined. The excitement of the House was such that no other speaker could obtain a hearing; and the debate was adjourned. The ferment spread fast through the town. Within four and twenty hours, Sheridan was offered a thousand pounds for the copyright of the speech, if he would himself correct it for the press. The impression made by this remarkable display of eloquence on severe and experienced critics, whose discernment may be supposed to have been quickened by emulation, was deep and permanent. Mr.

Windham, twenty years later, said that the speech deserved all its fame, and was, in spite of some faults of taste, such as were seldom wanting either in the literary or in the parliamentary performances of Sheridan, the finest that had been delivered within the memory of man. Mr. Fox, about the same time, being asked by the late Lord Holland what was the best speech ever made in the House of Commons, assigned the first place, without hesitation, to the great oration of Sheridan on the Oude charge.

When the debate was resumed, the tide ran so strongly against the accused that his friends were coughed and scraped down.[1] Pitt declared himself for Sheridan's motion; and the question was carried by a hundred and seventy-five votes against sixty-eight.

The opposition, flushed with victory and strongly supported by the public sympathy, proceeded to bring forward a succession of charges relating chiefly to pecuniary transactions. The friends of Hastings were discouraged, and having now no hope of being able to avert an impeachment, were not very strenuous in their exertions. At length the House, having agreed to twenty articles of charge, directed Burke to go before the Lords,[2] and to impeach the late Governor-General of High Crimes and Misdemeanors. Hastings was at the same time arrested by the Serjeant-at-arms, and carried to the bar of the Peers.

The session was now within ten days of its close. It was, therefore, impossible that any progress could be made in the trial till the next year. Hastings was admitted to bail; and further proceedings were postponed till the Houses should re-assemble.

When Parliament met in the following winter, the Commons proceeded to elect a committee for managing the impeachment. Burke stood at the head; and with him were associated most of the leading members of the Opposition. But when the name of Francis was read a fierce contention arose. It was said that Francis and Hastings were notoriously on bad terms, that they had been at feud during many years, that on one occasion their mutual aversion had impelled them to seek each other's lives, and that it would be improper and indelicate to select a private enemy to be a public accuser. It was urged on the other side with great force, particularly by Mr. Windham, that impartiality, though the first duty of a judge, had never been reckoned among the qualities of an advocate; that in the ordinary administration of criminal justice among the English, the aggrieved party, the very last person who ought to be admitted into the jury-box, is the prosecutor; that what was wanted in a manager was, not that he should be free from bias, but that he should be able, well informed, energetic, and active. The ability and information of Francis were admitted; and the very animosity with which he was reproached, whether a virtue or a vice, was at least a pledge for his energy and activity. It seems difficult to refute these arguments. But the inveterate hatred borne by Francis to Hastings had excited general disgust. The House decided that

Francis should not be a manager. Pitt voted with the majority, Dundas with the minority.

In the meantime, the preparations for the trial had proceeded rapidly; and on the 13th of February, 1788, the sittings of the Court commenced. There have been spectacles more dazzling to the eye, more gorgeous with jewelry and cloth of gold, more attractive to grown-up children, than that which was then exhibited at Westminster; but, perhaps, there never was a spectacle so well calculated to strike a highly cultivated, a reflecting, and imaginative mind. All the various kinds of interest which belong to the near and to the distant, to the present and to the past, were collected on one spot, and in one hour. All the talents and all the accomplishments which are developed by liberty and civilization were now displayed, with every advantage that could be derived both from co-operation and from contrast. Every step in the proceedings carried the mind either backward, through many troubled centuries, to the days when the foundations of our constitution were laid; or far away, over boundless seas and deserts, to dusky nations living under strange stars, worshipping strange gods, and writing strange characters from right to left. The high Court of Parliament was to sit, according to forms handed down from the days of the Plantagenets, on an Englishman accused of exercising tyranny over the lord of the holy city of Benares, and over the ladies of the princely house of Oude.

The place was worthy of such a trial. It was the

great hall of William Rufus,[1] the hall which had resounded with acclamations at the inauguration of thirty kings, the hall which had witnessed the just sentence of Bacon [2] and the just absolution of Somers, the hall where the eloquence of Strafford had for a moment awed and melted a victorious party inflamed with just resentment, the hall where Charles had confronted the High Court of Justice with the placid courage which has half redeemed his fame. Neither military nor civil pomp was wanting. The avenues were lined with grenadiers. The streets were kept clear by cavalry. The peers, robed in gold and ermine, were marshalled by the heralds under Garter King-at-arms. The judges in their vestments of state attended to give advice on points of law. Near a hundred and seventy lords, three-fourths of the Upper House as the Upper House then was, walked in solemn order from their usual place of assembling to the tribunal. The junior Baron present led the way, George Eliott, Lord Heathfield, recently ennobled for his memorable defence of Gibraltar against the fleets and armies of France and Spain. The long procession was closed by the Duke of Norfolk, Earl Marshal of the realm, by the great dignitaries, and by the brothers and sons of the King. Last of all came the Prince of Wales, conspicuous by his fine person and noble bearing. The gray old walls were hung with scarlet. The long galleries were crowded by an audience such as has rarely excited the fears or the emulation of an orator. There were gathered together, from all parts of a great, free, enlightened, and prosperous empire, grace and female loveliness, wit and learning, the representatives of every science and of every art. There were seated round the Queen the fair-haired young daughters of the house of Brunswick. There the Ambassadors of great Kings and Commonwealths gazed with admiration on a spectacle which no other country in the world could present. There Siddons,[1] in the prime of her majestic beauty, looked with emotion on a scene surpassing all the imitations of the stage. There the historian of the Roman Empire thought of the days when Cicero pleaded the cause of Sicily against Verres, and when, before a senate which still retained some show of freedom, Tacitus thundered against the oppressor of Africa. There were seen, side by side, the greatest painter and the greatest scholar of the age. The spectacle had allured Reynolds from that easel which has preserved to us the thoughtful foreheads of so many writers and statesmen, and the sweet smiles of so many noble matrons. It had induced Parr to suspend his labors in that dark and profound mine from which he had extracted a vast treasure of erudition, a treasure too often buried in the earth, too often paraded with injudicious and inelegant ostentation, but still precious, massive, and splendid. There appeared the voluptuous charms of her to whom the heir of the throne had in secret plighted his faith. There too was she, the beautiful mother of a beautiful race, the Saint Cecilia whose delicate features, lighted up by love and music, art has rescued from the common decay. There were the members of that brilliant society which quoted, criticised, and exchanged repartees, under the rich peacock-hangings of Mrs. Montague. And there the ladies whose lips, more persuasive than those of Fox himself, had carried the Westminster election against palace and treasury, shone round Georgiana Duchess of Devonshire.

The Serjeants made proclamation. Hastings advanced to the bar, and bent his knee. The culprit was indeed not unworthy of that great presence. He had ruled an extensive and populous country, had made laws and treaties, had sent forth armies, had set up and pulled down princes. And in his high place he had so borne himself, that all had feared him, that most had loved him, and that hatred itself could deny him no title to glory, except virtue. He looked like a great man, and not like a bad man. A person small and emaciated, yet deriving dignity from a carriage which, while it indicated deference to the court, indicated also habitual self-possession and self-respect, a high and intellectual forehead, a brow pensive, but not gloomy, a mouth of inflexible decision, a face pale and worn, but serene, on which was written, as legibly as under the picture in the council-chamber at Calcutta, *Mens æqua in arduis;*[1] such was the aspect with which the great Proconsul presented himself to his judges.

His counsel accompanied him, men all of whom were afterwards raised by their talents and learning to the highest posts in their profession, the bold and strong-minded Law, afterwards Chief Justice of the King's Bench; the more humane and eloquent Dallas, afterwards Chief Justice of the Common Pleas; and Plomer who, near twenty years later, successfully conducted in the same high court the defence of Lord Melville, and subsequently became Vice-chancellor and Master of the Rolls.

But neither the culprit nor his advocates attracted so much notice as the accusers. In the midst of the blaze of red drapery, a space has been fitted up with green benches and tables for the Commons. The managers, with Burke at their head, appeared in full dress. The collectors of gossip did not fail to remark that even Fox, generally so regardless of his appearance, had paid to the illustrious tribunal the compliment of wearing a bag and sword.[1] Pitt had refused to be one of the conductors of the impeachment; and his commanding, copious, and sonorous eloquence was wanting to that great muster of various talents. Age and blindness had unfitted Lord North for the duties of a public prosecutor; and his friends were left without the help of his excellent sense, his tact, and his urbanity. But, in spite of the absence of these two distinguished members of the Lower House, the box in which the managers stood contained an array of speakers such as perhaps had not appeared together since the great age of Athenian eloquence. There were Fox and Sheridan,[2] the English Demosthenes and the English Hyperides. There was Burke, ignorant, indeed, or negligent of the art of adapting his reasonings and his style to the capacity and taste of his hearers, but in amplitude of comprehension and richness of imagination superior to every orator, ancient or modern. There, with eyes reverentially fixed on Burke, appeared the finest gentleman of the age, his form developed by every manly exercise, his face beaming with intelligence and spirit, the ingenious, the chivalrous, the high-souled Windham.[1] Nor, though surrounded by such men, did the youngest manager pass unnoticed. At an age when most of those who distinguish themselves in life are still contending for prizes and fellowships at college, he had won for himself a conspicuous place in Parliament. No advantage of fortune or connection was wanting that could set off to the height his splendid talents and his unblemished honor. At twenty-three he had been thought worthy to be ranked with the veteran statesmen who appeared as the delegates of the British Commons, at the bar of the British nobility. All who stood at that bar, save him alone, are gone, culprit, advocates, accusers. To the generation which is now in the vigor of life, he is the sole representative of a great age which has passed away. But those who, within the last ten years, have listened with delight, till the morning sun [2] shone on the tapestries of the House of Lords, to the lofty and animated eloquence of Charles Earl Grey, are able to form some estimate of the powers of a race of men among whom he was not the foremost.

The charges and the answers of Hastings were first read. The ceremony occupied two whole days, and was rendered less tedious than it would otherwise have been by the silver voice and just emphasis of Cowper, the clerk of the court, a near relation of the amiable poet. On the third day Burke rose. Four sittings were occupied by his opening speech, which was intended to be a general introduction to all the charges. With an exuberance of thought and a splendor of diction which more than satisfied the highly raised expectation of the audience, he described the character and institutions of the natives of India, recounted the circumstances in which the Asiatic empire of Britain had originated, and set forth the constitution of the Company and of the English Presidencies. Having thus attempted to communicate to his hearers an idea of Eastern society, as vivid as that which existed in his own mind, he proceeded to arraign the administration of Hastings as systematically conducted in defiance of morality and public law. The energy and pathos of the great orator extorted expressions of unwonted admiration from the stern and hostile Chancellor, and, for a moment, seemed to pierce even the resolute heart of the defendant. The ladies in the galleries, unaccustomed to such displays of eloquence, excited by the solemnity of the occasion, and perhaps not unwilling to display their taste and sensibility,[1] were in a state of uncontrollable emotion. Handkerchiefs were pulled out; smelling-bottles were handed round; hysterical sobs and screams were heard; and Mrs. Sheridan was carried out in a fit. At length the orator concluded. Raising his voice till the old arches of Irish oak resounded, "Therefore," said he, "hath it with all confidence been ordered by the Commons of Great Britain, that I impeach Warren Hastings of high crimes and misdemeanors. I impeach him in the name of the Commons' House of Parliament, whose trust he has betrayed. I impeach him in the name of the English nation, whose ancient honor he has sullied. I impeach him in the name of the people of India, whose rights he has trodden under foot, and whose country he has turned into a desert. Lastly, in the name of human nature itself, in the name of both sexes, in the name of every age, in the name of every rank, I impeach the common enemy and oppressor of all!"

When the deep murmur of various emotions had subsided, Mr. Fox rose to address the Lords respecting the course of proceeding to be followed. The wish of the accusers was that the Court would bring to a close the investigation of the first charge before the second was opened. The wish of Hastings and of his counsel was that the managers should open all the charges, and produce all the evidence for the prosecution, before the defence began. The Lords retired to their own House to consider the question. The Chancellor took the side of Hastings. Lord Loughborough, who was now in opposition, supported the demand of the managers. The division showed which way the inclination of the tribunal leaned. A majority of near three to one decided in favor of the course for which Hastings contended.

When the Court sat again, Mr. Fox, assisted by Mr. Grey, opened the charge respecting Cheyte Sing, and several days were spent in reading papers and hearing witnesses. The next article was that relating to the Princesses of Oude. The conduct of this part of the case was intrusted to Sheridan. The curiosity of the public to hear him was unbounded. His sparkling and highly finished declamation lasted two days; but the Hall was crowded to suffocation during the whole time. It was said that fifty guineas had been paid for a single ticket. Sheridan, when he concluded, contrived, with a knowledge of stage effect which his father might have envied, to sink back, as if exhausted, into the arms of Burke, who hugged him with the energy of generous admiration.

June was now far advanced. The session could not last much longer; and the progress which had been made in the impeachment was not very satisfactory. There were twenty charges. On two only of these had even the case for the prosecution been heard; and it was now a year since Hastings had been admitted to bail.

The interest taken by the public in the trial was great when the Court began to sit, and rose to the height when Sheridan spoke on the charge relating to the Begums. From that time the excitement went down fast. The spectacle had lost the attraction of novelty. The great displays of rhetoric were over. What was behind was not of a nature to entice men of letters from their books in the morning, or to tempt ladies who had left the masquerade at two to be out of bed before eight. There remained examinations and cross-examinations. There remained statements of accounts. There remained the reading of papers, filled with words unintelligible to English ears, with lacs and crores, zemindars and aumils, sunnuds and perwannahs, jaghires and nuzzurs. There remained bickerings, not always carried on with the best taste or with the best temper, between the managers of the impeachment and the counsel for the defence, particularly between Mr. Burke and Mr. Law. There remained the endless marches and countermarches of the Peers between their House and the Hall; for as often as a point of law was to be discussed, their Lordships retired to discuss it apart; and the consequence was, as a Peer wittily said, that the judges walked and the trial stood still.

It is to be added that, in the spring of 1788, when the trial commenced, no important question, either of domestic or foreign policy, occupied the public mind. The proceeding in Westminster Hall, therefore, naturally attracted most of the attention of Parliament and of the country. It was the one great event of that season. But in the following year the King's illness, the debates on the Regency, the expectation of a change of ministry, completely diverted public attention from Indian affairs; and within a fortnight after George the Third had returned thanks in St. Paul's for his recovery, the States-General of France met at Versailles. In the midst of the agitation produced by these events, the impeachment was for a time almost forgotten.

The trial in the Hall went on languidly. In the session of 1788, when the proceedings had the interest of novelty, and when the Peers had little other business before them, only thirty-five days were given to the impeachment. In 1789, the Regency Bill occupied the Upper House till the session was far advanced. When the King recovered the circuits were beginning. The judges left town; the Lords waited for the return of the oracles of jurisprudence; and the consequence was that during the whole year only seventeen days were given to the case of Hastings. It was clear that the matter would be protracted to a length unprecedented in the annals of criminal law.

In truth, it is impossible to deny that impeachment, though it is a fine ceremony, and though it may have been useful in the seventeenth century, is not a proceeding from which much good can now be expected. Whatever confidence may be placed in the decision of the Peers on an appeal arising out of ordinary litigation, it is certain that no man has the least confidence in their impartiality, when a great public functionary, charged with a great state crime, is brought to their bar. They are all politicians. There is hardly one among them whose vote on an impeachment may not be confidently predicted before a witness has been examined; and, even if it were possible to rely on their justice, they would still be quite unfit to try such a cause as that of Hastings. They sit only during half the year. They have to transact much legislative and much judicial business. The law-lords, whose advice is required to guide the unlearned majority, are employed daily in administering justice elsewhere. It is impossible, therefore, that during a busy session, the Upper House should give more than a few days to an impeachment. To expect that their Lordships would give up partridge-shooting, in order to bring the greatest delinquent to speedy justice, or to relieve accused innocence by speedy acquittal, would be unreasonable indeed. A well-constituted tribunal, sitting regularly six days in the week, and nine hours in the day, would have brought the trial of Hastings to a close in less than three months. The Lords had not finished their work in seven years.

The result ceased to be a matter of doubt, from the time when the Lords resolved that they would be guided by the rules of evidence which are received in the inferior courts of the realm. Those rules, it is well known, exclude much information which would be quite sufficient to determine the conduct of any reasonable man, in the most important transactions of private life. These rules, at every assizes, save scores of culprits whom judges, jury, and spectators firmly believe to be guilty. But when those rules were rigidly applied to offences committed many years before, at the distance of many thousands of miles, conviction was, of course, out of the question. We do not blame the accused and his counsel for availing themselves of every legal advantage in order to obtain an acquittal.

But it is clear that an acquittal obtained cannot be pleaded in bar of the judgment of history.

Several attempts were made by the friends of Hastings to put a stop to the trial. In 1789 [1] they proposed a vote of censure upon Burke, for some violent language which he had used respecting the death of Nuncomar and the connection between Hastings and Impey. Burke was then unpopular in the last degree both with the House and with the country. The asperity and indecency of some expressions which he had used during the debates on the Regency had annoyed even his warmest friends. The vote of censure was carried; and those who had moved it hoped that the managers would resign in disgust. Burke was deeply hurt. But his zeal for what he considered as the cause of justice and mercy triumphed over his personal feelings. He received the censure of the House with dignity and meekness, and declared that no personal mortification or humiliation should induce him to flinch from the sacred duty which he had undertaken.

In the following year the Parliament was dissolved; and the friends of Hastings entertained a hope that the new House of Commons might not be disposed to go on with the impeachment. They began by maintaining that the whole proceeding was terminated by the dissolution. Defeated on this point, they made a direct motion that the impeachment should be dropped; but they were defeated by the combined forces of the Government and the Opposition. It was, however, resolved that, for the sake of expedition, many of the articles should be withdrawn. In truth, had not some such measure been adopted, the trial would have lasted till the defendant was in his grave.

At length, in the spring of 1795, the decision was pronounced; near eight years after Hastings had been brought by the Serjeant-at-arms of the Commons to the bar of the Lords. On the last day of this great procedure the public curiosity, long suspended, seemed to be revived. Anxiety about the judgment there could be none; for it had been fully ascertained that there was a great majority for the defendant. Nevertheless many wished to see the pageant, and the Hall was as much crowded as on the first day. But those who, having been present on the first day, now bore a part in the proceedings of the last, were few; and most of those few were altered men.

As Hastings himself said, the arraignment had taken place before one generation, and the judgment was pronounced by another. The spectator could not look at the woolsack,[1] or at the red benches of the Peers, or at the green benches of the Commons, without seeing something that reminded him of the instability of all human things, of the instability of power and fame and life, of the more lamentable instability of friendship. The great seal was borne before Lord Loughborough, who, when the trial commenced, was a fierce opponent of Mr. Pitt's government, and who was now a member of that government, while Thurlow, who presided in the court when it first sat, estranged from all his old allies, sat scowling among the junior barons. Of about a hundred and sixty nobles who walked in the procession on the first day, sixty had been laid in their family vaults. Still more affecting must have been the sight of the managers' box. What had become of that fair fellowship, so closely bound together by public and private ties, so resplendent with every talent and accomplishment? It had been scattered by calamities more bitter than the bitterness of death. The great chiefs were still living, and still in the full vigor of their genius. But their friendship was at an end. It had been violently and publicly dissolved, with tears and stormy reproaches. If those men, once so dear to each other, were now compelled to meet for the purpose of managing the impeachment, they met as strangers whom public business had brought together, and behaved to each other with cold and distant civility. Burke had in his vortex whirled away Windham. Fox had been followed by Sheridan and Grey.

Only twenty-nine Peers voted. Of these only six found Hastings guilty on the charges relating to Cheyte Sing and to the Begums. On other charges, the majority in his favor was still greater. On some he was unanimously absolved. He was then called to the bar, was informed from the woolsack that the Lords had acquitted him, and was solemnly discharged. He bowed respectfully and retired.

We have said that the decision had been fully expected. It was also generally approved. At the commencement of the trial there had been a strong and indeed unreasonable feeling against Hastings. At the close of the trial there was a feeling equally strong and equally unreasonable in his favor. One cause of the change was, no doubt, what is commonly called the fickleness of the multitude, but what seems to us to be merely the general law of human nature. Both in individuals and in masses violent excitement is always followed by remission, and often by reaction. We are all inclined to depreciate whatever we have overpraised, and, on the other hand, to show undue indulgence where we have shown undue rigor. It was thus in the case of Hastings. The length of his trial, moreover, made him an object of compassion. It was thought, and not without reason, that, even if he was guilty, he was still an ill-used man, and that an impeachment of eight years was more than a sufficient punishment. It was also felt that, though, in the ordinary course of criminal law, a defendant is not allowed to set off his good actions against his crimes, a great political cause should be tried on different principles, and that a man who had governed an empire during thirteen years might have done some very reprehensible things, and yet might be on the whole deserving of rewards and honors rather than of fine and imprisonment. The press, an instrument neglected by the prosecutors, was used by Hastings and his friends with great effect. Every ship, too, that arrived from Madras or Bengal, brought a cuddy full of his admirers. Every gentleman from India spoke of the late Governor-General as having deserved better, and having been treated worse, than any man living. The effect of this testimony unanimously given by all persons who knew the East, was naturally very great. Retired members of the Indian services, civil and military, were settled in all corners of the kingdom. Each of them was, of course, in his own little circle, regarded as an oracle on an Indian question; and they were, with scarcely one exception, the zealous advocates of Hastings. It is to be added, that the numerous addresses to the late Governor-General, which his friends in Bengal obtained from the natives and transmitted to England, made a considerable impression. To these addresses we attach little or no importance. That Hastings was beloved by the people whom he governed is true; but the eulogies of pundits, zemindars, Mahommedan doctors, do not prove it to be true. For an English collector or judge would have found it easy to induce any native who could write to sign a panegyric on the most odious ruler that ever was in India. It was said that at Benares, the very place at which the acts set forth in the first article of impeachment had been committed, the natives had erected a temple to Hastings; and this story excited a strong sensation in England. Burke's observations on the apotheosis were admirable. He saw no reason for astonishment, he said, in the incident which had been represented as so striking. He knew something of the mythology of the Brahmins. He knew that as they worshipped some gods from love, so they worshipped others from fear. He knew that they erected shrines, not only to the benignant deities of light and plenty, but also to the fiends who preside over smallpox and murder; nor did he at all dispute the claim of Mr. Hastings to be admitted into such a Pantheon. This reply has always struck us as one of the finest that ever was made in Parliament. It is a grave and forcible argument, decorated by the most brilliant wit and fancy.

Hastings was, however, safe. But in everything except character, he would have been far better off if, when first impeached, he had at once pleaded guilty, and paid a fine of fifty thousand pounds. He was a ruined man. The legal expenses of his defence had been enormous. The expenses which did not appear in his attorney's bill were perhaps larger still. Great sums had been paid to Major Scott. Great sums had been laid out in bribing newspapers, rewarding pamphleteers, and circulating tracts. Burke, so early as 1790, declared in the House of Commons that twenty thousand pounds had been employed in corrupting the press. It is certain that no controversial weapon, from the gravest reasoning to the coarsest ribaldry, was left unemployed. Logan defended the accused Governor with great ability in prose. For the lovers of verse, the speeches of the managers were burlesqued in Simpkin's letters. It is, we are afraid, indisputable that Hastings stooped so low as to court the aid of that malignant and filthy baboon John Williams, who called himself Anthony Pasquin. It was necessary to subsidize such allies largely. The private hoards of Mrs. Hastings had disappeared. It is said that the banker to whom they had been entrusted had failed. Still if Hastings had practised strict economy he would, after all his losses, have had a moderate competence; but in the management of his private affairs he was imprudent. The dearest wish of his heart had always been to regain Daylesford. At length, in the very year in which his trial commenced, the wish was accomplished; and the domain, alienated more than seventy years before, returned to the descendant of its old lords. But the manor house was a ruin; and the grounds round it had, during many years, been utterly neglected. Hastings proceeded to build, to plant, to form a sheet of water, to excavate a grotto; and, before he was dismissed from the bar of the House of Lords, he had expended more than forty thousand pounds in adorning his seat.

The general feeling both of the Directors and of the proprietors of the East India Company was that he had great claims on them, that his services to them had been eminent, and that his misfortunes had been the effect of his zeal for their interest. His friends in Leadenhall Street proposed to reimburse him the costs of his trial, and to settle on him an annuity of five thousand pounds a year. But the consent of the Board of Control was necessary; and at the head of the Board of Control was Mr. Dundas, who had himself been a party to the impeachment, who had, on that account, been reviled with great bitterness by the adherents of Hastings, and who, therefore, was not in a very complying mood. He refused to consent to what the Directors suggested. The Directors remonstrated. A long controversy followed. Hastings, in the meantime, was reduced to such distress, that he could hardly pay his weekly bills. At length a compromise was made. An annuity for life of four thousand pounds was settled on Hastings; and in order to enable him to meet pressing demands, he was to receive ten years' annuity in advance. The Company was also permitted to lend him fifty thousand pounds, to be repaid by instalments without interest. This relief, though given in the most absurd manner, was sufficient to enable the retired Governor to live in comfort, and even in luxury, if he had been a skilful manager. But he was careless and profuse, and was more than once under the necessity of applying to the Company for assistance, which was liberally given.

He had security and affluence, but not the power and dignity which, when he landed from India, he had reason to expect. He had then looked forward to a coronet, a red riband,[1] a seat at the Council Board, an office at Whitehall. He was then only fifty-two, and might hope for many years of bodily and mental vigor. The case was widely different when he left the bar of the Lords. He was now too old a man to turn his mind to a new class of studies and duties. He had no chance of receiving any mark of royal favor while Mr. Pitt remained in power; and, when Mr. Pitt retired, Hastings was approaching his seventieth year.

Once, and only once, after his acquittal, he interfered in politics; and that interference was not much to his honor. In 1804 he exerted himself strenuously to prevent Mr. Addington, against whom Fox and Pitt had combined, from resigning the Treasury. It is difficult to believe that a man so able and energetic as Hastings can have thought that, when Bonaparte was at Boulogne with a great army, the defence of our island could safely be intrusted to a ministry which did not contain a single person whom flattery could describe as a great statesman. It is also certain that, on the important question which had raised Mr. Addington to power, and on which he differed from both Fox and Pitt, Hastings, as might have been expected, agreed with Fox and Pitt, and was decidedly opposed to Addington. Religious intolerance has never been the vice of the Indian service, and certainly was not the vice of Hastings. But Mr. Addington had treated him with marked favor. Fox had been a principal manager of the impeachment. To Pitt it was owing that there had been an impeachment; and Hastings, we fear, was on this occasion guided by personal considerations, rather than by a regard to the public interest.

The last twenty-four years of his life were chiefly passed at Daylesford. He amused himself with embellishing his grounds, riding fine Arab horses, fattening prize-cattle, and trying to rear Indian animals and vegetables in England. He sent for seeds of a very fine custard-apple, from the garden of what had once been his own villa, among the green hedgerows of

Allipore. He tried also to naturalize in Worcestershire the delicious leechee, almost the only fruit of Bengal which deserves to be regretted even amidst the plenty of Covent Garden. The Mogul emperors, in the time of their greatness, had in vain attempted to introduce into Hindostan the goat of the table-land of Thibet, whose down supplies the looms of Cashmere with the materials of the finest shawls. Hastings tried, with no better fortune, to rear a breed at Daylesford; nor does he seem to have succeeded better with the cattle of Bootan, whose tails are in high esteem as the best fans for brushing away the mosquitoes.

Literature divided his attention with his conservatories and his menagerie. He had always loved books, and they were now necessary to him. Though not a poet, in any high sense of the word, he wrote neat and polished lines with great facility, and was fond of exercising this talent. Indeed, if we must speak out, he seems to have been more of a Trissotin than was to be expected from the powers of his mind, and from the great part which he had played in life. We are assured in these Memoirs that the first thing which he did in the morning was to write a copy of verses. When the family and guests assembled, the poem made its appearance as regularly as the eggs and rolls; and Mr. Gleig requires us to believe that, if from any accident Hastings came to the breakfast-table without one of his charming performances in his hand, the omission was felt by all as a grievous disappointment.

Tastes differ widely. For ourselves, we must say that, however good the breakfasts at Daylesford may have been,—and we are assured that the tea was of the most aromatic flavor, and that neither tongue nor venison-pasty was wanting,—we should have thought the reckoning high if we had been forced to earn our repast by listening every day to a new madrigal or sonnet composed by our host. We are glad, however, that Mr. Gleig has preserved this little feature of character, though we think it by no means a beauty. It is good to be often reminded of the inconsistency of human nature, and to learn to look without wonder or disgust on the weaknesses which are found in the strongest minds. Dionysius in old times, Frederic in the last century, with capacity and vigor equal to the conduct of the greatest affairs, united all the little vanities and affectations of provincial blue-stockings. These great examples may console the admirers of Hastings for the affliction of seeing him reduced to the level of the Hayleys and Sewards.

When Hastings had passed many years in retirement, and had long outlived the common age of men, he again became for a short time an object of general attention. In 1813 the charter of the East India Company was renewed; and much discussion about Indian affairs took place in Parliament. It was determined to examine witnesses at the bar of the Commons; and Hastings was ordered to attend. He had appeared at that bar once before. It was when he read his answer to the charges which Burke had laid on the table. Since that time twenty-seven years had elapsed; public feeling had undergone a complete change; the nation had now forgotten his faults, and remembered only his services. The reappearance, too, of a man who had been among the most distinguished of a generation that had passed away, who now belonged to history, and who seemed to have risen from the dead, could not but produce a solemn and pathetic effect. The Commons received him with acclamations, ordered a chair to be set for him, and, when he retired, rose and uncovered. There were, indeed, a few who did not sympathize with the general feeling. One or two of the managers of the impeachment were present. They sate in the same seats which they had occupied when they had been thanked for the services which they had rendered in Westminster Hall; for, by the courtesy of the House, a member who has been thanked in his place is considered as having a right always to occupy that place. These gentlemen were not disposed to admit that they had employed several of the best years of their lives in persecuting an innocent man. They accordingly kept their seats, and pulled their hats over their brows; but the exceptions only made the prevailing enthusiasm more remarkable. The Lords received the old man with similar tokens of respect. The University of Oxford conferred on him the degree of Doctor of Laws; and in the Sheldonian Theatre the undergraduates welcomed him with tumultuous cheering.

These marks of public esteem were soon followed

by marks of royal favor. Hastings was sworn of the Privy Council, and was admitted to a long private audience of the Prince Regent, who treated him very graciously. When the Emperor of Russia and the King of Prussia visited England, Hastings appeared in their train both at Oxford and in the Guildhall of London, and, though surrounded by a crowd of princes and great warriors, was everywhere received with marks of respect and admiration. He was presented by the Prince Regent both to Alexander and to Frederic William; and his Royal Highness went so far as to declare in public that honors far higher than a seat in the Privy Council were due, and would soon be paid, to the man who had saved the British dominions in Asia. Hastings now confidently expected a peerage; but from some unexplained cause, he was again disappointed.

He lived about four years longer, in the enjoyment of good spirits, of faculties not impaired to any painful or degrading extent, and of health such as is rarely enjoyed by those who attain such an age. At length, on the twenty-second of August 1818, in the eighty-sixth year of his age, he met death with the same tranquil and decorous fortitude which he had opposed to all the trials of his various and eventful life.

With all his faults,—and they were neither few nor small,—only one cemetery was worthy to contain his remains. In that temple of silence and reconciliation where the enmities of twenty generations lie buried, in the Great Abbey which has during many ages afforded a quiet resting-place to those whose minds and bodies have been shattered by the contentions of the Great Hall, the dust of the illustrious accused should have mingled with the dust of the illustrious accusers. This was not to be. Yet the place of interment was not ill chosen. Behind the chancel of the parish church of Daylesford, in earth which already held the bones of many chiefs of the house of Hastings, was laid the coffin of the greatest man who has ever borne that ancient and widely extended name. On that very spot probably, fourscore years before, the little Warren, meanly clad and scantily fed, had played with the children of ploughmen. Even then his young mind had revolved plans which might be called romantic. Yet, however romantic, it is not likely that they had been so strange as the truth. Not only had the poor orphan retrieved the fallen fortunes of his line. Not only had he repurchased the old lands, and rebuilt the old dwelling. He had preserved and extended an empire. He had founded a polity. He had administered government and war with more than the capacity of Richelieu. He had patronized learning with the judicious liberality of Cosmo. He had been attacked by the most formidable combination of enemies that ever sought the destruction of a single victim; and over that combination, after a struggle of ten years, he had triumphed. He had at length gone down to his grave in the fulness of age, in peace, after so many troubles, in honor, after so much obloquy.

Those who look on his character without favor or

malevolence will pronounce that, in the two great elements of all social virtue, in respect for the rights of others, and in sympathy for the sufferings of others, he was deficient. His principles were somewhat lax. His heart was somewhat hard. But though we cannot with truth describe him either as a righteous or as a merciful ruler, we cannot regard without admiration the amplitude and fertility of his intellect, his rare talents for command, for administration, and for controversy, his dauntless courage, his honorable poverty, his fervent zeal for the interests of the state, his noble equanimity, tried by both extremes of fortune, and never disturbed by either.

NOTES

LORD CLIVE

23, 1. **Every schoolboy knows.** Rather a hyperbole, save in such rare cases as that of Macaulay himself who began his reading at the age of three.

2. **Montezuma Atahualpa.** See Prescott, *Conquest of Mexico*, Bk. IV, Chap. III, for an account of the defeat of Montezuma II, ninth King of Mexico, by Hernando Cortez; *Conquest of Peru* (Bk. II, Chap. VII, Prescott), for an account of the treachery of Pizarro, the Spanish conqueror of Peru, toward Atahualpa.

3. **The battle of Buxar,** where Sir Hector Munro defeated the forces of Meer Cossim, Nabob of Patna, and the Nabob of Oude, in 1764, thereby winning for the English the province of Oude.

4. **The massacre of Patna.** Meer Cossim captured the town of Patna in 1763, and massacred in cold blood two hundred defenseless English prisoners.

5. **Surajah Dowlah.** Nabob of Bengal. Oude and Travancore represent extreme ends of India.

6. **Holkar.** A Hindoo Mahratta chief, one of the most formidable enemies of the English, who died in 1811.

7. **The victories of Cortes were gained over savages.** Consult Prescott's *Conquest of Mexico*, and the article on "Mexico" in the *Encyclopedia Britannica* for information on the civilization of Mexico at this time.

8. **Harquebusier.** An arquebuss was a gun fired from a rest.

24, 1. **Buildings more beautiful.** Shah Jehan's palace at Shâh-Jehânpoor, the Jumna Mosque, the Temple at Ajmir.

2. **Ferdinand the Catholic.** A title given to Ferdinand V of Navarre, in whose reign the Inquisition was established in Spain, and the New World was discovered by Columbus.

3. **The Great Captain.** Gonsalvo Hernandez de Cordova, who won his title in the wars against the Moors, under Ferdinand and Isabella, and in the recovery of Naples from the French.

4. **One of the greatest empires in the world.** The area of Brit-

ish India, including Burmah, is 1,800,258 square miles, or nearly one half that of the United States, excluding Alaska.

5. **Mr. Mill's book.** *History of India*, 1818, by James Mill; father of John Stuart Mill, writer on economics.

6. **Orme, Robert.** Author of *History of British India 1763–1788*.

7. **Lord Powis, Edward.** Eldest son of Clive, Earl of Powis, 1804.

25, 1. **Whose love passes the love of biographers.** One of the many instances where Macaulay paraphrases Biblical diction. See 2 Sam. i, 26, for the original.

26, 1. **The old seat of his ancestors.** Styche, in the parish of Moreton Tay.

2. **One of his uncles.** A remark made by Mr. Bayle of Hope Hall, near Manchester, in a letter written 1732, Clive's seventh year.

27, 1. **From school to school.** Lostock in Cheshire, Merchant Taylors' school, and a private school in Hemel Hempstead, Hertfordshire.

2. **A writership.** The lowest office in the East India Company, a clerkship, or accountantship. For an account of the founding of the East India Company see Macaulay's *History of England*, Chap. XVIII. Originally a mere trading company, with fortified posts at Madras, Calcutta and Bombay; the Company determined, in 1689, to become "a nation in India," but until Clive's victory at Plassey nothing was done to realize this ambition.

3. **East India College.** Established by the Company to train men for the Indian Service. Made a public school when India came under the Civil Service System, 1858.

28, 1. **The prophet's gourd.** See Jonah iv.

29, 1. The **Carnatic.** The **Deccan.** Rich provinces of Southern India.

2. **There is still a Nabob.** In 1857 the Sepoy Mutiny broke out. After it had been suppressed Parliament transferred the government of India to the Crown, and in 1877 the Sovereign took the title, Empress of India, thus occupying the position formerly held by "the Great Mogul," as the hereditary rulers of India, descendants of Baber, were called.

31, 1. **Wallenstein.** The great general of the Imperialists in the Thirty Years' War, the hero of Schiller's great dramatic trilogy.

2. **War of the Austrian Succession 1740–1748.** England supported Queen Maria Theresa, daughter of Charles VI of Austria, in her attempt to claim the crown, against the Elector

of Bavaria, who was aided by Frederick II of Prussia and the Bourbon King of France.

32, 1. **Labourdonnais.** Bertrand François Mahé de la Bourdonnais entered the service of the French East India Company at the age of nineteen, and soon rose to distinction. In 1734 he became Governor of Ile de France. On his return to France he was arrested and imprisoned for three years in the Bastile on the charge of Dupleix that he had taken bribes at Madras. He was finally acquitted.

2. **Dupleix, Joseph.** Head of the factory at Chandernagore, who made this post of the French Company so prosperous that in 1742 he was made Governor of Pondicherry, and director general of the French factories in India. He was recalled to France in disgrace, and died nine years later in poverty, 1763.

33, 1. **Major Lawrence.** For twenty years a distinguished soldier of the East India Company. The Company erected a monument to his memory in Westminster after his death, 1774.

2. **Peace.** By the treaty of Aix-la-Chapelle, 1748. England gained nothing by it.

34, 1. **"The House of Tamerlane."** Tamerlane, or Tamer the Lame, a Mongol Chief, invaded India in 1398, and his descendants formed the Mongol or Mogul dynasty; the power weakening with the death of Aurungzebe the last really "Great" Mogul.

2. **The beauty and magnificence of the buildings.** The imperial palace at Delhi, the Taj Mahal and the Pearl Mosque at Ogno are among the best known. Sir Thomas Roe (1580–1644) gives an interesting account of the splendors he witnessed in his embassy to Jehangir, 1615.

35, 1. **Aurungzebe.** The last of the great rulers of India.

2. **Theodosius.** The last great emperor of the East. After his death the boundaries of Rome steadily receded, while queen mothers and barbarian generals ruled in turn the enfeebled princelings who bore the name of emperor.

3. **Carlovingians.** The name given to the descendants of Charlemagne, who proved as incapable of ruling as the descendants of Theodosius, and were known, not as their great ancestor had been, by deeds, but by such physical or mental attributes as "The Bald," "The Fat," "The Simple."

36, 1. **Pirates of the Northern Sea.** The Northmen or Vikings, under Rollo, or Rolf the Ganger, invaded Normandy and later penetrated to the Mediterranean.

2. **The Hungarian.** Attila the Hun, "The Scourge of God," who in 432–452 ravaged Central Europe,

Gog and Magog. Used by Ezekiel xxxviii–xxxix as the symbol of earthly violence arrayed against the people of God.

3. **Campania.** The present site of Naples and its environs.

37, 1. **Bang,** or hasheesh. A Turkish drug, made of dried hemp leaves, producing intoxication and deep stupor.

2. **A Persian Conqueror.** Nadir Shah in 1739, carried off over fifty million dollars' worth of plunder, including the Peacock Throne built for Shah Jehan in his palace at Delhi, at a cost of six and a half million sterling. It was ornamented with the figure of a peacock with outspread tail, the colors being imitated in gems. Shah Nadir also carried off the Kohinoor, or "Mountain of Light," a famous diamond. It was given by Runjert Sing, "Lion of the Punjâb" to the idol Jagannâth or Juggernaut at Orissa, but in 1849 came into the possession of the East India Company, who in 1850 presented it to Queen Victoria.

38, 1. **Mahrattas.** A warlike tribe of India, the bitter foes of the English.

2. **Redeemed their harvests.** An annual ransom, equal to one-fourth the revenue, termed the *chout*, was levied by Siraji, founder of the Mahratta power.

3. **The Mahratta ditch.** Made at Calcutta in 1742 as a defense against the Mahrattas who, under Meer Hubert, were laying waste Bengal.

40, 1. **Burrampooter.** Now spelled Brahmaputra. **Hydaspes.** The Jhilam, a tributary of the Indus, one of the five rivers of the Punjab.

2. **Dictate terms of peace at Ava.** The treaty ceding Aracan was signed at Ava in central Burmah, February 24, 1826. It typifies the eastern extremity as Candahar in Afghanistan does the western.

3. **Saxe or Frederic.** Maurice, Comte de Saxe, Marshal of France, one of the most famous generals of the eighteenth century, as was also Frederick the Great, of Prussia.

41, 1. **Nizam al Mulk.** The son of a favorite of Aurungzebe, who had managed to make himself independent as Nizam of Hyderabad.

42, 1. **Anaverdy Khan.** Through the murder of a young prince entrusted to his care, he seized the power in the Carnatic. For years he played fast and loose with the French and English, but was finally killed by the latter in a battle near Arcot, 1750.

2. **Sepoy.** A corruption of Sipoohi, the Hindâstanee for soldier.

3. **The eloquence of Burke.** The speech on the Nabob of Arcot's debts, delivered by Edmund Burke in 1785, ranks as one of his finest efforts, for wealth of imagery, invective and sarcasm.

44, 1. **Mirzapha Jung.** He was killed soon after, while fighting against three Nabobs who had been discontented with his manner of rewarding them.

48, 1. **Tenth Legion of Cæsar.** The legion on whom Cæsar most relied.

2. **The Old Guard of Napoleon.** A division of the Imperial Guard, formed by Napoleon, 1809. No soldier could enter it till he had served with distinction four campaigns in the line or as a member of the Young Guard. It served with distinction at Waterloo, was disbanded by Louis XVIII in 1815, reorganized by Napoleon III, 1854, and served in the Crimean War.

49, 1. **Hosein, the son of Ali.** Ali was the cousin of Mohammed, and his first disciple. He married Fatima, the favorite daughter of Mohammed, hence his followers and descendants were called Fatimites. He was killed in 661. His adherents claimed that he was the first rightful Caliph. His son, Hosein, was murdered in 680. The anniversary of his death is kept on September 14, and is known as the "Muharrem."

2. **Prophet of God.** The Mohammedan creed declares "There is no God but God and Mohammed is His prophet."

50, 1. **The Houris.** Those who die in defense or practice of the Moslem faith pass at once to Paradise.

54, 1. **Captain Bobadil.** See Ben Jonson's play *Every Man in His Humor*, in which this bragging coward is a leading character.

2. **Bussy.** Charles Joseph Palissier, Marquis de Bussy-Castelnan, died at Pondicherry 1785.

55, 1. **Chunda Sahib.** Deserted by his own officers. Chunda Sahib surrendered to the general of the Tanjore troops, expecting to escape in disguise. He was betrayed and claimed by the English, Mahomet Ali, and the Mahrattas. To escape from the difficulty of decision, the general put him to death.

56, 1. **Crimps and flash-houses.** Crimps were kidnappers of men, who entrapped them and held them till they could sell them to the army or navy. Flash-houses were kept by persons of low character as a store house for stolen goods.

2. **Maskelyne, the eminent mathematician.** Dr. Nevil Maskelyne, best known for his *Astronomical Observations* of which it has been said that these volumes contain all the essentials of modern astronomy.

59, 1. **Newcastle.** The Prime Minister, and First Lord of the Treasury was so incompetent, that, when in 1756, the Seven Years' War was plainly inevitable, there were only three regiments in England fit for service. It is no wonder that defeat followed until he resigned and Pitt, the "Great Commoner" took his place.

2. **Cornish boroughs.** Until the Reform Act of 1832, ended the evil, many little hamlets or even farms that had once been villages, sent one or two representatives to Parliament, while the great modern cities sent none. These were called "rotten" or sometimes "pocket" boroughs as they were practically in the pocket of the owner of the land to give or sell at will.

60, 1. **Committee of the whole House.** Similar to our American "Committee of the Whole."

2. **Division after division.** In order to ascertain a vote, the members of Parliament are separated into sides.

63, 1. **Chandernagore.** Twenty miles above Calcutta, at one time a French post, taken by the English in 1757, restored to France 1763, retaken by English in 1794, again restored to France in 1816.

2. **Chowringhee.** At the time Macaulay wrote, one of the chief suburbs of Calcutta.

3. **The Course.** A noted pleasure drive in Calcutta.

64, 1. **Aliverdy Khan.** A Tartar adventurer, Mohammed Ali, who managed, by plot and conspiracy, to get control of Bengal, Bahar, and Orissa, three of the chief native states. He was one of the most remarkable men of his age, intelligent in all affairs, encouraging the deserving of every profession, affable in manner, wise in statecraft, courageous in warfare, and possessed of every noble quality.

65, 1. **Fort William.** The chief defense of Calcutta.

66, 1. **The fort was taken.** For forty-eight hours Mr. Holwell directed the defense of the fort. Repeated signals of distress were made to the vessels anchored below the town, any one of which might with perfect safety have attempted a rescue; but not a vessel moved to the assistance of the fort.

67, 1. **Ugolino.** Count Ugolino of Pisa was starved to death with his children by Archbishop Ruggieri, a fellow-conspirator and later a bitter enemy. Dante represents him frozen with Ruggieri in a lake of ice, gnawing his murderer's skull.

69, 1. **The expedition sailed.** It arrived at Fulta, twenty miles from Calcutta, December 10, after traversing a distance nearly as great as that from London to Liverpool.

79, 1. **The furies.** In the Greek theology the Furies or Eumenides represented the avenging forces of the moral order of the world, and were believed never to rest till the expiation for every crime had been made.

2. **The army of the Nabob.** It consisted almost entirely of Rajputs, soldiers from childhood, and for centuries the most distinguished warriors of Hindoostan.

81, 1. **An empire larger than Great Britain.** To-day England possesses practically the entire peninsula, having an area equal to nearly half that of the United States, exclusive of Alaska, and a population more than one-fifth that of the world.

84, 1. **Machiavelli.** An unscrupulous Italian statesman whose name has become a synonym for the use of craft rather than honest means.

2. **Borgia.** Cesare Borgia, an Italian primate of the church; one of the most evil men that ever lived.

87, 1. **The shower of wealth.** Clive gives the following details in his letter to the directors:—"The substance of the treaty with the Nabob is as follows: (I) Confirmation of the mint and all other grants in the treaty with the late Nabob. (II) An Alliance, offensive and defensive, against all enemies. (III) The French factories and effects to be delivered up, and they were permitted to resettle in any of the provinces. (IV) One hundred lacs of rupees, (£ 1,000,000) to be paid to the Company in consideration for the losses at Calcutta and the expenses of the campaign. (V) Fifty lacs to be given to the English sufferers at the loss of Calcutta. (VI) Twenty lacs to Gentoos, Moors and black sufferers at the loss of Calcutta. (VII) Seven lacs to the Armenian sufferers. These last three donations to be distributed at the pleasure of the Admiral and gentlemen of the council, including me. (VIII) The entire property of lands within the Mahratta ditch which runs round Calcutta to be vested in the Company; also 600 yards all round without said ditch. (IX) The Company to have the Zemindary (power to collect revenue) to the south of Calcutta lying between the lake and the river and reaching as far as Culpee, they paying the customary rents paid by former Zemindars to the government. (X) Whenever the assistance of the English troops shall be wanted, their extraordinary charge to be paid by the Nabob. (XI) No forts to be erected by the government on the riverside from Hooghly downward. (XII) The foregoing articles to be performed without delay as soon as Meer Jaffier becomes Bubahdai." This secured to the Lords of Fort William the monoply of trade in all districts watered by the Ganges.

2. **Florin.** A coin made by the Florentines, worth about six shillings. The modern English florin is worth about two shillings.

3. **Byzant,** or bezant. A gold coin first struck at Byzantium, worth about fifteen pounds sterling in English money.

4. **Before any European ship.** After the Latin conquest of Constantinople, in which Venice took part, she received for her services many islands and important trading posts on the coast of Asia Minor, which formed the starting point of her great eastern trade.

88, 1. **The biographer.** Mill claims, and Malcolm reiterates, that there was no law to forbid Clive's acceptance of the money. Marlborough, for his victory at Blenheim, was made Prince of Mindelheim, by the Emperor Joseph I; Nelson, for the battle of the Nile, was made Duke of Bronte by King Ferdinand of Naples; Wellington, for the battle of Vittoria, was made Duke of Vittoria by King Ferdinand VII of Spain, yet all were English generals.

91, 1. **The viceroy . . . of Oude. Surajah Dowlah.** The Nabobs of Oude, independent since 1753, had long been hereditary viziers of the empire. The power of Oude was broken by the battle of Buxar, 1764.

92, 1. **The tract . . . north of the Carnatic.** Four provinces called the Northern Circars had been ceded to Bussy by the Nizam of Hyderabad, 1753.

94, 1. **Quit-rent.** Money paid in discharge of services which would otherwise be due.

95, 1. **Batavia.** Capital of the Dutch possessions in Java.

97, 1. **Raised to the Irish peerage** as Baron Plassey.

2. **Pitt.** Grandson of a governor of Madras and therefore especially interested in Clive's work.

3. **That memorable period.** The year 1759 saw the defeat of the French at Minden, and off Cape Lagos; the capture of Quebec, and the annihilation of the French fleet off Quebec Bay. While in India Forde and Corte wrested from them the Four Circars.

4. **The admiration of the King of Prussia.** Frederick the Great, foremost soldier of his day, is reported to have said of a young volunteer who had asked to join the Duke of Brunswick's division, "What can he get by attending the Duke of Brunswick? If he desires to learn the art of war, let him go to Clive."

5. **No reporters.** The publication of debates was considered a breach of privilege until 1771. A gallery for reporters was erected in the House after the fire of 1834.

6. **His single victory** over the Young Pretender at Culloden.

98, 1. **Conway, General Henry,** who served during the Seven Years' War.

2. **Granby, John Manners,** who served in the continental wars.

3. **Sackville, Lord George Germain,** refused to charge the retreating French at Minden. In consequence he was court-martialled and declared forever unworthy to serve his country as a soldier.

4. **A foreign general.** Duke Ferdinand of Brunswick led the allied German and English forces.

99, 1. **Wilkes.** See Greene's *History of the English People,*

Bk. IX, Chap. I. He established the right of the press to discuss public affairs.

100, 1. **Board of Control.** Established by Pitt's India Bill, 1784, and invested with authority over the Company. Before this the Court of Directors, twenty-four in number, chosen by the Proprietors from their own number, had supreme control. Any man who held £500 or more of stock in the Company was a Proprietor.

102, 1. **Leadenhall Street.** A street in London where the East India Company's House was situated.

2. **South Sea year.** Founded in 1711, for trade with South America, the South Sea Company in expectation of immense profits, inflated its stock to enormous values, leading many poor people to invest in it. The bubble burst in 1720, ruining great numbers.

103, 1. **As Clive once said.** In his speech on East India Judicature bill, Clive says, "The native trader lays his bags of silver before the Company's servant to-day; gold to-morrow; jewels the next day; and if all these fail he then tempts him in the way of his profession, which is trade. In short, flesh and blood can not bear it."

2. **The Roman proconsul.** Lucius Licinius Lucullus. In Roman provinces the chief officer was termed proconsul or proprætor; having served in the highest offices at Rome, he was sent to a province to command the legions there and usually to act as greedy despot, though supposed to rule for the safety and enrichment of Rome.

104, 1. **Spanish viceroy.** Possibly Pizarro, or Cortes.

105, 1. **Thicker than the loins.** See I Kings xii, 10.

106, 1. **The Mussulman historian.** Seid Ghilam Hoslin Khan, author of the *Sujar-ul-Muta-Okharim* or *Manners of the Moderns*, an account of the last seven emperors of Hindoostan and the wars of the English in Bengal until 1783.

107, 1. **The Sepoys.** The first Sepoy mutiny took place in 1764, at Patna. It was put down by Major Munro, who blew twenty men from the guns.

2. **Verres and Pizarro.** Caius Verres, Prætor of Sicily, 74–72 B. C., so misgoverned that the Sicilians brought accusations against him before the Roman Senate. Cicero pleaded their cause against Verres.

113, 1. **Accused by historians.** Mill, with unusual narrowness, calls Clive's arrangement "A proceeding in its own nature shameful."

114, 1. **Cashiered.** Dismissed from service in a manner amounting almost to disgrace.

115, 1. **One of the conspirators.** Lieutenant Stainsforth was reported to Clive as having expressed an intention of killing Clive rather than have the conspiracy broken up.

116, 1. **Ricimers and Odoacers.** Count Ricimer, commander of barbarian forces in the service of Rome, was Patrician of Rome during the fifth century. Odoacer, son of one of Attila's officers, was elected King of Rome by his army in 476.

2. **Theodoric,** after the downfall of Odoacer, forced Zeno, Emperor of the East, to acknowledge him as ruler of the West.

3. **The last drivelling Chilperics.** The latest Merovingian kings, many of whom bore the name of Chilperic or of Childeric, were mere shadow kings,—do-nothing kings they were called,—puppets in the hands of their nominal servants, the mayors of the palace, Charles Martel, hero of the battle of Tours, and his son, Pepin le Bref, father of Charlemagne, and founder of the Carlovingian line.

120, 1. **Farmer-general.** One of the class of tax-collectors in France who acquired enormous wealth by oppression and extortion. They were of plebeian birth and despised by the nobility.

121, 1. **Domesday Book.** After the Norman Conquest William I, in 1086, had a census made out of every estate in England.

2. **Turcaret.** The hero of a comedy, written by Le Sage 1709; he is an unprincipled, stupid financier, the dupe of a clever baroness.

3. **Monsieur Jourdain.** The hero of Molière's *Le Bourgeois Gentilhomme*, a newly rich commoner, who makes himself ridiculous by aping the manners of the nobles.

122, 1. **The dilettante.** A society established in 1734, by several widely traveled noblemen and gentlemen, who were anxious to introduce into England a taste for the fine arts.

2. **The maccaroni.** The name given to men of fashion, or dandies, especially those who had completed the Italian tour where maccaroni was the favorite dish.

3. **Foote, Samuel.** Author of many comedies popular in the eighteenth century.

4. **Chairmen.** Bearers of the Sedan chair, a covered chair, carried by two men, a favorite means of conveyance at this time.

5. **Jaghires.** Land revenue, given by the Indian government to an individual, for government purposes or for his own use,—in the latter case usually a reward for some service.

6. **Mackenzie.** A Scotch writer, novelist and dramatist, as well as critic.

7. **Cowper.** See Cowper's poem *Expostulation*, lines 364–375.

123, 1. **Spartan temperance.** The supremacy of Sparta over the other Greek cities was largely due to the plainness, temperance and simplicity of the life of her citizens. In this they were the exact opposite of the people of Sybaris, a town of Italy, who gave themselves up to all luxury, and so have given us the word Sybarite.

124, 1. **Sir Matthew Mite.** A returned East India merchant in Foote's play *The Nabob*.

125, 1. **William Huntington, S. S.** An eccentric man, half sincere, half charlatan, who after a wild life, became a Methodist minister, giving himself the degree S. S., "Sinner Saved."

127, 1. **Adam Smith.** Author of the *Wealth of Nations*. See Bk. IV, Chap. V.

128, 1. **Strange malady.** A sort of melancholy, in which for nearly three years he remained aloof from the world; terminating after a brief return to Parliament, in apoplexy.

2. **Middlesex election.** In 1769 Middlesex sent John Wilkes to Parliament. The House refused to receive him; the Middlesex electors insisted that they could send whom they chose to Parliament. After a hot struggle the House finally conceded the right.

129, 1. **His spurs chopped off.** He had been created a Knight of the Bath; to chop off his spurs would mean to degrade and expel him from the order.

131, 1. **The House rose.** Adjourned.

132, 1. **Bruce.** Who stabbed a suspected foe, John Comyn, in a church; **Maurice,** who deserted the Protestants for Charles V to become Elector of Saxony, and then deserted the emperor for the Protestants; **William the Silent,** suspected of the murder of his wife; **William III** of England, his fame marred by the Massacre of Glencoe; **Murray,** who plotted his own sister's downfall; **Cosimo de' Medici,** suspected of murder; **Henry IV,** twice a traitor to his faith; **Peter the Great,** a mighty ruler, and a bloodthirsty murderer.

133, 1. **Henry VII's Chapel.** One of the most beautiful chapels of Westminster, the home of the insignia of the Knights of the Bath.

2. **Burgoyne.** Of Revolutionary fame.

134, 1. **The previous question.** A usual means of putting an end to debate is to move "the previous question."

136, 1. **Rejoiceth exceedingly.** Job iii, 22.

138, 1. **Ghizni.** Captured in 1839 by the English, thus enabling them to maintain Afghanistan as a barrier against Russia.

2. **Alexander the Great,** victorious at twenty-two; **Condé** of France, at twenty-one; **Charles XII** of Sweden at eighteen.

139, 1. **The Sacred Way.** Roman triumphs passed along the Via Sacra.

2. **Antiochus** of Syria, defeated by Scipio Asiaticus; **Tigranes** of Armenia, defeated by Pompey.

140, 1. **Munroe.** Governor of Madras, 1820; **Elphinstone** of Bombay 1819–1827, one of the most celebrated British Indian statesmen; **Metcalfe,** acting Governor General 1835.

2. **Lucullus.** One of the conquerors of Tigranes; **Trajan,** Emperor of Rome, conqueror of Dacia; builder of Column of Trajan.

3. **Turgot.** Minister of France under Louis XVI; he might have averted the Revolution, but for the folly of Louis.

4. **Bentinck.** Governor General of India 1828–1835. He introduced many noteworthy reforms; and was the first to rule India for the Hindoo people.

WARREN HASTINGS

143, 1. Like most of Macaulay's Essays, this was called forth by the appearance of a book on the subject, one of which, as in the case of the essay on Addison, he did not approve. It is interesting to remember, in studying his comments on what Hastings was and did, his own admission that he had little gift for interpreting a man's inner nature; that he judged, as a critic says, by deeds rather than by motives; by facts rather than by theories.

2. **Uncovered.** A sign of honor usually reserved for royalty.

144, 1. **Danish sea-king.** Hastings was one of the sea-kings finally defeated and driven from England by Alfred, 896.

2. **Renowned Chamberlain.** Famed in Shakespeare's Richard III.

3. **White Rose.** In the English Civil War 1455–1485 the house of York chose the White Rose, that of Lancaster the Red Rose as its emblem. It was ended by the accession of the Tudor Henry VII.

145, 1. **Mint at Oxford.** Oxford was the Royalist headquarters as London was the Parliamentary.

2. **Living.** A term used in England to signify position of clergymen in a parish; usually a part of some great estate whose owner presented the "living" to a friend, or even at times sold it; a condition largely responsible for placing over a parish a man in no way fit for the office.

3. **Tithes.** Originally a tenth part of one's substance, given, in accordance with God's command to the Israelites, for the sup-

port of the Church. Now, money or supplies given for church support.

147, 1. **Westminster school.** Founded by Queen Elizabeth, having in its gift three two-year scholarships at Christ Church, Oxford, given annually, valued at $400 each.

2. **Cowper.** As famous, perhaps, in literature as Hastings in history.

148, 1. **His spirit had been severely tried.** Cowper was subject to fits of melancholy in which he believed his soul irretrievably lost.

2. **Choice between innocence and greatness.** Bear this in mind, to show wherein Hastings had to make the choice and what it was.

149, 1. **Hexameters.** An English education sets high value on Latin, regarding proficiency in its use, especially in writing Latin verse, as the final mark of scholarship.

2. **Writership.** Each trading center in India employed **merchants,** senior and junior, who conducted the trade; **factors,** who ordered and inspected and dispatched goods; **writers,** who were clerks and bookkeepers. In five years a writer became a factor, in three more a merchant. The senior merchants were chosen the members of the Council, and from these the president who directed affairs at the **factory,** as the place was called where the factors did business.

3. **East India Company.** Original charter granted to a company of London merchants by Elizabeth in 1600, giving exclusive right to trade in the whole of the Indian and Pacific Oceans. In 1612 the Company obtained permission from several native princes, to establish trading posts or factories on the coast of Hindoostan. Madras was established in 1640, Calcutta in 1645, and Bombay in 1665 as the chief posts. In 1662, Charles II gave the Company permission to make war on the native princes, a permission used for nearly two centuries. A constitution was established in 1702, and the charter several times renewed, but with steadily lessening powers, until by the Act of 1858, its powers were transferred to the crown.

4. **Dupleix.** Governor of French possessions in Southern India. (Consult map for places mentioned.) *Clive,* pp. 32, 40.

5. **Carnatic.** A name given to the southeastern part of the peninsula; war of succession. *Clive,* pp. 40–43.

6. **Bengal.** Now largest and most populous of twelve great divisions of British India. Then, the region between the Boglipoor and the sea.

150, 1. **Hoogley.** The only one of the delta branches of the Ganges held sacred by the Hindoos.

2. **A prince.** The Nabob of Bengal.

3. **The Mogul.** A name given to ruling Emperor of India by Baber, a descendant of Tamerlane.

4. **Black Hole.** The Nabob confined 146 prisoners in a room twenty feet square, June 18, 1756. The room had but two small windows, these opening on a verandah. Of the prisoners only twenty-three survived the night. See *Clive*, pp. 66–68.

151, 1. **"Treason."** Meer Jaffier, rival of Surajah Dowlah, was afterward aided by Clive to become Nabob of Bengal when Surajah Dowlah was defeated at Plassey, 1757.

2. **Expedition commanded by Clive.** See *Clive*, p. 69.

153, 1. **Rotten boroughs.** Until well into the nineteenth century parliamentary representation was so unfairly adjusted that an old tree might send a representative to parliament, while a large city, if of modern growth, was absolutely unrepresented. See accounts in English history of various reform bills of nineteenth century.

156, 1. **Pagodas.** A gold coin, valued at $1.94.

157, 1. **The long voyage in an Indiaman.** The trip around Good Hope took the ships for India seldom less than six months, often nearly a year.

159, 1. **Clive.** See Macaulay's *Essay on Clive*, a man even greater than Hastings, founder of the British Empire in India.

Two governments. Clive had left the nominal power in the hands of the Nabob, who was, however, tributary to the Company, the actual ruler, having absolute power, while feigning to be vassals.

160, 1. **Augustulus to Odoacer.** The last Roman Emperor, a weakling in the hands of his great general Odoacer. The last Merovingian Kings of France dominated by the great Carlovingian generals, Charles Martel and Pepin, founders of Carlovingian line of kings.

2. **Cadet.** A junior clerk or employee.

166, 1. **Agents in Leadenhall Street.** The home of the East India Company.

172, 1. **Rupee.** A silver coin worth about two shillings.

2. **The Great Mogul.** Ruler of India.

3. **Oude.** One of the rich provinces of Northern India, now a British province.

173, 1. **Nabob.** Originally a native prince; later used of any one who had amassed wealth in India.

174, 1. **The cross of Saint George.** The flag of England, carried beyond the Punjab to Ghesni in 1839.

175, 1. **Catherine's claim to Poland.** A lasting blot on the fame of Russia was her partition of Poland without a shadow of right in 1772–1795. In Catherine's phrase Poland became her "door mat" upon which she stepped when visiting the West.

182, 1. Letters of Junius. A series of brilliant and intensely bitter attacks upon the government, which appeared in the *Public Advertiser*, 1769–1772. Their author is not known.

2. **Lord Chatham.** William Pitt, one of England's greatest statesmen. See Greene's *History of the English People.*

184, 1. Woodfall. A printer and parliamentary reporter, prosecuted for publishing the *Letters of Junius.*

185, 1. Old Sarum. One of the "rotten boroughs" before mentioned, sending two representatives to parliament, though uninhabited. Disfranchised by the Reform Bill of 1832.

186, 1. Elijah Impey. An old acquaintance of Hastings. See p. 193.

2. **Twenty-one guns.** A royal salute.

187, 1. The disputes of the Mahratta government, bringing about the first Mahratta war.

189, 1. Oates, inventor of an alleged plot to kill King Charles II; Oates and his accomplices were proven perjurors but not till many innocent people had been executed. Known in history as the Popish Plot.

190, 1. The Munny Begum. The queen mother. See p. 239.

194, 1. A Brahmin of the Brahmins. A member of the highest caste among the Hindoos; one whose person was sacred, no matter what his offense.

195, 1. The Mahommedan historian. Hardly any one but Macaulay would have investigated so far. Only one instance in many of his untiring efforts to secure historical accuracy by examining every possible authority.

197, 1. Impey. The tool of Hastings in this conviction.

200, 1. Jones' Persian Grammar. See p. 251 for mention of Hastings' interest in the study of Oriental languages.

201, 1. Lord North. Minister who lost the American Colonies to England.

208, 1. Mayor of the palace. A term originally used to designate the officials who, under the Merovingian kings, held the real power in France.

209, 1. A treaty between France and the Mahrattas. See *Essay on Clive* for account of former troubles with French in India.

210, 1. The brave and unfortunate Lally. A French general, defeated at Pondicherry, unjustly condemned and executed in France.

213, 1. English law is neither cheap nor speedy. See Dickens' *Bleak House* for a full exposure of this fact.

215, 1. **Alguazil.** A Spanish term for an inferior officer of justice.

218, 1. **"Rich, quiet and infamous."** An excellent definition of Impey's character.

2. **Jeffreys.** The brutal judge who conducted the trials after Monmouth's rebellion, 1685, in the "Bloody Assizes."

3. **Regulating Act.** Passed by Parliament in 1773. Provided for a new law court at Calcutta, called the Supreme Court; made the Governor of Bengal (Warren Hastings) Governor-General of India and named a council of four to advise him. This act was thought necessary in order to prevent mismanagement in India and the evils attending it.

221, 1. **"A far more formidable danger."** For the second time this is hinted at, but not yet explained.

222, 1. **Lewis the Eleventh.** One of the greatest French kings (1461–1483), "a perfect Ulysses in craft and deceit," who finally broke the power of the great nobles.

2. **"The most formidable enemy,"** not only in his own ability but also in the fact of alliance with France, thus uniting the powers of Southern India against the English stations of Madras, Calcutta and Bombay.

228, 1. **"The House of Tamerlane."** See note **34,** 1.

2. **"No such constitution."** India was a vast agglomeration of states, each nominally independent, yet some tributary to each other and most bound by some agreement or understanding to the Company; but ready at any moment to dissolve or ignore the agreement.

3. **Hugh Capet.** Duke of France, founder of the Capetian dynasty. Consult French history for an explanation of conditions at that time. Anderson's *A New Manual of General History*.

4. **Charles X.** A blind, stubborn Bourbon, exiled for his despotism. His conduct gave rise to the saying "A Bourbon learns nothing and forgets nothing."

230, 1. **This legerdemain.** Trickery and deception.

233, 1. **Benares.** On the Ganges River, 390 miles northwest of Calcutta. One of the most ancient and renowned cities of the world.

245, 1. **"The time was approaching."** Pitt's India Bill of 1784, brought the Company directly under a Board of Control in England, and gave Parliament a right to interfere when such disgraceful acts as the Rohilla War and the treatment of the Begums blackened the name of England. Heretofore the Company had been a private enterprise and so practically beyond reach so long as it was guilty of no crime against the government.

249, 1. **Downing Street.** The principal building in this street was given by George I to Sir Robert Walpole who accepted it for his office of First Lord of the Treasury. It has since been the official residence of successive Prime Ministers, and has made the street in which it stands the official street of the English government.

2. **Somerset House.** A building in the Strand, London, devoted to the accommodation of government and semi-public offices.

252, 1. **A far more virtuous ruler.** The Sir William Bentinck so highly lauded in the last sentence of the *Essay on Clive.*

253, 1. **Pundits.** Brahmin scholars.

256, 1. **Zemindars.** Revenue officers.

2. **Carlton House.** Residence of the Prince of Wales.

257, 1. **Lac.** Hindoo numeral equivalent to one hundred thousand.

258, 1. **Sir Charles Grandison.** The immaculate hero of Richardson's novel by that name; a favorite book of Macaulay's.

259, 1. **Burke gave notice.** No statesman was ever more devotedly the champion of the oppressed than was Edmund Burke. India and America alike owe much gratitude to him.

260, 1. **In India he had a bad hand.** A good example of Macaulay's use of analogy to explain conditions.

264, 1. **The opposition.** A term used to designate the members of Parliament opposed to the ministry. At the beginning of a ministry the minority.

2. **Brooks's.** A Whig club.

265, 1. **Pharisaical ostentation.** Macaulay never liked Philip Francis.

266, 1. **Fall of the coalition.** The friends of Fox and those of Lord North joined in forming what is known as the coalition ministry; but this did not last long, as it proposed a law about the government of India which offended many people and led the King to turn it out of office.

267, 1. **His knowledge of India.** Few other men, possibly none save Macaulay himself, possessed so vast a fund of information on all subjects, or so great a power of vivid presentation, as did Burke.

268, 1. **Mecca.** The holy city of the Moslems in Arabia; the birthplace of Mohammed.

2. **St. James's Streeet.** A fashionable London street.

3. **Lord George Gordon.** The leader of a mob which pillaged London in 1780. See Dickens' *Barnaby Rudge;* **Dr. Dodd,** a fashionable London preacher, executed for forgery in 1771.

270, 1. **Sensibility.** Meaning emotion or sympathy.

2. **Made a bridge of gold.** Used money.

273, 1. **The star of the Bath.** A high order, ranking almost with that of the Garter, given in appreciation of special service was a mark of royal favor.

2. **Sworn of the privy council.** Made a member of the king's personal advisory body.

276, 1. **Works of supererogation.** Voluntary deeds or works of piety or charity, beyond one's duty, in hopes that they may serve to cancel former sins.

277, 1. **Wilberforce.** A friend of Pitt; a bitter opponent of the slave trade.

279, 1. **Prorogation.** Adjournment of Parliament.

2. **Spoliation of the Begums.** See p. 239.

3. **Sheridan.** Richard Brinsley Sheridan, a brilliant orator and author of the well-known plays, *The Rivals* and *The School for Scandal.*

280, 1. **Coughed and scraped down.** The members of Parliament take care that an offensive measure shall not get a fair hearing, even though its proposer may have the floor.

2. **To go before the Lords.** The House impeaches, the Lords try the case. (This is the most famous portion of the speech, and one of the finest historical word pictures ever written.)

283, 1. **The great hall of William Rufus.** Westminster Hall, one of the noblest examples of early Roman building, was erected by William II, called Rufus. It is now a part of the new hall of Parliament.

2. **Bacon.** Impeached and convicted for taking bribes, in the reign of James I; **Somers,** Chancellor under William III, acquitted, not on his merits, but through a difference between the Lords and Commons as to methods of procedure; **Strafford,** unjustly executed under Charles I, who afterward met the same death.

284, 1, **Siddons.** Sarah Siddons, the greatest tragic actress of her day, then at the height of her fame; **Historian of the Roman Empire,** Gibbon, author of *The Decline and Fall of the Roman Empire;* **Cicero against Verres,** the great Roman orator impeached Verres, Prætor of Sicily, on charges not unlike those against Hastings, though of far graver nature; **The greatest painter,** Sir Joshua Reynolds, famous for his portraits of beautiful women; **The greatest scholar,** Dr. Samuel Parr, who, though now forgotten, had an extraordinary reputation for scholarship. See DeQuincey's *Essay on Dr. Samuel Parr;* **Heir to the throne had plighted his faith,** Mrs. Fitzherbert, morganatic wife of the Prince of Wales. Her Catholic faith made the marriage contrary to law by the Royal Marriage Act, 1772. (Note Macaulay's use of particular terms to support his general statements.) **Beauti-**

ful mother of a beautiful race, Mrs. Sheridan, painted by Reynolds as St. Cecilia, the patron saint of music; **Mrs. Montague,** a famous English hostess, whose salon was frequented by the foremost men of the day; **Duchess of Devonshire,** one of the loveliest women of the day; a friend of Fox for whom it is said she bought votes by kisses.

285, 1. **Mens æqua in arduis.** A mind unmoved amid difficulties.

286, 1. **Wearing a bag and sword.** No gentleman of fashion considered himself dressed for any ceremonious occasion unless he wore his sword, and a wig with a bag to hold the back hair.

2. **Fox and Sheridan.** Among the greatest debaters and orators of the day. Cicero ranks Hyperides, whose name alone now survives, as second only to Demosthenes.

287, 1. **William Windham.** A man of great talents and rare gifts, yet one who made no mark in history; **The youngest manager,** Grey, head of the Ministry which carried the Reform Bill of 1832, of whom it was said that no more honorable man ever lived.

2. **The morning sun.** All night sessions are by no means uncommon, as the session does not begin till 4 P. M.

288, 1. **Their taste and sensibility.** Only natural in an age which enjoyed the sentimentality of *Clarissa Harlowe* and *Sir Charles Grandison.*

294, 1. **In 1789.** When Burke alone opposed the French Revolution.

295, 1. **Woolsack.** In order to keep well in mind the fact that wool was one of the sources of natural wealth, sacks of wool were placed in the House of Lords as seats for the Judges. To this day the seat of the Lord Chancellor is called "the woolsack."

301, 1. **A coronet and a red riband.** Distinguished services were ordinarily rewarded by knighthood, and investment with some honorary order.

EXAMINATION QUESTIONS

LORD MACAULAY

LIFE AND WORKS

1. Give some details of Macaulay's early life. 2. Anecdotes illustrating his precocity. 3. Incidents showing his early love for books and reading. 4. Some details of his wonderful memory and his capacity for taking in at a glance the contents of a printed page. (*Trevelyan's Life*, Vol. I, ch. i.) 5. His career at Cambridge University. 6. The study of law and his literary work for Knight's *Quarterly Magazine.* 7. Incidents which led Macaulay to write his essay on Milton for the *Edinburgh Review*—its success. 8. Mention the subjects of Macaulay's most important essays contributed for many years to the same periodical. 9. What are the chief characteristics of these celebrated essays? 10. What political honors were conferred upon Macaulay? 11. His appointment to an office in India and his residence in that country. 12. His return to England and subsequent career in Parliament. 13. What fine martial ballads were published in 1842? 14. When was his *History* first published?—its success? 15. Give some details of the scope of this work. 16. What can you tell of Macaulay's career as a public speaker? 17. The death of the great historian in 1859? 18. Macaulay's style—its prominent characteristics? 19. What adverse criticisms have been made on his writings? 20. How will you account for the remarkable popularity of all that Macaulay has written? 21. Personal life of Macaulay—its chief characteristics? 22. Incidents and anecdotes to illustrate the same. 23. Macaulay's opinion of famous men and books. (Cf. Trevelyan.)

ESSAY ON CLIVE

Occasion for Writing Essay

1. What was the actual civilization in Mexico and Peru at the time of their conquest by Spain?

2. Give illustrations from these paragraphs of Macaulay's preference for specific details rather than the abstract statement under which these details come. What does he gain by it?

3. Judging from the fault he finds with Orme and Mill, what do you consider to be his belief as to the requisites of a good history?

4. What are the essentials of a good biography? Compare your opinion with that stated by Carlyle in the opening paragraphs of his *Essay on Burns*.

Ancestry and Character

1. What is the topic sentence of the paragraph beginning on page 26? How is it developed?

2. Explain the term "such slender parts" (page 27).

The East India Company

1. Read Chap. XVIII in Macaulay's *History of England* and from that and the account given here write an account of the early history of the East India Company.

2. "Infringe the monopoly"; explain.

3. "The rapidity of the prophet's gourd"; explain the significance of this allusion.

4. "The voyage by the Cape." How is the journey from England to India made to-day?

Clive's Early Experiences

1. Select from these paragraphs, examples of balanced structure and explain why they are used.

2. What is shown of his character in these early days?

The Struggle for India

1. "Even then the first of maritime powers." What naval battles had England won? How does her navy, to-day, compare with ours?

2. "On parole"; explain.

3. What right had Dupleix to overrule the orders of Labourdonnais? Locate Mauritius.

4. Does page 34 disprove the assertions made elsewhere by Macaulay and others that India is poor? Reasons for your answer.

5. Point out examples of explanation by comparison with known objects.

6. "The vices of Oriental despotism." What are they?

7. "The vices inseparable from the dominion of race over race." Give examples of these from the history of the United States.

8. What is the purpose of the paragraph at the bottom of page 35?

9. "Feudal privileges"; explain.

10. From pages 37 and 38, comment on Macaulay's sentence structure, and especially on his use of long and short sentences.

11. What is the purpose of the questions in the last half of page 39?

12. "From Cape Cormorin to the eternal snows of the Himalayas." State in other words. Which is the better form? Why? Give other examples of the same usage in this paragraph.

13. "Confounded the confusion." Explain meaning, and state in your own words how it was done.

14. What is Dupleix's ambition? Why does Macaulay speak so harshly of him and not of Clive, who does practically the same things?

15. Analyze the paragraph beginning at the foot of page 44. Purpose of the last sentence?

16. In the last paragraph on page 47 what is the topic? Where stated? how developed? What, in Clive, won his men?

17. Page 52, "Induced . . . by a just and profound policy." Explain what it was.

18. Page 56, sentence beginning line 16. Rearrange to secure better order.

19. Sum up Clive's work in a well-constructed paragraph, imitating, as far as possible, Macaulay's style, both as to choice of words, and as to sentence structure.

First Return to England

1. What traits of character were displayed by his actions in his relations with the Company, with his family, in his private life, his public career?

2. How had he fulfilled the promise of his boyhood?

3. "Calumny and chicanery" (page 61); explain.

The Subjugation of Bengal

1. What is the topic of paragraph beginning on page 62? Analyze the paragraph, indicating the method of development.
2. Explain the Castilian proverb. Show how it applies to the Bengalese.
3. "Oriental despots are the worst class of human beings." Why? Give other proof of the truth of this statement.
4. Criticise the sentence structure in paragraphs beginning on pages 66 and 67. Why are so many short sentences used?
5. Criticise Clive's action in making terms with Surajah Dowlah, instead of punishing him.
6. "The substituting of documents and the counterfeiting of hands"; explain. To what episode does Macaulay refer?
7. What excuse is there for Clive's treatment of Omichund? Is the excuse a justification? Why?
8. Why is Plassey ranked among the decisive battles of the world?
9. What, in Macaulay's opinion, is the real secret of British power in India? Is he right? Read Kipling's *The White Man's Burden.*
10. Explain the figure in sentence beginning line 29, page 85. What is the purpose of making the next paragraph separate instead of uniting it with the previous one?
11. Does the paragraph at the middle of page 87 prove India a rich colony? Why?
12. What does Macaulay find to blame in Clive's conduct?
13. Page 90, "By implication at least"; explain.
14. Page 90, "So unfortunate as to be born in the purple." Explain.
15. Page 94, "The great army . . . melted away." What figure is used? What is signified by it?
16. Why does Macaulay justify Clive for accepting the quit-rent?

Second Return to England

1. Page 97, "Since the death of Wolfe." When and where?
2. What cause had England to be proud of Clive, rather than of the other generals mentioned?
3. Page 100, "The power of the Company is an anomaly." Explain. When and how was this anomaly brought to an end?
4. "Mounted by the regular gradations" (page 101). What were they?
5. "Above a year and a half" (page 103). What is the present usage for this idea?

6. Show how the Company was responsible for the misdeeds of its servants.
7. "Cruelty was not among the vices of the Company" (page 104). Comment on this in the light of the rest of the paragraph.
8. Explain lines 11–12, page 105; line 17.
9. What progress has England made toward the ideal nation spoken of by the Mussulman historian on page 106?
10. What was the real cause of the directors' anxiety about India?

Final Work in India

1. Was Clive in any way responsible for the conditions in India?
2. Explain lines 23–25, page 110.
3. Page 111, "A mistaken policy." Why mistaken?
4. Page 111, "This practice had been seriously injurious to the commercial interests of the corporation." How?
5. State in your own words Clive's reasons for appropriating to the support of the service the monopoly of salt.
6. Page 117, last sentence. Criticise the order.

Final Return to England

1. What is the structure of the last sentence, page 120? How is it kept a unit?
2. Page 120, "Raised the price of rotten boroughs." Explain.
3. Why was Clive so well hated?

Retrospect

1. Give examples of parallel structure.
2. In what respects has his name a right to a place "in the list of those who have done and suffered much for the happiness of mankind?"

GENERAL TOPICS FOR PARAGRAPHS

1. Show how Clive's career in India fulfilled the promise of his boyhood.
2. Tell the story of the Sepoy Mutiny, after which the Company's power came to an end.
3. Explain the present government of India.

4. How do conditions in India differ from those in England's other colonies?
5. Compare the work and character of Clive and of Hastings.
6. Prove that England is or is not justified in holding India.
7. Compare conditions in India with those in the American colonies prior to the Revolution.
8. Discuss Macaulay's style.
9. Discuss Macaulay's power of making a vivid picture.
10. Sketch the rise and fall of the East India Company.

ESSAY ON HASTINGS

Occasion for the Essay

1. What does Macaulay state as his opinion of Hastings' character?
2. What does he consider the fault of Mr. Gleig's biography? What should his own sketch contain?

Hastings' Ancestry

1. What characteristics does he find in the Hastings' ancestry?
2. What sort of character would you expect from such parentage?

Education

1. What were the chief traits of character shown in his childhood?
2. Give an account of Cowper, his schoolmate.
3. Explain "the doctrine of human depravity" (page 148).
4. What is implied in lines 6–10, page 148?
5. What do lines 11–17 suggest as to Impey's character?
6. What evidences, in his boyhood, of traits which might lead to greatness?

Beginning of His Work for the Company

1. Locate on the map the various places mentioned.
2. Sketch the history of the East India Company.
3. Give an account of the trouble with the French in India.
4. Give an account of the various peoples making up the inhabitants of India.
5. Explain the caste system among the Hindoos.

6. Who was the "Mogul," and why so called?
7. Give a brief account of the work done by Clive in India.
8. From bottom of page 151 to top of 154, what is the theme? Criticise the unity of the paragraph.
9. Point out examples in above of Macaulay's use of the concrete, the particular, instead of the abstract, general statement.
10. Explain why a statesman would not be a freebooter; a plunderer of the people.

First Return to England

1. What traits of character are shown during his stay in England?
2. Give brief account of Dr. Johnson.

The Meeting with "Fair Marion"

1. What excuse is there for Baroness Imhoff?
2. What means does Macaulay use to justify Hastings?

Rise of Hastings' Power

1. How had "the servants of the Company ceased to be clerks, and had become warriors and negotiators"?
2. State, in your own words, the nature of the government of Bengal at this time.
3. What are the powers of the Viceroy in India to-day?
4. Explain the meaning of "political" and "diplomatic," showing why they are not synonymous.
5. Explain the words "important, lucrative and splendid" as they apply to the office of native minister of Bengal.
6. Explain the term "Maharajah."
7. Explain the term "high and pure caste."
8. State in your own words the meaning of lines 7–9, page 163. Why has Macaulay chosen this way to state it? Give another instance of the same method in this paragraph.
9. Describe the character of the Bengalee, showing why the English find it so difficult to comprehend.
10. Why does Macaulay consider India a poor country? What is your opinion as to what makes a nation rich? For what do the colonies of England spend their revenues to-day? What use was the Company making of India?
11. Why were "the Company's instructions in perfect conformity with his own views" on the matter of removing Mahommed Reza Khan?

12. Explain the change made by Hastings in the government of Bengal. Show where it was for the better.
13. Explain why Nuncomar was so angry.

Sale of Allahabad and Lorah

1. What is implied as to Hastings' character by his "fundamental proposition"? Does Macaulay's excuse justify him for it?

The Infamy of Rohilcund

1. What does history show as to the character of mountaineers?
2. Locate Rohilcund, and describe the Rohillas.
3. What figures of speech are used in lines 2–10, page 176?
4. What justification is there for Hastings' conduct?
5. Why does Macaulay consider this infamous?
6. What rhetorical device does Macaulay use in the paragraph at the bottom of page 176?
7. Would it have been possible to obtain money by honest means?

The Regulating Act and Its Results

1. State in your own words the terms of the Act.
2. Show how it altered existing conditions.
3. Characterize Philip Francis.
4. What do you gather to be Macaulay's feeling toward him?
5. What were the *Letters of Junius?*
6. What caused the rivalry between Francis and Hastings?
7. Justify by results Hastings' unwillingness to give over to the Council the government of Bengal.
8. Why does Macaulay lay so much stress on "Asiatic mendacity" on page 188?

Struggle Between Hastings and Nuncomar

1. What had caused Nuncomar's grudge of seventeen years?
2. Had the terms of the Regulating Act given the Council control over the Governor?
3. Explain Nuncomar's mistake.
4. "Idiots and biographers excepted." To whom is the reference? What is its implication?
5. Why was Nuncomar's execution illegal?
6. What made his execution so terrible, in the eyes of the Bengalese?

7. Why does Macaulay blame Impey for that for which he excuses Hastings?
8. What justification does he find for Hastings?

Trouble in England

1. Point out the injustice in the Directors' conduct.
2. What had been the terms on which Hastings gave his resignation to Macleane? How far was Macleane justified?
3. Justify Hastings in his refusal to withdraw.
4. Why is Hastings so confident of the verdict of the Supreme Court? Show the wisdom of his act.
5. Criticise his action toward Clavering.

Foreign Complications

1. In what wars was England engaged at this time?
2. Characterize the Mahrattas.
3. Explain line 12, page 208.

Evils of the Supreme Court

1. What had been the powers given this court by the Regulating Act?
2. Explain why a code of laws for one country cannot be transplanted to another?
3. Justify Hastings in bribing rather than fighting Impey.
4. What analogy does Macaulay use to justify Hastings' conduct?
5. What excuse had Hastings for his opinion of Francis?

Trouble with Hyder Ali

1. What were the measures he had taken to break the power of the Mahrattas?
2. What rhetorical device is used in paragraph starting line 15, page 221?
3. Locate on the map the places mentioned.
4. "The struggle with Hyder was a struggle for life or death." Give reasons.

Subjugation of Cheyte Sing

1. Describe Benares.
2. Describe the condition of government in India at this time.
3. Explain "a government *de facto* and a government *de jure.*"

4. What is the ultimate effect of such action as that mentioned in paragraph beginning at the middle of page 229? Has it been proven so in the case of India?
5. What was Hastings' plan with regard to Cheyte Sing?
6. Why was Benares particularly hostile to the English?

The Extortion from the Begums

1. Compare the robbery of the Begums with the affair of Rohilcund. Are these two stains on Hastings' name in any way to be excused or justified?
2. Why did not Hastings torture the women themselves, instead of their innocent servants?
3. Compare the crimes of Hastings with those of Impey. Why has Macaulay no excuse for Impey?
4. Why had not the English government interfered?
5. Have we any case in our own century where a so-called civilized country has perpetrated like crimes?

Summary of Hastings' Work

1. Enumerate the grave crimes of Hastings' administration against the public service. Had he committed any crimes against the Company or done any public service for India? Could a service for one compensate for a crime against the other?
2. What grounds has Macaulay for considering him one of the most remarkable men in English history?

Return to England

1. What right had the government to impeach a servant of a private company?
2. What claims had Hastings on the government?
3. Give a brief sketch of the career of Edmund Burke. Why was he especially fitted to lead the attack on Hastings?
4. What debt do Americans owe him?

The Impeachment and Trial

1. Explain in your own words the inconsistency of Pitt's action.
2. Why should Pitt be jealous of Hastings?
3. Give brief account of Sheridan.
4. Explain why the paragraph starting at the bottom of page

282 has received so much praise. Point out its merits in point of style. What evidence does it afford of Macaulay's scholarship?

5. Comment on Hastings' conduct at the trial.
6. What was the real punishment?

Outcome of the Trial

1. Comment on the means used by Hastings to win public favor.
2. How much better off "in character" was he by reason of his acquittal?

Last Days

1. What had been his boyhood ambition?
2. What traits of his boyhood reappear in his old age?
3. Why does Macaulay think him worthy of a place in Westminster?
4. Compare Macaulay's estimate of him with your own.

GENERAL

I. Subject-Matter

1. Outline work done by Hastings in India.
2. Give proof of his statesmanship.
3. Give proof that he believed that the end justified the means.
4. Explain the nature of the East India Company; locate their chief stations; tell how their power was brought to a close.
5. Explain the divisions and governments of India at the time of Hastings, naming and locating chief states.
6. Why has not England given India the same government as Australia or Canada?
7. Describe government of India of to-day.
8. Explain what England owed to Hastings.
9. Characterize Hastings as a man.
10. Explain why he failed in England.
11. Justify his impeachment.

II. Style

1. Cite instances proving that Macaulay is at his best in portraying dramatic scenes.
2. Cite instances showing his vast information.

3. Cite instances showing his personal knowledge of India.
4. Cite instances showing his partiality.
5. Discuss his sentence structure, his favorite type of sentence, his use of long and short sentences.
6. Quote passages showing his use of particulars.
7. Quote passages showing his power of vivid presentation.
8. Outline and criticise one of his argumentative passages.
9. Discuss his use of figures.
10. What makes his style so clear?